A PREDATOR IN WAIT

Brenda and her mother got out of the car. They each grabbed a suitcase from the backseat of the vehicle before they shut the doors to the car, and on the life that they had both once cherished.

They walked forward and Mary slid her key into the lock of the front door. Inside the house, an intruder sat waiting. He wore a blue bandana over his face so that just his eyes and the top of his head were visible. He expected the return of Mary Parsh, a fifty-eight-year-old woman who wouldn't be able to put up much of a fight, and therefore become an easy victim. Instead, he got Mary, as well as her young and physically fit daughter Brenda. He would have to deal with Brenda first in order to eliminate any problems that might occur due to her unexpected presence.

When he heard the car pull into the driveway, the intruder moved to the front door. Adrenaline coursed through his body as he listened to the key enter the lock to release the bolt. The door opened and he confronted Mary and Brenda as soon as they stepped inside. Mary never even had an opportunity to pull the keys out of the front door's lock.

Also by Steven Walker

BLOOD TRAIL

PREDATOR

STEVEN WALKER

PINNACLE BOOKS
Kensington Publishing Corp.
http://www.kensingtonbooks.com

PINNACLE BOOKS are published by

Kensington Publishing Corp.
119 West 40th Street
New York, NY 10018

All Kensington Titles, Imprints, and Distributed Lines are available at special quantity discounts for bulk purchases for sales promotions, premiums, fund-raising, and educational or institutional use. Special book excerpts or customized printings can also be created to fit specific needs. For details, write or phone the office of the Kensington special sales manager: Kensington Publishing Corp., 119 West 40th Street, New York, NY 10018, attn: Special Sales Department, Phone: 1-800-221-2647.

Pinnacle and the P logo Reg. U.S. Pat. & TM Off.

ISBN-13: 978-0-7860-2018-8
ISBN-10: 0-7860-2018-0

First printing: January 2010

10 9 8 7 6 5 4 3 2 1

Printed in the United States of America

Dedicated to Mary and Brenda Parsh, Sheila Cole, Virginia Witte, Myrtle Rupp, Marjorie Call, Deborah Sheppard, Mildred Wallace, and Joyce Tharp. None of them deserved to die by the hands of a brutal murderer. May they be remembered for all time for the lives they led, not just for the way they died.

I dropped a single tear in the ocean. When you find it, that's when I'll stop missing you.

—Years of Tears Web site,
www.yearsoftears.org

Acknowledgments

I'd like to thank the victims' surviving friends and relatives for allowing me to get to know their loved ones through their stories and pictures. Special thanks go out to Don Call, Sue Sewing, Rosebud Call, Teresa Haubold, Mike Stafford, Richard McGougan, and Vicki Abernathy. I'd also like to thank the Cape Girardeau Police Department, and, in particular, Henry Gerecke, Jimmy Smith, Carl Kinnison, and especially John Brown. I also appreciate the assistance of Adrian Schuka, of the Berks County District Attorney's Office, and I promised to acknowledge Noah Bond, of WPSD.

I need to give credit to Michaela Hamilton for having enough confidence and patience to allow me to write another book for Kensington. Mike Shohl deserves credit for his invaluable feedback, encouragement, and editing skills. Mike's boot needs equal credit for kicking my butt whenever I fell asleep at the keyboard.

Without Kindra's loving patience and support, this project would never have been accomplished.

As an additional note: If Morley Swingle started wearing a cape, he could put Batman out of business. The bad guys don't have a chance against him.

Prologue

Missouri is often referred to as the "Show Me" state. People have to prove themselves to a Missourian, just as the residents of this state have been proving themselves to the rest of the country since the mid-eighteenth century when a French trading post was first established in what is present-day St. Louis.

Lewis and Clark were famous frontiersmen who began their expedition west from the city of St. Charles, in 1804. The famous Gateway Arch rises majestically above the St. Louis skyline as a symbol of Missouri's role as the "Gateway to the West" and the opening of a new frontier. Today, visitors to the state can follow in the footsteps of daring adventurers of the past by retracing their paths along the California, Santa Fe, and Oregon Trails.

Samuel Langhorne Clemens, better known as Mark Twain, was born in the town of Florida, Missouri, and based the adventures of Tom Sawyer and Huckleberry Finn on his own childhood in the town of Hannibal, where he grew up.

The infamous Pony Express was headquartered in

Missouri and began its short-lived run from St. Joseph, Missouri, to Sacramento, California, in 1860.

If you've ever walked along Main Street U.S.A. in Disneyland, you might be interested to know that it was modeled after Walt Disney's hometown of Marceline, Missouri.

In 1860, a St. Louis businessman, Eberhard Anheuser, and his son-in-law, Adolphus Busch, recognized an opportunity to make a profit from the country's growing taste for beer, culminating in the creation of Anheuser-Busch, the world's largest brewery.

A Kansas City, Missouri, resident, Harry S. Truman, guided our country out of the world's largest and most horrific conflagration of the twentieth century and steered us along the path to postwar prosperity.

If you think about pioneers of the music world, Scott Joplin, Chuck Berry, Duke Ellington, and Miles Davis have to be on your greatest list. They all resided in Missouri.

All of the above-mentioned people and an almost endless list of others have led the way in their specific field of expertise without waiting for somebody else to come along to show them how. That is why it is fitting that a resident of this state has many reasons to feel proud. It's no wonder they want others to prove themselves and "show me" what you're made of.

Greatness, however, is not reserved solely for those individuals who have become famous for their deeds. It can be found in the lives and actions of ordinary people who offer a kind word, a helping hand, or encouragement to others. Such is the case of nine women whose lives were needlessly cut short at the hand of confessed serial killer Timothy Krajcir. Five of these women were from Cape Girardeau, Missouri.

Mary Parsh, Brenda Parsh, Sheila Cole, Margie Call, and Mildred Wallace all lived in this town of about thirty-five thousand people, which is situated along the Mississippi River in the southeast portion of the state. The friends and family members of these women know that they all possessed a sense of greatness, because these ladies had a positive impact on the lives of others.

Ten miles north of Cape Girardeau, on Route 177, is the Trail of Tears State Park. Just across the Mississippi River, in Illinois, is the Trail of Tears State Forest. The Trail of Tears refers to the sad and often fatal journey that the defeated Cherokee Indians were forced to walk after their land in the East was seized by the United States government. The parkland and forest encompass thousands of acres of wooded hills, valleys, and high bluffs that overlook the Mississippi River. This scenic area is home to deer, wild turkeys, hawks, foxes, and bald eagles.

Although the area is beautiful, the Trail of Tears name is fitting for another reason besides that of the suffering of the Cherokee people. The park and the forest are spread out on both sides of the Mississippi between Cape Girardeau and the town of Carbondale, Illinois. Carbondale is the location of another murder committed by Krajcir. It was the home of Deborah Sheppard, a young woman one month away from earning her bachelor's degree. Her life was just beginning when it was abruptly and brutally cut short. Now the world will never benefit from the potential of this individual.

Also in Illinois, northeast of Carbondale along Interstate 57, just on the edge of Crab Orchard National Wildlife Refuge, is the town of Marion. It was there that David Witte discovered the body of his wife, Virginia, stabbed to death in their Westernaire Estates home.

The trail of tears and fear spread like wildfire throughout the area. A short distance south, just across the Ohio River, is the town of Paducah, Kentucky. A florist was making a delivery when he found the nude body of Joyce Tharp beside some trash cans behind the Park Avenue Baptist Church.

Krajcir's trail of tears continued to grow. It was not connected until many years later, but that trail extended all the way to Pennsylvania. Just outside of Reading, Pennsylvania, is the town of Temple. It was there that the body of Myrtle Rupp was found strangled to death in her home, where she had been recovering from a recent surgery.

It took twenty-eight years to link all nine women to the same murderer. Family members and friends of the victims anguished for nearly three decades as the case files of unsolved murders swelled in state after state. As the years passed, some of those loved ones passed away themselves without ever finding answers. Who would kill my wife, my daughter, my sister, my niece, my friend? Why? Finally, with advancements in forensic technology, closure came to those who remained alive in 2007. Timothy Krajcir, a murderer who described himself as a "twisted individual," confessed to the nine murders, and the process of indicting him began.

Suddenly authorities nationwide began to scrutinize files of cold cases as they looked for links to Krajcir in unsolved murders, rapes, and sexual assaults. The quest was on, and the nation's eyes and ears were all pointed in the direction of one man—Timothy Wayne Krajcir.

1

Deborah Sheppard
August 2007

The rusting wheels of justice were given a shot of oil and slowly began to turn. A statement of probable cause and a motion for arrest warrant was signed August 28, 2007, by Michael L. Wepsiec, state's attorney for Jackson County, Illinois. There were four counts of murder while committing forcible rape brought against the defendant in connection with the death of Deborah Sheppard.

The next day, the warrant of arrest commanded all peace officers of the state of Illinois to arrest Timothy Wayne Krajcir, and bring him without delay before the presiding judge of the First Judicial Circuit Court in the Jackson County Courthouse, in the city of Murphysboro. The amount of bail was already determined to be set at no less than $1 million.

Adrenaline was stirred. Lieutenant Paul Echols, of the Carbondale Police Department (CPD), couldn't help but feel alive; to feel like he had made a difference and had a positive impact. He knew that he had played an integral part alongside the co-ordinated efforts of many others that finally helped to bring the case to a point where it might finally be solved. It was a cold case that had been pursued relentlessly for years without resolution. Echols was confident that Krajcir was guilty, but unless Krajcir confessed, his guilt or innocence would have to be determined by a judge or a jury based on the evidence.

Carbondale, Illinois, is smaller than Cape Girardeau, Missouri. Give or take a couple of thousand people, its population has hovered around the twenty-five thousand mark since 1970. There is one Muslim temple, one Jewish synagogue, two Catholic churches, and forty-seven Protestant churches located within the city limits. Carbondale is the epitome of the stereotypical White Anglo-Saxon Protestant (WASP) environment. Carbondale was selected as "Best Small City in Illinois" in 1990, and again in 1997. It was also awarded the Governor's Hometown Award in 1991 and 1992. There is a central business district in the downtown area. There are several strip mall centers, and the University Mall is the single enclosed shopping area. There are two high schools and there is the nearby John A. Logan Community College in Cartersville. Carbondale is also home to Southern Illinois University (SIU), a comprehensive teaching and research institution with approximately sixty-one graduate programs and professional schools of law, medicine, and engineering. With about 6,800 employees, it is the area's largest employer.

Being allotted the time to investigate cold cases,

Lieutenant Echols had recently been responsible for helping to convict Daniel Woloson for the murder of Susan Schumake. She was a Southern Illinois University student who was murdered August 17, 1981. Her body was found along a trail, commonly referred to as the "Ho Chi Minh Trail," which was frequented by students on their way back to the residence halls. The trail cuts across US 51 where the southernmost overpass walkway currently exists on the campus. Today the walkway contains a plaque that commemorates the current walkway in memory of Susan Schumake. As a communications major, Schumake was walking home at night from a WIDB radio station employee meeting in the Communications Building and was killed. Her roommates reported her missing that night, and her body was found two days later—apparently dragged about thirty yards off the trail.

Susan's brother, John, described her as someone who was quiet in large groups or with people she didn't know very well.

"If you knew her really well, she could be really funny and very engaging," he said. "She was a very kindhearted person. I would say that one of the words that describe her best is peacemaker."

John said that his sister enjoyed writing poetry and that she wanted to pursue a career in radio journalism. He had a lot of tapes of her preparing vocal spots for on-air journalistic reports.

About a month after Schumake's body was discovered, Timothy Krajcir, who was deemed a sexually dangerous person and recently paroled, became a viable suspect in the homicide. Police investigators interviewed Krajcir but they had no solid evidence to connect him to the crime, and he denied having any involvement with Schumake.

Echols had just joined the force seven days before Schumake was murdered, and he did not become involved in the investigation. Now he had the opportunity to look into the case, which had remained unsolved for over twenty years. Before Woloson, the primary suspect in the case was John Paul Phillips, who was sentenced for the 1981 rape and murder of Joan Wetherall and was a suspect in the murders of at least two other women. While serving a forty-year sentence, Phillips died of a heart attack in 1993. He was posthumously eliminated as a suspect in the murder of Schumake in 2002 after his body was exhumed and a DNA sample taken from the marrow of his thighbone did not match preserved vaginal swabs taken from Schumake.

Echols began to look at the history of previous suspects and spent time attempting to procure DNA samples from them. Two previous suspects in the case voluntarily provided DNA samples, and the results eliminated them from suspicion. When initially contacted, Woloson refused to provide a DNA sample, but through a twist of events his DNA was obtained. With the assistance of the Michigan State Police (MSP) and the Washtenaw County Sheriff's Department (WCSD), DNA samples were obtained from cigarette butts found in a vehicle that Woloson had recently owned. Media sources provided conflicting reports regarding the vehicle in question. One report stated that the butts were recovered from a vehicle that Woloson recently sold. Another reported that Woloson loaned his car to a prostitute, but it was never returned—the car was involved in a crime and traced back to Woloson. The first cigarette butts tested were found to be smoked by a woman. Several months later, a second set of butts were tested and the DNA proved to be a definitive match to Woloson, who was arrested on September 23, 2004. That was the date of Frank Schumake's birthday—Susan's father—but he died seven years earlier and never had the gratification of seeing justice for his daughter's murder. The evidence led to Woloson's conviction in connection with Schumake's murder. In his closing argument, Jackson County state's attorney Michael Wepsiec said that "the DNA in this case doesn't lie. The defendant is the person in this great whodunit. Daniel Woloson is the person who killed Susan Schumake."

Woloson received a forty-year sentence, but credit for good behavior and time served may mean that he could be released in less than twenty years. He continues to claim that he is innocent and is currently appealing his conviction.

It was new technology that prompted Echols to look into other unsolved cases like that of Deborah Sheppard, who was also an SIU student. According to Carbondale police chief Jeff Grubbs, Echols didn't pick Sheppard's case because of any specific reason. Grubbs said that it was part of Echols's job to investigate any open cases that remained unsolved, and the one involving Sheppard's murder was just one of several.

It was DNA evidence from Sheppard's purple shirt that Echols resubmitted for examination that linked the murder to Timothy Wayne Krajcir. According to an article in the *St. Louis Post-Dispatch,* Echols said that investigators who worked on the Sheppard crime scene twenty-five years earlier were not initially going to collect the shirt because it didn't appear to be linked to the crime. But when they turned her body over, fluid spilled out from her mouth and got on the shirt, so they decided to take it as evidence. The stained shirt was stored and preserved well enough that Echols was able to submit the evidence to the Illinois State Police Forensic Science Laboratory. A forensic scientist was able to develop a DNA profile from the stain on the shirt, which was found to contain seminal fluid. The profile that the lab technician developed was compared to the DNA profiles in the Combined DNA Index System (CODIS).

CODIS is a federally funded computer system that stores DNA profiles created by federal, state, and local crime laboratories throughout the United States, and authorities have the ability to search the database of profiles to identify suspects in crimes. In its original form, CODIS consisted of two indexes, the Convicted Offender Index and the Forensic Index. The Convicted Offender Index contains profiles of individuals already convicted of crimes. All fifty states have passed DNA legislation authorizing the collection of DNA profiles from convicted offenders for submission to CODIS. The Forensic Index contains profiles developed from biological material found at crime scenes.

A DNA profile was able to be developed from seminal fluid on the piece of clothing, and on August 9, 2007, a computerized search of CODIS revealed a match to Krajcir, who was already incarcerated at the Big Muddy River Correctional Center.

On August 21, 2007, Lieutenant Echols and Sergeant Michael Osifcin drove to Ina, Illinois, to question Krajcir in regard to the offense. During the interview, Krajcir denied having anything to do with Sheppard's murder. The next day, Echols and Osifcin pursued their questioning at a second interview. This time, knowing that the DNA evidence against him was irrefutable, Krajcir finally broke down and admitted that he had committed the crime.

Deborah Sheppard was from Olympia Fields. Deborah was the firstborn child in her family and served as a surrogate mother to her two younger siblings. She loved animals and had an interest in pursuing a career in veterinarian medicine, but when she moved to Carbondale to attend SIU, she majored in marketing.

On April 8, 1982, she was a twenty-three-year-old African American senior who looked forward to her upcoming graduation. Sheppard didn't know who Krajcir was at the time, but he was also a student at SIU, who was recently paroled despite objections from the Jackson County Prosecutor's Office. The state's attorney feared that if Krajcir was released, he had the potential to commit violent, sexual criminal offenses. His intuition proved correct.

Krajcir confessed that he broke into Sheppard's apartment and then attacked her as she came out of the shower. He said that he threw her down on the living-room floor and raped her. He said that he wore a blue bandana to cover his face, but Sheppard managed to pull it down. After the rape, he strangled her to death. Krajcir told Echols that he had to kill her because she had seen his face, and he didn't want her to be able to identify him.

In the late evening hours of April 8, Edward Cralle found the front door to Sheppard's apartment left slightly ajar. Upon entering, he found her naked body lying on the floor, and the phone cord had been cut. After her body was discovered and an autopsy was performed by Dr. Steven Nernberger, of Anderson Hospital in Maryville, Illinois, the Carbondale Police Department issued a statement that there was no indication of foul play connected with her death. Deborah's father, Bernie Sheppard, was not convinced. His daughter was happy, young, and healthy. He claimed that the original report filed by officers at the scene ruled the death as "suspicious" and a probable homicide. Bernie Sheppard also claimed that the initial report was changed under the orders of Edward Hogan, the Carbondale police chief. Sheppard said that when he asked for an explanation, he was told that it was decided that mistakes made on the initial report were subsequently corrected. Sheppard believed that it was a conspiratorial attempt to cover up the murder. He said that the police did it deliberately because there were a growing number of unsolved homicides in the area at the time, and they did not want to absorb another one.

Over the last decade, there have been many allegations made against police departments for manipulating crime statistics in order to reduce the number in incidents of violent crime. It has been documented that the Patrolmen's Benevolent Association (PBA) in New York City accused officials in 2004 of reclassifying felonies as misdemeanors, logging in rapes as "inconclusive incidents," and labeling incidents of attempted murder as simple criminal mischief. In Los Angeles, the Los Angeles Police Department (LAPD) showed a 28 percent reduction in violent crime in 2005 after they reclassified domestic assaults in which the victims suffered minor or no injuries. Several police officers in New Orleans were fired in 2003 after they were accused of downgrading incidents of violent crimes. There is no doubt that this type of unethical and often illegal behavior exists within law enforcement agencies across the country, but Sheppard had no evidence that this was the case in Illinois.

Sheppard also said that because his daughter was black, racism probably played a role in the alleged cover-up. Whether that was true or not, the fact remains that this was only conjecture on his part, and he had no proof to back up his accusation. At the time, he told the *Chicago Tribune* that he did not care how much time, money, or heartache was involved, he was going to do whatever he could to make sure that his daughter's killer was found and convicted.

Sheppard's family had her body flown to Chicago and paid to have Cook County medical examiner Robert Stein perform a second autopsy. Stein determined that she had suffered several blows to the head and was strangled to death. He also found evidence of seminal fluid inside her mouth. Sheppard's death was now considered a homicide.

Bernie Sheppard said that if it had not been for the fact that he had access to people in prominent positions, his daughter's death would have been swept under the rug as a natural-death situation, and it would have been forgotten about. Sheppard's theory of conspiracy and racism is only speculative, and during an interview in 2008, former Carbondale police chief Hogan provided a different version of the events that took place twenty-five years earlier.

Hogan said that precinct sergeant Jim Rossiter was the first police officer to arrive on the scene. After finding Sheppard's body, Rossiter called a police dispatch operator who, in turn, contacted Hogan. When Hogan arrived at the apartment building, he noted that there was no indication of a struggle. "There were no broken dishes, no broken furniture, and no injuries to the body that were discernable to the naked eye. It was a clean scene," Hogan stated.

There were four apartments in the two-story building and Sheppard lived on the ground floor on the east side of the structure. A window to the living room was found open. After Sheppard's death was ruled to be a homicide, Hogan changed his story and said that he initially suspected that the intruder entered through the open window and then waited for Sheppard to come home. He said that Carbondale police investigators collected all the evidence they could find and spent several days questioning other residents in the building and around the neighborhood.

"We did as extensive of an investigation as possible at the time, but, of course, we didn't have the expertise or equipment that is available today. No fingerprints were found at the scene, and we kept running into blind alleys with nothing breaking in our favor," Hogan said.

When asked about Sheppard's accusation that racism contributed to the hindrance of the investigation, Hogan replied that there was no prejudice on the side of the police department.

"If you know Illinois, you'll know that there are areas in and around Chicago, and then there is the rest of the state. They are two different worlds. Sheppard comes from one of the 'colored counties' and much of what he believes is just a figmentation of his hostility. I have no doubt that it appeared like that to him. He called us a bunch of hick country bumpkins that didn't know what we were doing. The fact is that we did everything we could. If we would have had the technology that exists today, things might have been different at the time, but we did collect all the evidence we found, and we were able to preserve it well enough to allow it to be used when the technology did finally become available," Hogan said. Despite Hogan's insistence that there was no element of racism that played a role, his comment about the "colored counties" might indicate otherwise. The real truth of the matter regarding racism and a possible intentional cover-up of the homicide probably lies somewhere between the perspectives of both Bernie Sheppard and Edward Hogan.

Evidence and leads may or may not have been compromised due to the passage of time between the discovery of Sheppard's body and the official declaration that it should be dealt with as a homicide, but the end result was that despite the efforts of the CPD, they were left with no suspects and no motive for the crime. A *Tribune* reporter quoted a Carbondale police officer at the time stating, "If we don't get a break and make an arrest now, we probably never will."

Once Krajcir was officially charged, Carbondale police chief Bob Ledbetter released a statement in which he quoted, "I must note that this investigation didn't sit in a box on the shelf as some might suspect. This case was always assigned to a detective over the years, and new leads would be investigated from time to time, always resulting in another frustrating dead end."

In 2007, when Echols informed Bernie Sheppard that they had at last found the man responsible for killing his daughter, Bernie said that he might finally get a bit of relief knowing who was responsible. Bernie Sheppard also said, "I want to see him executed. I want to sit right there and watch him take his last breath. . . . That's what I want."

Unfortunately for Sheppard, the state of Illinois didn't have capital punishment in 1982, so according to the statutes of law at the time the crime was committed, Krajcir would only be able to receive a maximum penalty of forty years if he was convicted.

A preliminary hearing for Krajcir was scheduled for September 28, 2007, and it was ordered that his bond remain at $1 million. The date to enter a plea actually took place on October 1, and the courtroom in the Jackson County Sheriff's Department (JCSD) fell silent as Timothy Krajcir was escorted into the room in handcuffs. Bernie Sheppard attended the hearing to see the man who had killed his daughter. He admitted that his real purpose for attending was to seek vengeance. He didn't care if it meant spending the rest of his life in prison—he wanted to kill Krajcir. Sheppard didn't bring a weapon to the hearing. He wanted to feel Krajcir die between his bare hands. The opportunity never presented itself, and with two bad legs, Bernie Sheppard probably wouldn't have been much of a match against the fit and athletic Krajcir.

Defense attorney Patricia Gross entered a tentative plea of not guilty to the judge. A pretrial date was set for November 13, when the presiding judge would decide if a bench trial or a jury trial would proceed unless a plea of guilty was entered before then. Plea negotiations could now be pursued by the prosecutor, and if an agreement could not be reached, a trial date of December 10 was scheduled.

Despite the new DNA evidence and Krajcir's confession during his interview with Echols and Osifcin, in the eyes of the law, his plea of not guilty made him innocent unless a judge or jury decided differently.

2

I've been twisted since I was a little kid. I can't blame it on anything else. The first six or seven years of my life, I was left alone too much. It twisted me. It just got worse when I grew up, I guess.

—Timothy Wayne Krajcir

Life and times of Timothy Krajcir

Despite Carbondale police chief Bob Ledbetter's efforts to suppress specifics to the media regarding the Deborah Sheppard case, Krajcir's arrest became headline news on the front page, above the fold, in newspapers across the Heartland. His history came under the scrutiny of law enforcement agencies, as well as the media. After learning of Krajcir's past, many people wondered how he could have been allowed to be free long enough to commit murder.

He was born in West Mahanoy City, Pennsylvania, on November 28, 1944, and was named Timothy Wayne McBride. His father, Charles McBride, was a WWII marine who abandoned his mother, Fern Yost, when Timothy was born. Krajcir had an unstable childhood, according to a 1983 psychological profile sent to Judge James Diefenderfer by Dr. Paul K. Gross, of Allentown, Pennsylvania. Yost moved about a dozen times while Timothy was a young boy, and she eventually gave birth to two half brothers, William and Bernie, by two different fathers.

The earliest record of crime committed by Timothy was on July 1, 1951, when he lived in Harrisburg, Pennsylvania, and was charged with petty theft for stealing a bicycle at the age of six. Yost got married again to Bernard Krajcir, who legally adopted Timothy in 1953 and gave him his last name. It was around this time that Timothy Krajcir said that he began engaging in voyeuristic activities, burglaries, fondling women in public, and secretly wearing feminine clothing. The family moved to New Milford, Pennsylvania, and fifteen-year-old Timothy was once again charged with petty theft. He was let go after making restitution for the $20 he stole.

Krajcir described his mother as cold and unaffectionate, but he recalled becoming sexually stimulated by her when she walked around the house in her negligee. During therapy he received in prison, Krajcir was told that he hated his mother, and he came to believe that those feelings were real. After further therapy, he also claimed that he had become shy and introverted during his adolescence.

The Krajcirs moved again to Wescosville, a small town just outside of Allentown, Pennsylvania. Timothy attended Emmaus High School, but he never made it to graduation. Instead, in 1962, he enlisted in the U.S. Navy Reserve at the age of seventeen. He was sent to Great Lakes, Illinois, for basic training.

During his short stint in the navy, Krajcir met Barbara Jean Kos, a seventeen-year-old girl from Milwaukee, Wisconsin. When Kos became pregnant, she married Krajcir on February 2, 1963, but continued to live with her parents. In May of that year, Krajcir was arrested in North Chicago for attempted rape. Three weeks later, Krajcir's daughter was born while he was still in jail. In July, Krajcir pleaded guilty to the rape of Joan Terrill in North Chicago, which took place just several weeks after he got married. He also pleaded guilty to the rape and stabbing of Joyce Erdal in Waukegan, Illinois. He was sentenced to serve twenty-five to fifty years inside Joliet Prison and given an undesirable discharge from the navy. During his 1963 interrogation, Krajcir also admitted to breaking into and robbing at least a half-dozen homes while he was a juvenile living in Wescosville.

Krajcir was transferred to Menard Correctional Center in 1969 and was allowed to take college classes free via a program offered through Southern Illinois University. He was transferred again in 1972 to the Vienna Correctional Center where taxpayer dollars allowed him to obtain an A.S. degree from Shawnee Community College. Krajcir utilized his education in 1974 to obtain work as an inmate emergency medical technician at Cairo PADCO Community Hospital. The next year, he worked as an inmate EMT at Union County Hospital in Anna, Illinois.

After serving thirteen years of his sentence, in 1976, Krajcir was paroled. He moved to Carbondale and began to attend classes in criminal justice and psychology at SIU. He acquired employment as an ambulance driver for the Jackson County Ambulance Service.

Robert Grove had an old, empty trailer behind his house on his property at North Springer Street. Krajcir rented it from Grove, and he seemed to live a quiet life with much of his time consumed by work and school. His coworkers used words such as "quiet," "gentle," and "a sweet guy" to describe him. Krajcir was discharged from parole on July 20, 1978.

Police records show that before the end of that year, Krajcir was arrested again. He was charged with public indecency at a Wal-Mart parking lot, but the case was dismissed and the details of his actions were not included in the records.

Carbondale police officers arrested Krajcir on February 20, 1979, and he was charged with indecent liberties with a child. Krajcir had been engaging in sexual activities with Maria, his landlord's thirteen-year-old daughter. These activities had taken place on several occasions, and on at least one occasion, they occurred in the presence of Grove's other daughter, Barbara, who was only twelve years old at the time.

Years later, Barbara explained the circumstances surrounding the incident. She said that their parents had split up in 1976 and that their mother had moved out of the house to live with their grandmother. She said that their father worked a lot of hours and was often not around. When Krajcir moved into the small trailer on the back of their property, the girls began to spend an increasing amount of time with him, especially Maria. Krajcir appeared harmless, friendly, and he paid attention to them. Maria was young, naïve and a bit impetuous. She enjoyed the attention of an older man. Barbara said that at the time, she and her sister suffered from physical but not sexual abuse by their father. Maria was able to confide in Krajcir and talk about her problems without fear of judgment. Because Krajcir seemed genuinely interested in what she had to say, Maria began to think of herself as an adult. She eventually gave in to his persistent sexual advances, which usually took place in Krajcir's trailer, but on occasion occurred in the basement of the house. According to her sister, Maria became enamored with Krajcir. Barbara said that there was one time when Maria saw a young woman with strawberry blond hair enter Krajcir's trailer, and she expressed strong feelings of jealousy. She was a love-struck teenager who was blind to the fact that she was being taken advantage of by a man who was nearly three times her age. Years later, Barbara speculated that the strawberry blonde was a college girl named Sheila Cole, whom Krajcir was eventually convicted of raping and murdering. The girls never saw her again after that one visit.

Barbara said that one day she and her sister were alone with Krajcir. Not only was he kissing and feeling up Maria, but he also began to touch Barbara in ways that made her feel uncomfortable. Barbara later told her mother about the incident and she reported it to the police after it came out that Krajcir had been having an ongoing sexual relationship with Maria for nearly two years. Their mother gained full custody of both girls in 1979 and they moved to Texas for a period of time.

According to Barbara, life did not improve much. Maria was allowed to date a nineteen-year-old boy when she was still thirteen. When she was fifteen years old, Maria dropped out of school because she became pregnant by a classmate. Her mother let her marry a man twice her age, and by the time she was twenty-one, Maria ended up having seven pregnancies and three miscarriages.

While Krajcir was in custody, a warrant to search the trailer he rented from Grove was issued. During a search of the bedroom closet, police recovered a .38-caliber five-shot Charter Arms revolver in a box, along with a receipt for the gun, which was sold to someone named Beverlee Pappas. Bullets for the gun were also discovered. Also found was a .25-caliber Raven Arms model P-25 handgun and an accompanying clip. Police also confiscated a glass jar, one-third full with what appeared to be cannabis. Under the conditions of his parole, it was unlawful for Krajcir to have possession of any guns.

With the aid of his employer, Krajcir was able to bond out of jail after only two days.

On April 25, 1979, Howard L. Hood, Illinois state's attorney of Jackson County, filed a petition to commit Krajcir as a "sexually dangerous person." The petition stated that Krajcir was a person suffering from a mental disorder coupled with criminal propensities to the commission of sexual offenses, which had included sexual assault and acts of sexual molestation of children.

The petition also asked the court to appoint two qualified psychiatrists to make a personal examination of Krajcir in order to ascertain whether he was a sexually dangerous person. It took four months to get through the bureaucracy of the justice system, but on August 23, 1979, Judge Richman officially declared Krajcir to be listed as the region's first "sexually dangerous person." After enjoying six months of freedom, Krajcir was committed to the Illinois Department of Corrections (DOC), where he was ordered to receive psychiatric treatment to help control his sexual deviancy.

During one psychotherapy session, Krajcir said that he enjoyed his sexual relationship with the thirteen-year-old girl because she would be pliable to his sexual demands and made him feel more masculine. Krajcir was told that his abuse of other women was his way of acting out his anger toward his own mother, and that he used violence to punish those who made him feel sexually inadequate.

Krajcir became an active and enthusiastic participant in group therapy sessions. On December 31, 1980, just sixteen months after being declared a sexually dangerous person, attorney John Ryan asked the court for Krajcir's release from incarceration. Dr. Frank M. Perez evaluated Krajcir for his potential release. He concluded that Krajcir was no longer prone to commit chronic violence, and that he was now able to exercise control over his behavior. His evaluation reported that the chance of Krajcir committing any future violent crimes was low.

Despite opposition from State's Attorney John Clemons, Krajcir was released from prison June 4, 1981, by order of Judge Richman. His release was dependent on certain conditions, one of which was that Krajcir was to attend SIU and complete his degree in criminal justice. Krajcir was paroled, but it was his later violation of the conditions of his parole that forced his return to the Illinois DOC in 1988, and allowed investigators to easily interview him and ultimately convict him of mulitiple rapes and murders, twenty-five years later.

In December, Krajcir graduated with a B.S. in administration of justice and a minor in psychology—taxpayer dollars hard at work. In April 1982, Deborah Sheppard was found dead. Twenty-five years later, Lieutenant Echols was convinced that he had finally found the man responsible for her murder. It was now up to a judge or jury to decide if he was correct.

3

Mary and Brenda Parsh
August 12, 1977

Floyd Parsh clutched his chest. He gasped for air. It felt like the weight of the world was pressing down on him. His life was being crushed out of his body. It was a heart attack. He knew it. It was something that was prevalent in his bloodline. It was inevitable and, of course, inconvenient. He knew that the consequences would be significant, even life-threatening. If he had lived a thousand more years, Floyd would never have anticipated just how much his life was about to change. As his heart failed to function, he feared the idea of losing his life and his connection with his loved ones. He did lose that connection, but not because he died. It was his wife and daughter that ended up losing their lives. Floyd's heart never recovered from that.

After receiving word that Floyd was hospitalized at the Southeast Missouri (SEMO) Hospital and was recovering from open-heart surgery, Brenda Parsh booked a flight from Milwaukee, Wisconsin, to St. Louis, Missouri. From there, she would travel south to Cape Girardeau so she could be with her father.

Brenda's boyfriend, Richard McGougan, lived in St. Louis at the time. He said that Brenda called him to let him know that she would be flying in on Friday, and if time permitted, they might be able to get together for dinner before she went to Cape Girardeau.

"I wasn't sure what time her flight was getting in, so Brenda called me when she arrived at the airport. She said that she had just talked with her mother, who expressed that she was very concerned about Floyd's condition," McGougan said. "Brenda decided that we would not have time to meet because she wanted to take the next commuter flight out to Cape as soon as possible."

It was the last conversation that Richard had with Brenda.

It was a short hop between St. Louis and Cape Girardeau, only 120 miles. Her plane arrived at 9:38 P.M. It took less than ten minutes to retrieve her luggage and then Brenda met her mother, Mary, who had come to pick her up.

Due to the situation they were now confronted with, the usual banter between mother and daughter was replaced by a long, uncomfortable silence during the short drive to Floyd and Mary's house on Koch Street. Police reports estimate that they would have arrived at around 10:00 P.M., barring any stops or delays.

The blanket of night did little to stifle the heat of the August sun, which beat down with a vengeance for days and had elevated temperatures to the upper 90s.

Mary Parsh pulled her car into the driveway in front of her house. After turning the air-conditioning and fan dials on her dashboard console to the off position, she twisted the ignition key backward to stop the engine. Mary and her daughter Brenda unbuckled the seat belts that were strapped across their midsections and then took a deep breath of cool air before opening their doors to enter the lingering heat and humidity outside. Little did they know that someone was already waiting inside the house they were about to enter. The intruder was waiting for Mary to return home. He wasn't expecting a guest, but when they arrived, he altered his plans to accommodate both of them.

Brenda and her mother got out of the car. They each grabbed a suitcase from the backseat of the vehicle before they shut the doors to the car, and on the life that they had both once cherished.

They walked forward and Mary slid her key into the lock of the front door. With a slight twist of her wrist, the door opened and they both stepped inside. Neither Mary nor Brenda was prepared for the possibility that Floyd might die. They didn't know what to say to each other or how to act. The usual conversation between them that sometimes consumed hours and consisted of nothing pertinent at all seemed strained as they struggled for something to say to each other. It did not last long, though. As soon as they passed through the doorway, there was something else that they were not prepared for. Now they were confronted with something more immediate and even more terrifying than the thought of the death of Mary's husband and Brenda's father. It was the reality that their own lives were in jeopardy. More frightening was the possibility of what they might have to endure before they gave up their lives.

Inside the house, an intruder sat waiting. He wore a blue bandana over his face so that just his eyes and the top of his head were visible. He expected the return of Mary Parsh, a fifty-eight-year-old woman who wouldn't be able to put up much of a fight, and therefore become an easy victim. Instead, he got Mary, as well as her young and physically fit daughter Brenda. He would have to deal with Brenda first in order to eliminate any problems that might occur due to her unexpected presence.

When he heard the car pull into the driveway, the intruder moved to the front door. Adrenaline coursed through his body as he listened to the key enter the lock to release the bolt. The door opened and he confronted Mary and Brenda as soon as they stepped inside. Mary never even had an opportunity to pull the keys out of the front door's lock.

They were led to the master bedroom at gunpoint and their hands were tied behind their backs. Their assailant pulled his bandana down around his neck and forced Brenda to perform oral sex on him. Then he raped her on the bed while her mother lay beside her, helpless and scared. The gruesome details of what Mary and Brenda had to endure would never be fully known by anyone other than the man who committed the crimes.

The phone might have rung several times during the ordeal. It was certain that at least one phone call was made. Somehow, Brenda was able to convince her rapist to allow her to answer it. The caller on the other end of the line was Floyd. She barely got to speak for a full minute when the intruder hung up the receiver. At least she got to tell her father that she loved him.

The gun that was pointed toward Brenda's head blasted a bullet into the back of her skull. Her mother trembled beside her raped and murdered daughter. It is nearly impossible to imagine what thoughts must have been going through her mind. A second gunshot blurted out and penetrated the pillow that Mary's head rested on, but it did not hit her.

Thinking that he had just killed both women, the intruder went into the other room. He rifled through a purse and took some money out of a desk in the den. He heard Mary crying, came back into the bedroom, and then squeezed off a third round. This time he made sure that Mary was dead.

McGougan claims that he called the house sometime between 8:30 and 11:00 P.M. but got no answer, so he decided to go to sleep and try again in the morning. Floyd called from the hospital after Mary and Brenda failed to show up to visit him. His call was the one that did get answered.

Sergeant John Brown, of the Cape Girardeau Police Department (CGPD) said Floyd told him that when Brenda answered the phone, he sensed that something was wrong right away.

"Floyd said that Brenda's voice was shaky, nervous, and she spoke with too much formality," Brown related.

Police speculate that during the time of the phone conversation, Brenda was already tied up and probably had a gun pointed at her head. Brenda told her father that they would not be able to visit him then because she was too tired. Floyd remembered asking, "Where is your mother?"

Without answering the question, Brenda told her father that she loved him. Floyd heard a click, which was replaced by the ominous sound of a dial tone.

As the hours passed on Saturday, and then through the entire day of Sunday, Floyd became increasingly worried that he had not heard from his wife and daughter. He called the house several times after they had not turned up to visit or even make contact with him. Brenda's boyfriend, Richard, called the house periodically throughout those two days without response. Floyd and Mary's other daughter, Karen, also called multiple times, and she became worried when nobody answered. She finally contacted her mother's neighbor and asked her to check in on Mary.

Mary's neighbor walked next door and found that the front door to the Parsh house was slightly ajar, with a set of keys still dangling from the lock. An overpowering stench of death filled the small house. The neighbor found two bodies inside, which were later identified as Mary and Brenda Parsh. A call to the police department was made.

"We received a call from a concerned neighbor very early on Monday, August fifteenth, when she noticed that there was a set of keys still inserted into the lock of Mary Parsh's front door, but nobody answered to repeated knocks on the door or ringing the doorbell," said Henry Gerecke. He was the Cape Girardeau police chief at the time.

Floyd was recovering from open-heart surgery and had been told not to become overly stressed emotionally just before he received the news that his wife and daughter had been murdered while he was in the hospital. A cardiologist, Dr. C. R. Talbert Jr., was not the physician who was treating Floyd at Southeast Missouri Hospital, but he was working there that day and was left with the unpleasant task of delivering the news.

"Mr. Parsh sat there quietly and took it in. He was obviously very upset, but he held it all inside. I believe that he already knew," Talbert said.

It was early Monday morning when Brenda's sister, Karen, called McGougan's father to tell him what happened, and, in turn, Richard's father called him to relay the news. Richard said that he was devastated and became almost dysfunctional. He ended up moving back to his parents' house while he struggled to deal with the circumstances.

When Chief Gerecke and his team arrived at the scene, they weren't prepared for what they were about to find when they entered the Parsh home. Just inside the front door were several suitcases, which were identified as belonging to Brenda.

"We entered the house and I remember that the stench was intolerable. I immediately opened up lines with the press and asked them to film the crime scene because we didn't have the capability to do that. They were gracious enough to do it for us and give us the tape without exposing it to the public," Gerecke said.

The victims were found naked and lying side by side on a bed with their hands tied behind their backs. Their clothes were neatly folded on a nearby chair. Their bodies were extremely bloated, black, and full of flies and maggots. During the August heat wave, nearly three days of exposure to extreme temperatures accelerated the decomposition process so rapidly that their insides began to turn to gelatin and their tongues protruded through swollen lips.

"I spent thirty-five years in the military and studied criminal justice, but I never encountered anything like this. I'm not ashamed to admit that I was out of my element and needed help," Gerecke said.

Evidence technician Ron Thomas took over the crime scene to collect evidence, while Gerecke, Brown, and other police officers canvassed the neighborhood to gather any information they could.

Brown said that they questioned everyone in the neighborhood but didn't receive much useful information other than the fact that nobody had seen Mary in a couple of days. They were told that Mary expected a visit from her daughter, which was helpful in identifying Brenda's body.

On several occasions throughout the day, Brown returned to the Parsh home to see if any new developments were discovered by the evidence technician.

"I can look at just about anything, and have seen hundreds of autopsies, but this was unbearable. The smell was intolerable. I would make it as far as the middle of the living room, and then I'd have to turn around and go out to the front yard to throw up. This happened several times, until there was nothing left to come up except dry heaves," Brown recalled.

When Brown was finally able to make his way into the back bedroom, Thomas, the evidence technician, was standing over the bodies and eating a sandwich without any difficulty at all.

It was discovered that a bedroom window was broken and then left open. It was determined that this was the intruder's point of entry into the house. A faint partial print of a tennis shoe on the hardwood floor of the bedroom was captured on film by cross-lighting the dust on the floor. Both bodies had their hands tied behind their backs with an electrical cord, which was cut from a clock in the bedroom. An electrical burn on the cord indicated that the clock must have been plugged in when the cord was cut. Investigators later duplicated this procedure and discovered that when cutting a cord from a plugged-in appliance with a pocketknife, an arc would burn a mark into the blade. This was a minor detail, but if a suspect was found possessing a knife with a similar mark, it might be able to be used as evidence.

Mary's keys were still in the front door. Saturday's mail was still in the mailbox. The Friday newspaper was inside the house, but the Sunday paper was still outside. The contents of Mary's purse were dumped on the living-room couch so the intruder probably stole anything valuable that he might have found in it, but no other jewelry in the house or on the bodies was disturbed, indicating that robbery was probably not the killer's motivation. The hall light was left on. A large floor fan situated in the doorway of the bedroom was left on, and the airflow was directed toward the bed, where Mary and Brenda were found.

There was a large amount of blood on the bedding beneath the heads of each of the victims, and a large amount of blood had soaked through to form pools of dry blood on the floor beneath the bed. There was a single bullet wound in the back of each victim's head. An additional bullet was found, which had penetrated the pillowcase beside Mary's head. Ligature marks were also burned around Brenda's neck, as if she had been strangled at some point during the assault.

After Thomas completed his investigation, the bodies were removed and transported to the Ford and Sons Funeral Home for autopsy.

One neighbor, Mr. Blattel, who lived about two blocks away, said that he heard several gunshots fired on Friday night, sometime after eleven.

With the evidence collected at the crime scene, the testimony of neighbors, and Floyd's phone call, police attempted to re-create the horrific events that took place. It wasn't difficult to determine an approximate time of death. Eventually they decided that Mary and Brenda were confronted immediately upon entering the house. They were forced to undress. They speculated that one of them was forced at gunpoint to tie up the other, and then the intruder tied up the second one. Police believed that while both victims were bound beside each other, Brenda was raped and then shot in the back of her head in front of her mother. Krajcir fired a second shot, but missed Mary's head. It wasn't until later, police speculated, that Krajcir heard Mary crying. He came back into the bedroom and made certain that his third bullet accurately hit its mark at the back of her skull.

Because of the advanced decomposition of the bodies, an autopsy provided no further clues to help identify their killer. DNA technology did not exist at the time. Mary and Brenda Parsh received a closed-casket funeral service in Cape Girardeau and then were buried in Alton Cemetery.

Background checks on Mary and Brenda revealed nothing that would target them to be executed. They were liked by everyone who knew them, and neither of them had any steamy secrets or was involved in any

criminal activities. The evidence collected did little
more than determine the time of death and provided
no clues to a suspect in the murders.

Feeling overwhelmed, Gerecke contacted Lieutenant Colonel Dougherty, the chief of detectives at
the St. Louis Metropolitan Police Department
(SLMPD), on Tuesday. He explained the case and
asked for assistance. Captain Jacobsmeyer, chief of
the St. Louis Homicide Division, readily agreed to
send two men from his department to Cape Girardeau. Sergeant Tom Rowane and Detective Colin
McCoy traveled south to Cape on Wednesday, and
they stayed for about two weeks.

After reviewing the case file and accompanying
Cape investigators on interviews, the St. Louis homicide investigators were unable to solve the case.
They told Brown and Gerecke that they had done
everything that could be done and even more.

"They told us not to get too stressed out about it
because we were living this twenty-four hours a day.
They said we should put it aside, and that something would eventually turn up," Brown said.

With no other leads to pursue, Richard McGougan, Brenda's boyfriend, became the number one
suspect.

"Homicide investigators from both St. Louis and
Cape Girardeau came to interrogate me. It was gru-
eling. I asked for an attorney, but they denied me
the ability to contact one," McGougan claimed.

He said that he was rigorously grilled for more
than ten hours and forced to look at explicit
crime scene photos, which nearly made him sick.
McGougan claimed that he had to endure every
police interrogation trick in the book, including

the good cop/bad cop scenario. He said that in order to provoke an admission of guilt, he was told that the police had recovered the gun used in the crime and that his fingerprints were on it. (His interrogators don't recall using this tactic.)

McGougan told the police that he was living with his brother in St. Louis and spent Friday night there. He gave the names of his brother and four other men, who were visiting to make plans for an upcoming weight-lifting competition, as witnesses to his whereabouts during the time of the murders. He also agreed to take a lie detector test at the conclusion of his interrogation. The test showed no evidence of deception on McGougan's part. Several days later, McGougan's brother and his friends were questioned by police investigators. They confirmed that he was in St. Louis at the time of the murders.

When Floyd was released from the hospital, he did not return home directly. Instead, he spent some time in a convalescent home on Sprigg Street, across the street from the Cape Girardeau Police Department.

McGougan was emotionally devastated by Brenda's death. They had been in a relationship together for eight years since they met at Southeast Missouri State University, known as SEMO State University. They intended to get married and eventually move to New York City, where McGougan planned to pursue his acting career. Instead, Brenda was murdered, and Richard became an outcast when he became an object of suspicion and a target for the police and the media.

* * *

Brenda Parsh was an American beauty, with beautiful eyes. She had full lips, which framed a wide open smile of perfectly aligned teeth, which sparkled in ivory whiteness. Her long brunette locks accented the features of her oval face and fell down gently below her shoulders. Her longtime friend Vicki Abernathy described Brenda as the living embodiment of a Barbie doll.

"The thing about Brenda was that she was so strikingly beautiful without even trying, but she didn't even know it herself," said Abernathy. "She wasn't a wild partier and wasn't a snobbish girl hung up on her looks. She was a levelheaded humanitarian, who was nonjudgmental and pure as snow on the inside."

Brenda grew up as a child in a hardworking blue-collar family that struggled to make ends meet, but they kept the values of love, honesty, family, and friendship as a priority. Despite the Parsh family's meager lifestyle, Brenda developed a love for clothes and fashion. She was also very adept at accentuating her natural beauty with makeup, and she was not afraid to be seen without any.

By the time Brenda attended high school, it became obvious that she was destined to become noticed for her beauty—whether she wanted to or not. She took advantage of the situation by entering the world of local beauty contests. She easily won the local title of Cape Girardeau's Watermelon Queen.

She enrolled in classes at Southeast Missouri State University and majored in theater. It was there that Brenda met Richard McGougan, a fellow drama student. Richard was a freshman when they met in 1969 and Brenda was a year ahead of him. Brenda got a job at the University Shop with Vicki Abernathy, who was another theater major and beauty queen. Despite the fact that Vicki was from the neighboring town of Jackson, she said that she became friends with Brenda while they were still in high school. She described their union as "Brenda, the mysterious brunette, and Vicki, the wild blonde. We bonded instantly and worked together selling clothes, designing window displays, and modeling."

In a sense, Vicki and Brenda were pioneers in the modeling industry as some of the first women to pose as live models in the storefront windows. They would pose as still as logs for hours at a time, but Vicki admits to occasionally winking at a passerby or flashing a bit more skin than what was deemed appropriate. Eventually they even organized their own catwalk events for the University Shop.

While Brenda's father, Floyd, remained quietly proud of his daughter's accomplishment, staying in the background of the crowd, mother Mary remained outwardly supportive. As an unacknowledged but very talented seamstress, Mary designed and made by hand almost all of the gowns that her daughter Brenda wore for beauty competitions. Brenda advanced through the beauty queen path until she competed for the Missouri state title, which would qualify the winner to compete for the title of Miss America. She ended up as first runner-up, but Brenda would never have a chance to compete again.

"She never thought that she was beautiful. She loved clothes and the fashion world. She entered contests hoping to win scholarship money for school, not for some ego trip. One of the things that I loved most about Brenda was the fact that even though she was this tame, 'always do what's right' girl, who didn't have any desire to experiment with the party and sexual scene of the late 1960s, she was never judgmental. I could tell her anything and know that she would still be my friend. She was the greatest," Abernathy said.

Vicki Abernathy was two years older than Brenda. Although both girls were beautiful and interested in theater, fashion, and modeling, Vicki moved on to become a flight attendant for Braniff International Airways. Her beauty queen days were over, but not without fond memories. She was able to attend college on a twirling scholarship, and was so talented at it that she performed at the 1971 Super Bowl V, where the Baltimore Colts overpowered the Dallas Cowboys.

Brenda remained focused on her passion for fashion. After graduating from college, she obtained employment as a fashion buyer and designer of window displays for Famous-Barr department stores, now Macy's, in St. Louis. She continued to appreciate acting and the theater, but as a levelheaded realist, she did not expect to be able to make a living in that occupation. She loved performing on the stage. Hedda Gabler was a favorite play of hers, and one in which she performed during her college years. Although separated from the adventurous Vicki by time and distance, the two girls kept in touch. Brenda even attended Vicki's wedding, once Vicki finally settled down a bit and decided to create a lifetime union with one man.

Brenda was happy for Vicki and her newfound love, but Vicki was less enthusiastic about Brenda's choice for a mate.

"There is no doubt that Brenda's boyfriend loved her, but he became completely obsessed with her. If there was ever a fatal attraction, that was it," Vicki said.

According to Richard McGougan, this statement may have been an emotional reaction to his suspected involvement in Brenda's murder.

"Brenda had lots of friends. Vicki was one of them, but she certainly was not her best friend," McGougan said.

Richard said that he finished school and he and Brenda remained committed to each other. They intended to marry and eventually move to New York City, where Richard planned to pursue his acting career.

Brenda was offered a job at the Grand Department Store in Milwaukee and wanted to accept it. Richard and Brenda discussed their options and mutually agreed to postpone their wedding, but not indefinitely. Richard moved to Los Angeles to work as an actor and Brenda took the position in Wisconsin. For about a year and a half, they maintained a long-distance relationship with occasional visits. The strain became too much, and Richard moved back to St. Louis, where he still had contacts to continue acting and would have a closer proximity to Brenda. The fact that they had still not followed through with their marriage plans, and they continued to find reasons to live in different states from each other, decreased the validity of their intention to remain committed to each other. Still, Richard maintained that their love for each other was as strong as ever.

* * *

Floyd eventually recovered from the physical injuries to his heart and he left the convalescent home on Sprigg Street to return to his empty house. It was the emotional injury that Floyd could never recover from. According to Sergeant Brown, Floyd would spend much of his time sitting in a rocking chair with a loaded shotgun by his side, waiting and praying that the person who stole his family's lives would someday return.

Without any other evidence or leads, McGougan remained on the police investigator's short list as a possible suspect for years. Because of that, he removed himself from the life he was familiar with, and finally moved to New York in 1979 in an effort to escape suspicion, to pursue his acting career, and to try to put this episode of his life behind him.

Without placing blame on the incident or excusing self-responsibility, McGougan admitted that for the next several years he indulged in drug use and heavy drinking, which might have been a result of the depression that was brought on by Brenda's murder and the accusations that he might have been responsible for the crime. He wasn't raped or murdered, but McGougan—like Floyd, Vicki, and many others— became a victim of the real perpetrator's actions.

Floyd later died of complications related to his heart condition, and he was never able to have the satisfaction of finding out who was responsible for killing the people he loved most in his life. It was the phone call that he made long ago, in August 1977, that proved to be a critical piece of evidence for linking the killer to the crime.

Thirty years later, after the murderer confessed to the crime, police authorities kept saying that

they would not officially press criminal charges
in connection with the deaths of Mary and Brenda
Parsh unless there was positive proof that he was
guilty. It's the "Show Me" state. The killer was the
only surviving person who would have had knowledge about the phone call that Floyd made to Mary
from the hospital. It was his mention of this call
that sealed his confession of guilt. There was no
possible way that he could have known about that
call unless he was there. There was no longer any
doubt about the perpetrator of the crime. Unfortunately, because so much time had passed, the
number of living relatives who benefited from his
confessions of at least nine murders all across the
country has been reduced, but the number of people
that these victims have had an influence on may
be uncountable.

Floyd went to his grave without ever having the
satisfaction of discovering the identity of the person
who murdered his wife and daughter. He never saw
justice prevail, and he never had closure. He died
of a broken heart.

When investigators announced publicly in 2007
that Timothy Wayne Krajcir had confessed to the
crime, McGougan was relieved that closure would
finally take place. Still, he was disappointed that
Krajcir was able to escape the death penalty in exchange for his confession.

"Krajcir stole the lives of decent, wonderful people,
but there are other lives, the lives of those who lived
on, which were also negatively impacted because of
his actions. Justice would be best served if he (Krajcir) would be executed," McGougan stated.

4

Sheila Cole
November 1977

Cape Girardeau is often described as a big town or a small city, depending on one's point of view. It hosts a plentiful stock of hotels and motels, bars, and hundreds of choices of places to eat, from fast-food chains to fine-dining establishments. There is a downtown that caters to tourists with a desire to explore American history as well as to the college students who attend the Southeast Missouri State University. There is plenty of free downtown parking available for people who want to visit the unique shops, galleries, and pubs that are nestled along the banks of the Mississippi River. What was not generally plentiful were horrific crimes of murder.

On November 17, 1977, just three months after the Parsh murders, a SEMO State University student was found dead. She was discovered at a rest stop along Illinois Route 3, just south of McClure, Illinois. Her fully clothed body was lying faceup on the floor in the women's restroom, with two .38-caliber gunshot wounds in her head.

A passing motorist who pulled over at the rest stop discovered the body and anonymously called 911 to report it. Deputy Kenneth Calvert, of the Alexander County Sheriff's Department (ACSD) in Cairo, Illinois, was the first to arrive on the scene. He saw the body of a fully clothed white female lying faceup on the floor at the north side of the restroom. A wound was clearly visible on the victim's head, where a large quantity of blood had pooled around it. It did not take long for other officers from the sheriff's department to arrive.

The scene was photographed and processed by Special Agents Gary Ashman and Connell Smith, of the Illinois Division of the Federal Bureau of Investigation. One bullet was found lodged in the north wall of the restroom. A second was recovered from the floor underneath the victim. Two partial footprints were found near a trash container. A woman's purse was discovered inside the trash can. The purse contained a photo driver's license belonging to twenty-one-year-old Sheila Cole, of Crest Oak Lane in Crestwood, Missouri. Also inside the purse was a checkbook. The last entry, dated November 16, was in the amount of $8.97 for a purchase from a Wal-Mart store. Other items recovered from her purse included credit cards, traveler's checks, a small amount of cash, and some personal items. The motive for her murder was obviously not robbery. There was also a Wal-Mart sales catalog in the purse, which was addressed to Sheila Cole, residing on Sprigg Street, in Cape Girardeau, Missouri.

Once all the evidence was collected from the

scene, Alexander County coroner Thomas Bradshaw had the body removed and transported to the Crain-Barkett Funeral Home in Cairo, Illinois.

The Cape Girardeau police were notified of Cole's murder and were told that she had been living in an apartment located on Sprigg Street, directly across from the police department, and, coincidentally, next door to the convalescent home where Floyd Parsh temporarily lived after his wife and daughter were murdered.

Special Agents Ashman and Smith were accompanied to the Sprigg Street address by Cape Girardeau patrolman Ronald Thomas. When they knocked on the door, they were greeted by Joan Barnard. Barnard said that she shared the apartment with Sheila, Connie Walker, and Jan Gredizer. They were all students at Southeast Missouri State University.

Barnard told the investigators that the last time she saw Sheila was at about 3:30 P.M. the previous day in the apartment. Barnard said that Sheila left at that time to go see her boyfriend, Matthew Sopko, a student who lived in a dormitory on campus. She also told them that Sheila's bed had not been slept in, and her light blue Chevy Nova was gone.

Cape Girardeau police captain William Stover was able to get a thorough description of Sheila's car, along with its vehicle identification and license plate numbers, by contacting the university's security police. The Illinois State Police (ISP) then dispatched that information with a notice that the vehicle should be secured for fingerprints if it was found.

When Matthew Sopko was interviewed, he said that Sheila had picked him up at the dormitory at around 4:00 P.M. and that they went to get something to eat at McDonald's, and then did some shopping at the Kroger grocery store. Sopko told the investigators that Sheila dropped him back off at the dormitory about an hour later, and that he had not seen or heard from her since. His roommate, William Doyle, confirmed that story. He said that Sopko had been dropped off by Sheila at around 5:00 P.M., and he and Sopko were together until around midnight. Doyle stated that Sopko spent a lot of time at Sheila's apartment—sometimes as many as three or four nights a week. He also provided investigators with a note that he found on Sopko's desk. The note read, *Sheila, I love you with all my heart. There is nothing I wouldn't do for you, but there is nothing that I can do for you. I guess you need me like a hole in the head.*

John Boyce, who lived in an apartment in the same building as Sheila, said that he remembered seeing her car parked in front of the building sometime between five-thirty and six o'clock that evening.

Gredizer, Sheila's other roommate, said that she was studying at the kitchen table when Sheila left the apartment again, at around 7:30 P.M., to go to Wal-Mart and pick up some film she had developed there.

Throughout all of these and many other interviews, the timeline of Sheila's whereabouts remained unbroken. Every minute of November 16 was accounted for, until she had gone to pick up her photos. She was never seen alive again by anyone other than her killer. Sopko laid eyes on her one more time. He was asked to come to the Crain-Barkett Funeral Home to identify her corpse. Later that evening, Dr. Cornelio Katubig, of Marion, Illinois, performed an autopsy in front of the coroner and Special Agents Ashman and Smith.

DNA technology didn't exist in 1977. One of the main purposes of an autopsy was to determine the cause and time of death, not to collect other evidence to solve a murder. In Sheila Cole's case, the cause of death was determined to be a result of a gunshot wound to the back of the neck and one to the right side of the bridge of the nose. The autopsy report provided no other information except that there was no evidence of injury to her external genitalia.

Sergeant Brown, of the Cape Girardeau Police Department, said that the hurried process of the autopsy and the embalming of Sheila Cole's body were detrimental to discovering any possible physical evidence that might have led them to a suspect. He said that the body was embalmed even before some investigating authorities were notified of her death. As a result, physical evidence that would have been beneficial may have been lost.

Patrolman Sam Light reported for duty at 11:00 P.M. on November 17. During his shift, he reported that he observed a blue Chevy Nova in the Wal-Mart parking lot. Detective John Brown relayed this information to the Federal Bureau of Investigation (FBI), and late the next morning, on November 18, Special Agents Ashman and Smith located a light blue 1976 Chevy Nova in the Wal-Mart parking lot located on South Kings Highway in Cape Girardeau. (Today it is a Hobby Lobby store.) The serial number and license plate matched Cole's car. The keys were left in the ignition, and the driver's door was unlocked. It had rained during the evening of

November 16, and the windshield wipers were left in the on position. A paper bag in the trunk of the vehicle contained photographs that were recently developed at Wal-Mart and a sales receipt totaling $8.97, corresponding with the last notation in Sheila Cole's checkbook.

An employee at the nearby Service Laundromat told investigators that she left work at approximately 10:45 on the evening on November 16 and that she believed that the blue Nova was parked in the Wal-Mart lot at that time.

A Wal-Mart employee told Brown that at about 10:30 A.M. on November 17, she heard a page over the store's public-address system asking for the owner of a blue 1976 Nova to go to the service desk. Apparently, nobody showed up.

The entire car was processed for the collection of evidence. Items sent to the Southeast Missouri Crime Laboratory for examination included hairs found in the vehicle, the floor mats, a gum wrapper, and the contents of the ashtray. No fingerprints were found on the cigarette butts or the gum wrapper. There were only two brands of cigarettes found in the ashtray; the brand that Sheila smoked and that of her boyfriend, Matthew. Hair samples found in the car matched those of Sheila, Matthew, and Sheila's roommate Connie Walker.

Sergeant John Brown, of the Cape Girardeau Police Department, said that he had no reason to believe that the murder of Sheila Cole was related to the Parsh murders, but for good measure, bullets retrieved from the Parsh house were sent to the FBI lab in Washington, DC, for comparison.

A white pair of panties belonging to Cole was sent

to the Bureau of Scientific Services in DeSoto, Illinois, for analysis. No hair or fibers were found. The crotch area was heavily stained, but chemical tests failed to confirm if that was caused by seminal fluid.

No further lab work was authorized unless additional evidence became available. After dozens of additional interviews, up to this point, investigators in both Missouri and Illinois had exhausted their leads, and they still were no closer to discovering who was responsible for the murders. That did not deter them from continuing to investigate every avenue available, no matter how insignificant it appeared.

One witness, Jess Norton, claimed that he had been traveling north on Illinois Route 3 at around 11:00 P.M. after he crossed the Mississippi River from Missouri and entered Illinois. He said that the blue midsized car in front of him pulled into the rest stop where Cole was murdered. He described the passengers as a male and a female, and his description of the female was similar to that of Sheila Cole. He was subsequently hypnotized by an FBI investigator and repeated the same information.

There was no physical evidence at the time to prove that Cole was a victim of rape. Robbery was ruled out because the killer had not taken the traveler's checks from her purse. Because there was so little evidence left at the scene, authorities could not even confirm if Cole's assailant was a man or a woman. Special Agent Ashman was quoted by the Missourian newspaper as saying, "People must realize that we have to have something to work on. We're not miracle workers who can pull a suspect out of thin air."

With no apparent motive in the slaying, investigators said that locating the handgun and tracing it through its serial number might be the only link to discovering the coed's killer. It seemed like a long shot, but detectives from the Illinois Division of Investigation called in a septic tank cleaning service to pump out the waste matter from the pits under both the men's and women's toilets at the McClure rest area. Once the pits were emptied, investigators probed the debris with claw arms and long-handled shovels to search for a handgun. At best, this might have been considered an unsavory task, but Ashman explained that "it's just something we have to check out. Experience has taught us that you can't second-guess these killers." Unfortunately, the attempt to recover the gun used to kill Sheila Cole was unsuccessful. There was still hope that some useful information might be revealed from the bullets that were recovered at the scene.

Sheila's mother and father were obviously distraught at the news of their daughter's death. Sergeant Brown said that for a long time afterward, Harold Cole, Sheila's father, would drive to Cape Girardeau from his home in Crestwood almost on a weekly basis.

"He would just drive around, hoping that somehow he would be able to find Sheila's killer. I think he knew that he never would, but he couldn't just sit around feeling helpless. He needed to feel like he was doing something," Brown said.

According to everyone who knew Sheila, she was a sweet girl who got along well with just about anyone. She had a contagious smile and an optimistic attitude. As a senior at SEMO State University, Sheila was a member of the Pi Kappa Alpha Little Sisters at the university and she enjoyed school activities. All her life, she had a fondness and fascination with animals, so she majored in zoology with a minor in chemistry. Her chosen course of study was academically challenging, but Sheila was very studious. She was also a social person who liked to party with her roommates and circle of close friends, but she was conservative with her money. Her roommates said that Sheila never had any financial problems and always found some type of job to make money during the summer months when she returned to live with her family in Crestwood.

During a coroner's inquest on December 1, 1977, her father, Harold, testified that Sheila always acted conservatively and responsibly when it came to her possessions. "I'd like to make this point very strongly," he said. "If her keys were found in her car, then she did not leave the car voluntarily. She always took her keys and locked the car."

Her roommate Connie Walker also testified that Sheila was fastidious in her habits. Walker said, "Sheila's car was her pride and joy. She took good care of it. She was always telling me to lock the door."

Harold Cole said that the only enemy the family might have was a woman from Arcadia, Missouri, who was involved in a lawsuit over some money that his wife's uncle gave to her. He also said that Sheila dated a boy named Jerry Seegers during her first year of college at St. Louis Community College (STLCC)—Meramec in Kirkwood, but that he moved on to attend Southern Illinois University in Carbondale, Illinois, when Sheila moved to Cape Girardeau.

Dixie Gail Keena, a friend of Sheila's, told police about another former boyfriend named James Zeiser, who belonged to the Sigma Tau Gamma Fraternity. Each person that investigators interviewed led them to another interview, and another.

Lester Burchyett told investigators that Bob Lusk, of Ralph Edwards Realty, told him that Sheila had inquired about finding a house in McClure, Illinois. When police contacted Ralph Edwards, they were told that Sheila had not contacted their agency.

Round and round it went as dozens of interviews were conducted throughout the next month, and still, the police were no closer to solving the case. They did not even have a suspect or a motive.

Matthew Sopko agreed to submit to a polygraph examination December 2 at the Cape Girardeau Police Department. The results of that examination indicated that Sopko had no involvement in the murder of Sheila Cole.

During the course of the investigation, Illinois state troopers were told of women who claimed they had been stalked by strange men, a member of a mercenary group that killed "dirty women," and a drunk man who sat at the bar in the Down's Club and told the bartender he was going to kill somebody. It seemed that everyone knew somebody who might be the killer.

Special Agent Richard Evans, of the Illinois Department of Law Enforcement (IDLE), tracked down Sheila's former boyfriend Jerry Seegers in Carbondale. He lived at the Tan Tara Mobile Home Park and still attended Southern Illinois University, where he majored in photography.

Seegers told Evans that he had not seen Sheila since he last visited her about a year earlier. He said that they had dinner together, went to the Trail of Tears State Park, and then spent the rest of the evening watching television in his motel room. He added that they did not have sex.

Seegers said that Sheila told him that she did not care for one of her roommates (she was living in the dormitory at that time) and that she was becoming disillusioned with Sopko because he "hassled" her about her foul language. He added that Sheila was not too fond of her brother, either. Seegers told Evans that he had learned of Sheila's death from a television news report and that he would assist investigators in any way that he could.

Alexander County sheriff Donald Turner reported that a man named Charles Clifton told him that another man, Dean Bagby, came into the Hub Tavern on the morning of November 17 and said that he was in terrible trouble because he had shot someone. When Bagby was interviewed, he denied making that statement. Round and round it continued, but police were still no closer to the truth.

It was not until near the end of December that ballistic test findings determined that it was probable that the same type of gun used to kill Sheila Cole was also used in the Parsh murders. The lab examiner reported that in both cases the bullets appeared to be Remington-Peters .38-caliber 158-grain round-nose bullets that were probably fired from a Charter Arms undercover model pistol. On December 29, the cases were combined.

In a prepared statement, the Cape Girardeau Police Department released to the media that the Parsh and Cole murders might be linked to a single "psychotic" killer. The statement said that in addition to similarities in the ballistic test report, the apparent lack of a normal motive in the slayings—such as robbery, rape, or revenge—has led authorities to theorize that one psychotic individual could be responsible for all three murders.

Chief Gerecke said at the time, "We don't want to be alarmists, but I feel it is our duty to alert the public." He added that his own daughter was visiting during the holiday break from her school in Texas, and he had told her not to go out alone or pick anyone up while she was staying in the area.

The bodies of Mary and Brenda Parsh were so decomposed when they were discovered that no useful physical evidence could be recovered from their autopsies that would aid investigators to solve the case. In contrast to the longevity that contributed to the accelerated decomposition of Mary and Brenda Parsh as a detrimental factor, it may have been haste that contributed to a lack of evidence in the Sheila Cole case. According to Sergeant Brown, Cole's body was already in the process of being embalmed before some investigating authorities were even notified of her death.

While the ballistic test showed similarities in the bullets used in the Parsh and Cole murders, the report did not provide definitive proof that the same weapon was used in both cases. Federal, state, and local authorities worked together to search for another common thread that might link the victims.

Sheila Cole lived in an apartment building that was located next door to the nursing home where Mr. Parsh lived for several months after his wife and daughter were killed, but he said that he had never spoken to or even had known who Cole was.

Before moving to Milwaukee, Wisconsin, Brenda Parsh lived and worked in St. Louis. Cole's family lived in Crestwood, which is located outside of St. Louis, but there was no indication that they ever ran into each other or even knew each other. In considering any possible connection with the background of the victims, Brown said, "Nothing seemed close or to overlap at all." He added, "That was just about the time that 'Son of Sam' was prominent in the newspapers and maybe that triggered something. If we have a true psychotic here as well, he might strike again."

1978–1981

I just went nuts. Back in '77 and '78, I think I just went a little crazy.

—Timothy Wayne Krajcir

5

New Year's came and went. More interviews ensued. Most of them were full of "he said that she told him she heard this guy say that because he heard it from that girl," and it all led nowhere.

Several people who heard about the Cole murder called the Cape Girardeau Police Department. Emma Glass said that she was driving to Kentucky on November 17 and stopped at the rest area on Illinois Route 3, near McClure. She said that she walked into the restroom, saw someone lying on the floor, and quickly turned around and walked back to her car.

Cheryl Bonta called to say that Donald Charles, who parked cars at the Hush Puppy Tavern in McClure, Illinois, saw Sheila Cole leave there with three guys on the night she was murdered. She said that she lived near Charles, and also near Jim Farmer and Dean Abernathy. Bonta said that Beverly Mayberry told her that Farmer drove a van similar to the one that she saw at the rest area on Illinois Route 3 on the night that Sheila Cole was murdered.

A lead with the potential to break the case presented itself on January 5, 1978. A man who asked to remain anonymous because he was in fear for his life contacted the Cape Girardeau Police Department. He spoke with Sergeant Dennis Dolan and told him that Donald Charles had witnessed Cole's murder.

Harold Cole called Special Agent Smith to report that he received a phone call from a woman named Sandy, from St. Louis. Sandy told him that Sheila attended the Bethany Baptist Church on Koch Street, near the Parshes' house in Cape Girardeau. He told Smith that Sandy told him that the pastor of the church received two anonymous phone calls prior to Sheila's murder. The first time, the caller told the pastor that Sheila had been involved in a car accident and was hospitalized. The second time, the caller said that Sheila had been killed in Illinois.

Sergeant Brown followed up on this information by contacting the secretary of the church and was told that there were no records to indicate that Sheila ever attended services at the church. Sheila's roommates Barnard and Gredizer said that they had no knowledge of Sheila attending the church, either. They also told Brown that their other roommate, Connie Walker, had moved back to her home in California.

Special Agent Smith contacted Donald Charles on January 13 to follow up on the anonymous caller's tip from the previous week. Charles told Smith that he did not know Sheila Cole and had no information about her death. He said that at the time, he had to take his daughter to St. Judes Children's Research Hospital in Memphis, Tennessee, for treatment for leukemia and that he stayed at the Convention Center Hotel. Charles submitted to taking a polygraph examination. The results indicated that he had no involvement with Cole's murder.

And round and round it goes until it ends up back at square one—with no evidence, no leads, no suspects, and no end in sight.

The details of the Cole and Parsh cases were put into a new database developed for the Federal Bureau of Investigation. The Violent Criminal Apprehension Program (ViCAP) was a state-of-the-art behavior-based crime analysis and investigative tool that could be used by any law enforcement agency to collect, collate, and analyze their own violent crime information on a local level, and assist in identifying similar cases on a regional, state, or national basis. Based on the criteria submitted, other cases across the country would be searched to find links that might connect them to other cases with similar details. The purpose of this process is to detect repeated or identifiable patterns of modus operandi (MOs) that are often connected to the commission of multiple unsolved homicides, which will, in turn, allow ViCAP personnel to pinpoint those crimes that have been committed by the same offender. Law enforcement agencies that enter information into the database or are involved in an investigation can access the results to see if patterns of behavior might point to a specific individual who could become a suspect in the crimes committed. The law enforcement agency can then pursue the suspect based on the information that is gathered. Computer technology at the time was relatively new and not always effective, but today the program is a very resourceful tool that is often used to identify dead bodies that have been found where the manner of death is known or suspected to be a homicide. It is also useful for suggesting a suspect in unsolved homicides—especially those that involve an abduction, or are apparently random, motiveless, or sexually oriented, or are suspected to be part of a series of similar attacks. Once a case is entered into the ViCAP database, it is compared continually against all other entries on the basis of certain aspects of the crime. When a pattern of criminal activity is discovered—for example, a serial murder suspect has been identified—ViCAP can then assist law enforcement agencies by coordinating a multiagency investigative conference for case review.

6

Virginia Witte
May 12, 1978

Nine months after the Parsh murders took place, and just six months after Sheila Cole's body was discovered at the rest area on Illinois Route 3, near McClure, another murder took place not very far away. On May 12, 1978, David Witte discovered the body of his wife, Virginia, just after 1:00 P.M. in their Westernaire Estates home on Lakeview Drive. He found her naked body on their bed with a kitchen knife protruding from her chest.

The Wittes lived comfortably in a well-to-do neighborhood in West Marion. David was formerly a district manager for General Motors Corporation and had more recently begun operating his own financial investment firm. His financial success afforded his wife, Virginia, the opportunity to be a stay-at-home housewife. Virginia was born in St. Louis, Missouri, in 1926. She met David and they fell in love and were married in 1942, in Webster Groves, Missouri. She raised two sons, David Witte Jr., who was living in Jefferson City, Missouri, at the time, and Michael Witte, who was married and living in Denver, Colorado. The couple in Denver just had a daughter of their own, Monica Lee Witte, who shared Virginia's middle name.

The day before she was killed, David and Virginia had just returned home from visiting their son and newborn granddaughter in Colorado. At the age of fifty-one, Virginia was elated to finally become a grandmother. She looked forward to more frequent visits with baby Monica. Unfortunately, she would never get the chance to watch her granddaughter blossom into a young woman.

David decided to run a few errands and meet with a friend for lunch while his wife went to buy groceries. They both left their house in separate cars at around half past eleven o'clock in the morning. When David returned about an hour and a half later, he saw that his wife had already returned before him. Apparently, she had been attacked as soon as she arrived home because bags of groceries were still standing on the kitchen counter.

David called out his wife's name but received no reply. He walked through the house, looking for Virginia, and found her body lying across their bed with a knife sticking out of her chest. She was dead.

He immediately called the Williamson County Sheriff's Department (WCSD) and told them that he needed police and an ambulance at his house right away because he believed that his wife had been murdered. Uniformed officers from the Marion Police Department (MPD) arrived at the scene at approximately 1:15 P.M. followed by members of the Williamson County Sheriff's Department and investigators from the Williamson County Detective Unit.

After they arrived at the scene, Witte led investigators into the bedroom where they found the naked body of fifty-one-year-old Virginia lying across the bed with her hands bound together behind her back. On examination of the body, in addition to the knife that protruded from her chest, they also discovered a large wound across her abdomen, which appeared to be a slash caused by a knife. The knife that was still lodged in Witte's body matched the set of knives that were found in the kitchen cabinet.

Crime scene investigators sealed off a perimeter around the property and spent almost two hours going through the house and collecting evidence. They decided that there was no indication of a forced entry into the premises. There was also no sign of a struggle in the bedroom, where Virginia's body was found. Sheriff's detective William Henshaw said that "the nearest thing to evidence of a struggle was in the kitchen where Mrs. Witte's purse was found on the floor."

Henshaw also said that "valuable jewelry owned by Witte had not been taken, and her husband could not find anything missing from the home, but since a motive has not been determined, robbery has not been ruled out."

When coroner James Wilson was finally called out to the scene, he did a preliminary examination of the body and reported that there were several knife slashes across Witte's abdominal area, but that there were also indications that she had been strangled prior to being stabbed in the chest. He would not offer any further details until a formal autopsy could be performed. The body was removed and taken to the Herrin Hospital. Wilson had requested that a full autopsy be performed as soon as possible.

Investigators canvassed the neighborhood. They knocked on the door of Witte's neighbor Bonney Patterson and asked if she had seen anything suspicious take place in the subdivision. She asked them why, had there been a burglary? When they told her that they were investigating a homicide, she could hardly believe that such a thing could take place in the quiet, conservative, well-to-do neighborhood. Patterson told police that she hadn't noticed anything suspicious, and she described Witte as a well-spoken and attractive woman who was proud of recently becoming a grandmother.

Other people in the neighborhood who were questioned said that they remembered seeing a stranger in the area at the time. Descriptions varied depending on who was questioned, but for the most part, the unidentified stranger was described as a muscular man, in his thirties or forties, with very dark hair. Through their descriptions, police were able to create two composite sketches of the stranger. Michael Wiseman, director of the County Detective Unit, distributed the sketches to local law enforcement agencies throughout the area in hopes that they might assist in identifying the man. At the time, Wiseman said that while the pictures varied in detail to detail, they represented witnesses' recollections of the same man.

Witnesses who were interviewed also told investigators that the man was driving a late-model car. Some of them described it as a silver or white Chevrolet or Oldsmobile. After more people were questioned—who also provided coinciding details of the stranger's description—a police composite sketch artist created a third image of the man, which was believed to represent a more accurate likeness of him. This image, as well as information about the circumstances of the murder, was released to the media with a plea for help in identifying the suspect.

A few days after the murder, Jack Jones, Timothy Krajcir's parole officer, contacted the Williamson County Major Case Squad and told them that the composite sketch released by the media looked very much like Krajcir. Investigators followed up on Jones's hunch and drove to North Springer Street in Carbondale, where Krajcir was living at the time. They observed Krajcir walk from his car to his trailer and noted that the vehicle was similar to the one described by Witte's neighbors as the car that was used by the stranger. Investigators then visited the Grob car dealership in Murphysboro, where Krajcir purchased his car. Afterward, they drove to the Jackson County Ambulance Service, where Krajcir was employed. They spoke with his supervisor and discovered that Krajcir did not come to work on the date that Witte was murdered.

Nearly a hundred pieces of possible physical and forensic evidence was collected from the crime scene, including latent fingerprints that were sent to the FBI. Federal officers compared Krajcir's fingerprints with those that were collected at Witte's house. Since they did not find a match, investigators never contacted Krajcir for questioning and he was dropped from the list of suspects. This decision later proved to be a fatal error in judgment. Local authorities may have found it difficult to ignore the mounting evidence against Krajcir, despite the fact that his fingerprints were not discovered at the scene of the crime. However, when they were told by the federal government that he was no longer a suspect, they had no choice but to abandon their only lead and begin to look elsewhere.

At Herrin Hospital, resident pathologist Dr. A. S. Thompson performed the actual autopsy. Thompson established the time of death to be around noon or shortly thereafter. An examination of the body revealed that Witte had been sexually assaulted. Eventually it was concluded that although Witte had been sliced several times across the abdomen and was stabbed in the chest, the cause of death was determined to be due to strangulation.

Virginia Lee Witte was Catholic. Her viewing took place on Sunday, just two days after she was murdered. The Rosary was recited at 7:30 P.M. at the funeral home, and on Monday morning, at ten o'clock, her funeral service was held at St. Joseph's Catholic Church, where Witte was a member and regularly attended. She was buried in San Carlos Cemetery at Herrin. Tornadoes and high winds raced across the state at the time. Perhaps it was a premonition of the storm of murderous rampage that was about to be unleashed.

An investigation by the Marion Police Department and the Williamson County Detective Unit ensued, but a connection with the murders that took place just fifty-seven miles away in Cape Girardeau was not made, and the cases remained independent of each other.

* * *

Despite the best efforts of everyone involved, no other solid leads developed as time passed, and eventually it became a cold case. Years later, Lieutenant Echols spoke with Les Snider, a retired Marion police detective, about the Witte case. In a subsequent report, Echols wrote that Snider told him that he believed that a convicted serial killer by the name of Anthony Joseph LaRette was responsible for killing Virginia Witte. Evidently, while working on a different case, Snider interviewed LaRette while he was incarcerated. During their conversation, LaRette made statements that convinced Snider he was responsible for the murder, although he never openly confessed and he did not mention Witte specifically. Snider made his assumption based on LaRette's propensity for committing acts of sexual violence, and the fact that he was suspected of engaging in a killing spree during the same period of time that Witte was murdered. Snider's gut instincts played a more substantial role than solid evidence did.

When he was about six years old, LaRette sustained an electrical injury that rendered him unconscious and caused his head to fall against the side of a trailer hitch, which knocked out several of his teeth. After that incident, LaRette claimed to experience auditory hallucinations. He began to exhibit tendencies toward violence at a young age by attacking several other children at various times. During one of these attacks, he was struck in the head with a baseball bat when he was only nine years old. As a result, he was diagnosed as suffering from psychomotor epilepsy. Several weeks after he received that blow to his head, he attacked a female family friend, who was a St. Petersburg, Florida, detective. He exposed himself to her and then tried to tear her clothes off as well. As he grew older, his behavior included increasingly aggressive sexual overtones. The number of attacks against women increased with each passing year.

In 1974, LaRette was charged as an adult for raping and strangling a woman named Ms. Hecker. He was admitted to the Larned State Hospital in Kansas for a pretrial evaluation on the charges of rape and aggravated burglary. He was found competent to stand trial. He entered a guilty plea to the charge of rape and was incarcerated at the Kansas State Reformatory. During his stay there, he received psychiatric treatment. According to the Amnesty International Web site: *The doctor treating him reported that sexual offences [sic] such as indecent exposure, choking of older women and rape were possibly committed during black-out spells.*

LaRette was paroled in 1976 and married Janet Suther within the next year. He claimed that he stopped taking the medication that was prescribed to control his mental illness and replaced it with illegal drug use and alcohol. He said that he unsuccessfully tried to kill his wife on two separate occasions after he found her in bed with another man on their anniversary in 1980, and that his feelings of anger intensified. He remembered driving to St. Charles, Missouri, to stay with a friend, and it was at this point that he hallucinated killing his wife. He was actually accused of killing another woman, Mary Fleming, and then attempted to kill himself by stabbing himself several times in the chest and slashing his neck with a knife. After LaRette was charged with Fleming's murder, his attorney requested a psychological evaluation of his client based on his suicide attempt. LaRette was found to be mentally competent.

A jury found him guilty of murder, and he was subsequently sentenced to death. After spending thirteen years behind bars, he became Missouri's longest-serving death row inmate. According to a book, *She Had No Enemies,* by Mary's brother, Dennis Fleming, *The police placed the number of [LaRette's] victims—all women—at two dozen, but he later claimed to have raped and killed thirty.*

Echols did not report finding any past official records to confirm Snider's suspicions that LaRette was responsible for Witte's murder, and he could not interview LaRette in regard to the incident because he was executed by lethal injection in November 1995 under then-governor Mel Carnahan.

In the meantime, investigators in Cape Girardeau continued to pursue every single possible lead and open up interdepartmental communications between law enforcement agencies across the nation.

7

July 22, 1978

As the year unfurled, the quest for Sheila Cole's killer continued.

When Gregory Bowman was arrested for kidnapping a woman from a Laundromat in Belleville, Illinois, he became a subject of interest in other kidnappings and murders. After the police in Cape Girardeau were informed of Bowman's arrest, Sergeant Brown contacted the SEMO State University and the Missouri Utilities Company to find out if Bowman had lived in the area during the time of the Parsh and Cole murders. He was unable to find any useful information that would link Bowman to the crimes.

October 6, 1978

Jane Keller told investigators that she left her home in Anna, Illinois, and traveled to Cape Girardeau for a doctor's appointment. She said that she had stopped at the rest area on Illinois Route 3, near McClure. When she walked into the women's restroom, she saw a note nailed to the wall. Keller told police that the note was written in blue ink and stated, *If you want to fuck, I have eight inches and I am with you now. Sign your name and phone number and I will call.* She said that the note was signed *David,* but the last name was marked out.

Keller said that as she stepped out of the restroom, a man came out of the adjoining restroom and followed closely behind her as she walked toward her car. She recalled hearing about a girl being murdered at the rest area, and became frightened. An Illinois Department of Transportation (DOT) maintenance truck pulled into the parking lot and the man behind Keller got into a blue midsized late-model car with a Missouri license plate and drove away.

She described the man as being about thirty-five years old, with dark hair and a mustache, and a solid medium build. State Trooper George Eaker was dispatched to the rest area but was unable to find a note in the women's restroom.

October 10, 1978

Cape Girardeau police detective B. J. Lincecum was contacted by a woman named Linda Boyd. Boyd said that she had been at the Purple Crackle Club in East Cape Girardeau when she was approached by a man named Johnny, who was possibly in his fifties. She said that the man was employed at the Superior Electric Company. When she refused his advances,

Boyd said that the man told her that she might end up like the girl in the rest area.

Lincecum followed up on the report and was able to identify "Johnny" at the Superior Electric Company as John Paul Dalton. Lincecum also tracked down Charles Patterson, a witness who said he overheard the conversation between Dalton and Boyd. He confirmed that Dalton told Boyd that she could wind up like the girl in the rest area. Dalton's comment turned out to be nothing more than an idle threat made during a heated moment of frustration, and investigators soon dismissed him as a suspect because they had no fingerprints, no weapon, no motive, or any other evidence to support that he may have been responsible for killing Cole.

October 31, 1978

Jim Gregory, chief of security at Southeast Missouri State University, contacted Sergeant Brown to let him know that a SEMO student named Larry Haney was recently suspended for following and harassing two female students. Gregory also informed Brown that Haney was a suspect in a rape investigation at Western Illinois University (WIU). During a polygraph examination, Haney registered a response in reference to questions about a homicide in Cape Girardeau and a rape at Murray State University (MSU) in Kentucky.

Follow-up phone calls made by Special Agent Connell Smith confirmed that Haney had indeed submitted to a polygraph examination administered by Dennis Jenkins and Associates, of Peoria, Illinois.

Smith learned that the results from that examination indicated that Haney may have had involvement in, or at least knowledge of, two rapes and a homicide.

Haney voluntarily entered the Zeller Zone Center, a mental-health hospital in Peoria about a week earlier. Smith was told that Haney was scheduled to be released the next day, but due to a lack of evidence, Haney was never charged with the crimes.

Smith tracked down Connie Walker, one of Sheila Cole's former roommates, and questioned her about Haney. Walker told Smith that she did not know anyone by that name, and that she had no knowledge of any connection between Haney and Cole.

Soon, another year had come and gone. Despite the fact that investigators were no closer to solving the murders than they were in August 1977, they had at least eliminated countless possibilities. Their efforts were not diminished, and the joint interdepartmental cooperation between law enforcement agencies grew stronger.

January 19, 1979

Police investigators in Sikeston, Missouri, contacted Detective Edward Barker in Cape Girardeau to inform him that a man named Joe White had been arrested in Marion, Illinois, for exposing himself to a woman in the parking lot of a Kroger grocery store. Barker traveled to Sikeston with Special Agent Smith to interview him.

White told them that he was a SEMO student who graduated in December 1977 with a major in marketing management. He said that he lived in the town of New Madrid at the time and commuted daily to the university. White told Barker and Smith that he owned an H&R .22-caliber pistol, and it was the only gun that he had ever owned.

White said that he did not know Cole or have any contact with her when he was at SEMO State University, and he had no knowledge about or involvement with her murder.

March 12, 1979

Willing to look at anyone who might be a possible suspect, Smith followed up a phone call he received from the Union County State's Attorney's Office. Investigator Harry Johnson told Smith that he had arrested a man named Harry Coleson in May 1976 for impersonating a police officer and stopping women on Illinois Route 3 and Route 146 in Union County, Illinois.

Johnson had no reason to believe that Coleson was responsible for the murders in Cape Girardeau, but he knew that investigators wanted to leave no rock unturned. Johnson told Smith that Coleson would pull women over on the road. Then he would approach the car, identify himself as a police officer, and accuse them of driving above the posted speed limit. Johnson said that Coleson would then tell the women that he would let them go without citing them if they would give him a kiss.

After Coleson was arrested, he agreed to seek treatment at the St. Francis Mental Health Center in Cape Girardeau; at which time, the charges against him in Union County were dismissed.

Like everyone else who was questioned and investigated, there was no evidence to link Coleson to the Parsh and Cole murders.

8

Joyce Tharp
March 23, 1979

Paducah, Kentucky, was founded in 1827 by William Clark, of the famous Lewis and Clark team. It is the only major city in the Commonwealth of Kentucky that bears a reference to an American Indian name in honor of the Padouca tribe. Its origins and prosperity can be attributed to its strategic location at the confluence of the Ohio and Tennessee Rivers.

According to legend, the Chickasaw Indians settled there under the leadership of Chief Paduke. They welcomed the new white traders who traveled along the rivers, and lived in harmony among those who settled in an adjoining community. That mix of cultural harmony was compromised when explorer William Clark arrived with a deed to the Indian's land and made them move to what is now Mississippi. Clark named the settlement in honor of the Indian chief who died of malaria a short time later. Paducah was incorporated as a town in 1830.

After a period of rapid growth, Paducah was
chartered as a city in 1856. It became an important
supply juncture during the Civil War, and was bat-
tled over and controlled at various times by both
the Confederate and the Union forces. Today the
small city of just over twenty-six thousand inhabitants has become a point of destination for travel-
ers because of its thriving arts district.

Ten months after Witte's body was discovered in
Illinois, another murder took place in Paducah,
Kentucky. Once again, the crime was regarded as
an independent event that was unconnected with
the murders in Illinois and Missouri, so the concept
of a multistate serial killer was never addressed, and
a multiple-state law enforcement task force was not
initiated.

Joyce Tharp had been born in February 1950.
She became the younger sister to Rene, and the
older sister to three brothers that followed her over
the next seven years. The tiny town of Fulton, Kentucky, with only about five thousand inhabitants,
was home to the Tharp family. Fulton contained a
church, a petrol station, a couple of auto dealer-
ships, less than a handful of eateries, a movie theater, an A&P grocery store, and not much else.

Their father worked as an auto mechanic at an
Oldsmobile dealership, and for extra income, he
would mow people's lawns. Momma Tharp was a
beautician and also worked as a cook in a local café
to help make ends meet. They had no illusions
about their economic status. They were poor, and
they knew it. Joyce's brother Vernell, who was one

year her junior, said that despite their circumstances, they never went hungry.

"There was always food on the table for us and clothes on our back," Vernell said. He also recalled one thing that the Tharp family always had and cherished—a close relationship with each other.

"We couldn't afford a place of our own, so we lived in our grandfather's house, along with one of our first cousins. All of us children shared a single room. The girls slept in one bed, and all of us boys shared another," Vernell said.

In the summertime, the Tharp children would head out to an open field near their home to meet up with other kids from the neighborhood. They would choose up sides and then spend their afternoons playing baseball. A baseball and a wooden Louisville slugger were as essential to life as food, air, and water. Not everyone had a leather baseball glove, so they shared what they had amongst themselves. Pieces of wood, flattened cardboard boxes, or just about anything else that they could find were more than sufficient to be used as bases.

Joyce and Rene's gender did nothing to slow them down when it came to playing baseball. They could throw, catch, hit a ball; and run just as competently as any of the boys that they played with, and probably better than some.

These were summers of innocence, smiles, and exploration in a tight-knit community where people knew their neighbors, and freedom meant not having to worry about harm because people looked out for each other.

Vernell said of that time, "We were all happy children and our family was solid."

During that period in the not-so-distant past, America was not what it is today. Prejudice was still prevalent, especially in the South and in states like Kentucky. Civil rights did not belong to everyone equally, and biased laws only served the fair-skinned community.

Most Caucasian teenagers today have no realistic concept of what life was like for African-Americans during this recent period of history. The term "African-American" didn't even exist. Colored, Negro, or the more inflammatory nigger were still prevalent ways to refer to members of a dark-skinned ancestry. Segregation in education was the norm in many states, and the Tharp children were forced to attend an all-black school through the eighth grade.

When they finally were able to attend the integrated high school in Fulton, the Tharp children were in a definite minority, and many of the white students let them know that they weren't welcome there. As hard as they tried to fit in, Joyce and her siblings found life difficult, and acceptance almost impossible. Signs of NO COLOREDS were posted in many businesses and entertainment venues. Vernell spoke about when he would go to the local movie theater with his brothers and sisters.

"We weren't allowed to sit with the white folks then. We were segregated into our own section up in the balcony, where the worst seats for viewing the screen were," he said.

Despite all of these things, according to Vernell, his sister Joyce managed to make friends at school. She played on the softball team and became well-liked by nearly everyone that she came in contact with.

Joyce performed well academically. She liked to read and play sports. She loved music, especially R &B and gospel. Marvin Gaye and The Temptations were near the top of her list of favorite musical artists.

"We didn't attend school dances and stuff like that. They didn't really want us there," Vernell said. "Instead, we would go to house parties with our own kind in order to socialize, listen to music, and just hang out and have fun."

Vernell's understandable frustration at not being welcome at school functions or being accepted by the white population, in general, is still very evident. The dating scene for Vernell, or his sister Joyce, had also become a frustrating factor. As a minority, prospective mates were limited. Interracial relationships were strictly taboo at the time, and these could end up with violent or even fatal circumstances.

Joyce Tharp lived through this tumultuous period and continued to be optimistic. Her enthusiasm for life rubbed off on everyone who fell into contact with her. She studied diligently and did well academically. Her hard work and positive attitude paid off. She moved to Carbondale, Illinois, and began to attend classes at Southern Illinois University.

Joyce met a young man while she was in college and had a brief relationship with him. She became pregnant, and he became a ghost, according to Vernell.

"He didn't have anything to do with Joyce or their daughter, Debbie. He never provided any financial support, as far as I know, and never provided any other kind of presence, either. I never met him and I don't even know his name," Vernell said.

After graduating from SIU, Joyce moved to Paducah, Kentucky, and obtained employment with Union Carbide, a uranium-enrichment plant.

Vernell joined the U.S. Army and was lucky enough to avoid a tour of service in Vietnam. He trained at Fort Dix, New Jersey, and then he was sent to Germany for the duration of his enlistment. Vernell returned home to Fulton, Kentucky, in 1974, where he found economic depression and limited job opportunities. After nearly two years of struggling to find a steady form of sustenance, he contacted his sister Joyce in Paducah. She was doing well, rented a modest place of her own, and had a history of sustained employment at the uranium-enrichment plant, which was not in jeopardy in the foreseeable future.

Out of the goodness of her heart, Joyce invited her brother Vernell to live with her so he could have a better opportunity to obtain gainful employment in the larger town of Paducah.

The siblings shared Joyce's modest apartment, and Vernell quickly acquired the lay of the land in his new environment. He became involved in a relationship with a local girl, while Joyce became burdened with the responsibilities associated with raising a daughter without a father. Joyce decided that she could no longer give her daughter a life that provided for her best interests, so she asked her parents in Fulton to take care of her for a while. Fortunately, young Debbie was living with her grandparents when things took a turn for the worse in Paducah.

A killer patrolled the Forest Hills area of town when the figure of Joyce Tharp caught his eye through the window of her apartment, but the time wasn't right yet to move in on his newfound target.

A short time later, during the overnight hours of March 23, 1979, a man broke into a window of Joyce's apartment and threatened her with a knife. He told her that if she did what he said, she might live. He abducted her and drove across the state line to Carbondale, Illinois. He took her to his trailer at the Carbondale Mobile Home units—now known as the Crossings. It was there that he abused Joyce sexually in order to fulfill his compulsive need to dominate another individual. After the ordeal, he strangled her to death.

"I left to go visit my girlfriend that night," Vernell said. "She only lived about fifty feet across the yard, but I never heard anything to alert me that there might be something dangerous going on at home. I feel bad because I know that if I was there, I might have been able to do something to save her."

During a cool rainy morning, a deliveryman, who worked for a local florist, found Joyce's naked body lying beside some garbage cans behind the Park Avenue Baptist Church in Paducah. Jerry Beyer, the coroner, determined that the cause of death was due to ligature strangulation. He also noted that the victim had several head contusions, and there was an indication of sexual assault, but that couldn't be confirmed at the time.

9

Myrtle Rupp worked as a registered nurse at the Community General Hospital in Reading, Pennsylvania. Her house on Fifth Avenue in South Temple was located about twenty miles north of Allentown, and almost a thousand miles away from Cape Girardeau.

Rupp was on a three-month medical leave from her job while she recovered from recent foot surgery. After twenty-eight years of employment at the hospital, Rupp had advanced to the position of supervisor of the obstetrics and gynecology departments, and she looked forward to the time when she would be well enough to return to work.

On April 10, 1979, she had spent the evening with her mother, Ellie Aungst. They went shopping at around 6:30 P.M. and returned to Rupp's house about three hours later. They pulled into the garage, which was kept locked, and then entered the house through a door that led into the basement. They made their way upstairs and set their bags down in the living room, located at the front of the house. Immediately they noticed that the front door was left open and there were shards of glass scattered all over the floor near the entrance. Rupp turned and walked into the kitchen to call the police. When she picked up the handset, she discovered that the phone cord had been cut.

Rupp and her mother left the house and walked to the home of neighbors Wayne and Dorothy Huey, but nobody was home. They couldn't get in, so they went to another neighbor's house and knocked on the door. Robert McWilliams answered and invited the two ladies to come inside. He let them use his telephone to call the police and report the incident. Rupp and Aungst stayed at the neighbor's house to wait for the police to arrive.

During the subsequent walk-through of the house, Rupp found nothing of value missing, except for a bag of half-dollar coins that she had been collecting. After the incident was reported, McWilliams went to Rupp's house and saw the broken window in the front door. He thought that the opening was too small for someone to be able to reach a hand through to unlock the door. He guessed that the burglar may have had some kind of tool to accomplish the task, but he thought that it would be odd for somebody to make the noise and mess associated with breaking the glass but not bother to break it enough to reach inside.

McWilliams repaired the cut phone cord for Rupp, and as he looked through the house, he noticed an empty soda bottle on the kitchen counter and a cookie on a dresser in the bedroom. The re-

sponding officer did not initially take note of these
things, but he did make a point of writing down
that McWilliams had two sons, ages eighteen and
twenty, who still lived at home. Perhaps the officer
thought that the youths might be suspects in the
burglary, but there are no documents to support
any follow-up on that perspective.

Several days after the incident, people who were
close to Rupp knew that she was still very upset
about it. The reason that she felt uneasy for the
next few days was because although her home was
broken into, nothing of value other than the half-
dollar coins that she was collecting, worth $15, were
stolen, and it appeared that the thief knew right
where those coins were kept.

The next afternoon, Harold Geisinger, the owner
of a glass and window repair business, came out to
repair Rupp's broken window. Rupp also called a
locksmith to get an estimate of the cost to change all
the locks in her house. The locksmith came over to
look at what needed to be done and then he told
her that he could return on Saturday to complete
the job. Rupp had already made previous plans for
that day, so she told him that she would have to set
up another date that would be more convenient.
She never did get her locks changed.

One week later, on April 17, 1979, the Berks
County Communications Center received a call with
a request to send police and an ambulance to a Fifth
Avenue address. The call was forwarded to the Muh-
lenberg Township Police Department (MTPD) and
received by Detective Kermit Frantz. Officer Donald
Hamaker was dispatched to investigate the call.
When he arrived at the address, he noticed a man

standing outside near the residence. Hamaker asked what was going on, and as he pointed toward the Rupp residence, the man replied, "I think there is a dead body in there."

Hamaker cautiously entered the house and made his way to the side bedroom, where he saw a body lying facedown across the bed. She was nude but for her anklet stockings. Her hands were tied behind her back with a nylon cord, which led down her back, wound around her right ankle twice, and then over to her left ankle, where it was knotted. There was another cord of the same type tied around the woman's neck, and it was knotted very tightly. The nylon cords used to tie the victim up appeared to have been cut from the drapes in the bedroom.

Hamaker knew that it was pointless, but he checked for signs of life. There were none. There was a pool of blood on the bed and a trail of blood that appeared to have come from the victim's left ear. Her back was blue in color, and the sides of her body were turning red. Her hands and feet were purple.

Someone—presumably the killer—had placed a blue-and-red-striped jersey underneath the victim's head. A pillowcase had been taken off a pillow and appeared "strained," as if it was previously twisted tightly, and it may have been used to choke the victim or had been placed on the victim's face. Some of Rupp's clothes were lying in a pile next to her body. On the floor at the left side of the bed was a pair of blue slacks that were turned inside out, and they still had a pair of white panties attached to them at the crotch area. A black purse and a brown wallet were also beside the victim on the bed, and it appeared that somebody had rummaged through them. Except for the disarray around the area of the bed, the rest of the house appeared to be very neat and orderly. A radio was still playing in the corner of the living room.

Hamaker called the coroner. He told him that he believed that there was no possible way that the victim could have hanged or strangled herself. He was confident that foul play was involved and that the scene should be treated as a homicide. The coroner told him to make sure that the scene was photographed and that the body was both photographed and finger-printed. Hamaker next called the police chief Harley Smith to inform him of the incident. Then he went back outside to talk to the man that he met when he first arrived. Hamaker quickly discovered that the man was Rupp's neighbor, and that he was the one who called to report the incident after he discovered the body. His name was Wayne Huey.

Hamaker questioned Wayne Huey and his wife, Dorothy. The police chief soon arrived, as well as investigators from the Reading barracks of the state police department who were dispatched to process the crime scene.

In the basement, they found a load of laundry had been started, and the washing machine was stopped in midcycle with the tub still half full with water. Among the clothes that were in the machine was a pair of lavender slacks and a shirt with a lavender print on it. After Hamaker conducted his initial interviews, he discovered that these were the pieces of clothing that Rupp was last seen wearing on Sunday evening, according to a friend named Sara Wentzel.

Wayne Huey told Hamaker that he left for work on Monday at 6:35 A.M. and noticed that the front door of Rupp's house was open. He said that it was still open after four o'clock, when he returned home. Huey stated that he cleaned the windshield of his car and then walked down the pavement and saw that Rupp's car was in her garage, so he assumed that she was home. He said that he then went inside his own house and watched television until his wife, Dorothy, came home from work at about 5:10 P.M.

Huey said that he and his wife decided to go out for dinner that evening. As they were about to get into Dorothy's car, Wayne said that he felt uneasy about their neighbor and that they should check in on Rupp before they left. Huey told Hamaker that he knocked repeatedly without a response. Hesitantly they entered the house because they were concerned about the well-being of their fifty-one-year-old neighbor who lived alone since her husband had passed away several years earlier.

Dorothy Huey entered the house first and walked straight into the kitchen to leave a note about the front door being left open. Her husband walked down into the basement. He came back up to the first floor and then called upstairs but received no answer in response. Huey told Hamaker that while his wife was still writing a note in the kitchen, he opened the bedroom door and saw that Rupp was dead on her bed.

"I grabbed my wife and got her out of there and then we came back home and called you," Huey said to Hamaker.

Hamaker made a note that the drapes over the front windows of the house were closed. The Hueys reported that the window dressings in the front windows of Rupp's house were normally left open.

Dorothy Huey said that her daughter, Marcia Amoroso, dropped something off at their house on Monday afternoon. "She told me that she stopped by around two or two-thirty in the afternoon and she noticed Myrt's door was open. She told me that she thought about walking over to say hello but decided against it because she had other stops to make and didn't want to get tied up in a lengthy conversation," Huey said.

When asked if Rupp had any male acquaintances, Wayne Huey said that she had a friend named Harold, with whom she spent a lot of time. Huey added that Harold was a married man and that his wife was called "Scottie," but he wasn't sure if that was her real name or just a nickname.

A newspaper delivery boy, Chris Sassaman, told Hamaker that he noticed Rupp's front door was open when he delivered her paper at around three-thirty on Monday afternoon. He said that the front door to the house was still open on Tuesday and that he placed that day's newspaper on top of the previous day's edition, which had not been moved. Sassaman said that the last time he saw Rupp was around three-thirty on Saturday afternoon.

While State Troopers Gary Stiver and Chester Zalegowski took photographs of the scene and checked for fingerprints, Hamaker and Detective Frantz went from door to door to question the neighbors.

Mrs. Francis Vallonio told Hamaker that she didn't know Rupp well. They only had occasion to talk if they were both outside working in their yards at the same time. She said that she saw Rupp a few days earlier, but Vallonio wasn't sure exactly when.

She couldn't recall seeing any strange vehicles or people recently in the neighborhood.

Another neighbor, Edward Hollang, said that he last saw Rupp on Friday or Saturday. He only knew her well enough to say hello in passing. He said that Rupp mostly kept to herself, and that ever since her husband had passed away, she no longer took the time to bother with her neighbors.

Mrs. Robert Hesser told Hamaker that she didn't know Rupp very well at all and that she didn't see her through most of the winter. She believed that Rupp's mother had been staying with her for quite a while. Hesser said that she did not see anything out of the ordinary in the last few days.

When Rupp's mailman, Gerald Frymoyer, was questioned, he said that he delivered her mail at about 9:30 A.M. At the time, he believed that the front door of her house was closed.

After canvassing the neighborhood, Hamaker determined that Rupp was last seen alive on Easter Sunday, April 15, 1979. Rupp, her mother, and a friend, Sara Wentzel, attended a holiday service at St. Stephen's United Church of Christ in Reading. The service ran from 10:45 A.M. until 12:15 P.M. After the service, the three ladies went to Wentzel's house for lunch. Wentzel said that they all went back to Rupp's house at about 3:30 P.M. They only stayed long enough to gather some things that Rupp's mother had left there, and then they drove her mother to her home in Pine Grove. Wentzel said that they stayed at Aungst's home for about two hours, and then Rupp drove Wentzel back home. Wentzel said that it was around 7:30 P.M. when they arrived at her house. Rupp went inside to use the bathroom but refused to stay any longer because she wanted to get home in time to see the *Donny & Marie* variety show and a Pat Boone special, which was scheduled to air on television, beginning at eight o'clock.

Sara Wentzel told Hamaker that she and Rupp were close friends and that they spoke to each other over the telephone or in person every day. She said that Rupp was not romantically involved with any men at the time. Wentzel said that Rupp began dating a man named John Dospoly about two years ago, but they broke it off after a year. She said that Dospoly lived near Pottstown and worked at Firestone.

Frantz and Hamaker conducted interviews all day long and then returned to the scene of the crime. By the time the state police were finished processing the area, it was nearly 9:00 P.M. All the physical evidence, including the bedspread that Rupp was found lying on, was bagged and sent to the state police crime laboratory in Bethlehem. Frantz accompanied the Muhlenberg Area Ambulance Service as they transferred Rupp's body to Reading Hospital and Medical Center. Dr. Joseph Granito officially pronounced Rupp dead at 9:20 P.M. The police determined that Rupp was probably killed on April 16, sometime between 9:30 A.M. and 2:30 P.M. just after she started a load of laundry. They also suspected that her murder may have been connected to the break-in that she reported to the police a week earlier.

Investigators tracked down Geisinger to ask if Rupp had talked with him while he fixed the window in her front door after the robbery. Geisinger said that Rupp had a female visitor while he was there and that they were chatting in another room of the house while he worked. When he was finished with the repair, he said, Rupp promptly came out to pay him for his services. That was when Rupp told him that she had been robbed three or four times over the past few years, and she couldn't understand why her house kept getting targeted by thieves. She feared that someone might have a key to the front door.

The police chief Harley Smith said that officials had to search throughout the state to find a qualified pathologist to perform a postmortem examination on Rupp's body, and he feared that it might cause a delay in the investigation. An autopsy was performed on Wednesday, April 18, in the Reading Hospital and Medical Center, by Dr. Robert Catherman, a forensic pathologist from Philadelphia. Catherman determined that the victim had been sexually assaulted. Dr. John Focht, the Berks County coroner, indicated that the cause of death was due to ligature strangulation, and he issued a certificate of death by homicide.

Rupp confided to her mother that she had been somewhat afraid of living alone after her husband died, and that fear was greatly heightened after her home had been broken into. She revealed to her mother that she feared the person who had broken into her house may have stolen an extra key to the front door, which she could not locate. When she took her mother home after the Easter Sunday service, Ellie Aungst said that she had become afraid that something awful was going to happen to her daughter. Her intuition proved to be correct.

The funeral service for Myrtle Rupp was held on

April 21, 1979, at the Sanders Funeral Home on North Eleventh Street. Muhlenberg Township police set up surveillance outside to see who attended.

Other than being able to develop a probable time of death, interviews of neighbors, coworkers, and family members provided no leads to possible suspects in the crime.

Muhlenberg police chief Harley Smith said that members of his investigation team met with the district attorney's staff to discuss the leads that both groups had at this point, and that neither group had any leads worth investigating, according to the April 27 edition of the *Reading Eagle* newspaper. They reported that "there are no major breaks in this case." Everyone who could be questioned was questioned. All evidence that could be collected was collected. There was no discernable motive, and there were no obvious suspects.

Investigators were stumped, and it appeared that someone was going to get away with murder.

10

When I was four years old, I can remember pushing my younger brother off the porch and breaking his leg. When I was five years old, I went into somebody's house and trashed it.

—Timothy Wayne Krajcir

Marge Buchter was Myrtle Rupp's friend for nearly three decades. They both trained to become nurses together. Buchter said that their mutual friend Harold Knehtle was the one who introduced Rupp to John Dospoly. Knehtle and Dospoly worked together at Firestone. Buchter told investigators that Rupp and Dospoly seemed to get along well, but they broke up after about a year. She said that they parted as friends and still kept in touch with each other.

Buchter said that Harold Knehtle's wife, Scottie, had been ill for quite some time and that she would visit her at the Hassler convalescent home with Rupp and Harold.

When asked if she knew of any other men that

Rupp may have been acquainted with, Buchter said, "One day in February, a man named Fritz, about fifty years old, came by to fix Myrt's garage door. He stayed for coffee, but there was no indication that they were anything more than friends."

When police questioned Harold Knehtle about Rupp, his statement echoed that of Buchter's. He said that he introduced Dospoly to Rupp and that they saw each other regularly as a couple for about a year. Dospoly owned a boat and they would sometimes go out on the water together. "They seemed to get along okay, and I don't know the reason why they broke up. I know that she didn't think John was friendly enough with other people. John spoke very little about her, even at work," Harold Knehtle said.

Knehtle's wife, Alice "Scottie" Knehtle, had been friends with Rupp for many years, and they both worked as nurses at Community General Hospital. "We'd visit Myrt to keep her company after her husband died," Harold Knehtle said. Rupp's sister, Verna Hartman, told Chief Smith that Rupp confided to her that Knehtle had been stopping by to see her even before his wife became sick.

Detective Frantz received an anonymous phone call from a woman who stated that she was a nurse at Community General Hospital. The unidentified caller said that there was a doctor employed at the hospital who worked with Rupp and he hated her. The caller told Frantz that this doctor had also had made sexual advances toward nurses at the hospital. She added that this same doctor was committed to a state mental hospital for several months and had just returned to Community General Hospital about a month ago. Anonymous calls are often taken with a grain of salt, and this one proved to be absent of validity. There was no evidence to persuade investigators to believe that this was nothing more than a disgruntled employee with a personal grudge.

Frantz received another call in regard to the Rupp case. He was informed that Robert Fulton, a man convicted of rape and deviate sexual intercourse, was furloughed from Graterford Prison three days before Rupp was murdered. Fulton was supposed to have headed for a residence on Avenue A in Glenside, but he was not seen or heard from since his release. He was described as a stocky twenty-nine-year-old black male who was five feet, seven inches tall and weighed about 180 pounds.

Frantz decided to talk with Rupp's mother one more time, and the conversation soon turned toward Wayne Huey.

"He would come over and do things for Myrt, like take out the trash and such. I don't know how he would get in the house, but I remember Myrt said she had loaned the Hueys a key to her place during a time that their house was being repaired after a fire. I remember one time I was sitting in the kitchen and I didn't hear any knock or doorbell. Then, all of a sudden, I saw Mr. Huey standing there in the kitchen. I never had much to say to him. He just seemed to come and go.

"I also remember a couple of weeks ago, I was in the house alone and there was a phone call. When I answered it, a man asked for Mrs. Rupp. I said that she wasn't in and he hung up. Nobody calls her Mrs. Rupp anymore," Aungst said.

Because Dospoly, Knehtle, and Huey were the only three men who seemed to have an ongoing relationship with Rupp, they were all asked to submit to a polygraph examination to be conducted at the state police barracks in Limerick. During the examinations, they were all asked, "Did you strangle or do you know who strangled Myrtle Rupp? Were you in the house on April sixteenth or April seventeenth? Had you seen Myrtle Rupp on those dates? Did you ever cause bodily harm to Myrtle Rupp?"

Dospoly was the first to be administered the test and his results showed that he had answered all the questions truthfully. When asked where he was on April 16, Dospoly said that to the best of his recollection he was on his boat in Chesapeake City, Maryland.

Chief Smith and Detective Frantz drove to Harbour North Marina in Chesapeake City to verify Dospoly's alibi. The president of the marina, David Moerschel, wasn't sure if Dospoly was there or not, but William Marcus Jr., the marina's service manager, recalled seeing Dospoly in the area over the Easter weekend.

Several days later, state police corporal Richard Long set up his equipment to administer the polygraph examination to Knehtle and Huey. Knehtle's results confirmed that he also was truthful in his answers. After Huey submitted to the test, Long checked the results and decided that he could not reach a positive conclusion. He noted that Huey appeared to be very nervous during questioning. He also noted that the results may have been skewed because despite being told to abstain from the use of alcohol and drugs prior to the examination, Huey admitted to taking some nerve medication and that he had been drinking. Long recommended that

Huey submit to a reexamination at a later date. He also asked Huey to submit to being fingerprinted. Huey said that he would agree to submit to both requests, and he set up a date in the near future to return to the barracks. When that date arrived, Huey never showed up. Instead, he contacted the law office of Stevens & Lee and gave his attorney, David Eschelman, a retainer to represent him.

Eschelman drafted a letter to give notice to anyone working on the investigation that Mr. Huey would not submit his fingerprints to the police and would not take part in a second polygraph examination. From that point on, no law officer could make contact with Huey in regard to the investigation without first going through Eschelman.

Frantz received a call on August 2 regarding the arrest of Michael Sustello, a teacher of vehicle maintenance at Reading Muhlenberg Vocational Technical School. Allegedly, Sustello attempted to rape a woman, but she was able to scream and fight him off until help arrived. There was also a report of a recent assault on another woman near Heister Lanes, where Sustello worked part-time as a bartender.

When police picked up Sustello, they found a loaded chrome-plated H&R .32-caliber pistol in his truck. A background check revealed that Sustello had been arrested by Reading police in 1966 for disorderly conduct and molesting women.

Detective Frantz checked with administrators at the school where Sustello was employed to see if he showed up for work there on Monday, April 16, when Rupp was killed. Frantz was told that Sustello had a good reputation at the school and a very good attendance record. Records showed that he was at the school from 8:00 A.M. until 3:15 P.M. that day; however, there was no record to account for his whereabouts during the lunchtime period. That did not seem to be too relevant, though, because it would not have afforded enough time to travel to Rupp's house, kill her, and then return to conduct afternoon classes. Sustello did not know who Rupp was and had no motive to commit the crime. Most important, there was no physical evidence to link Sustello to Rupp's murder.

Frantz turned his full attention toward Wayne Huey, whose refusal to cooperate only strengthened the detective's desire to pursue him as a suspect in the investigation. As that investigation continued, Frantz noticed that Huey showed signs of increased paranoia. He drank excessively. He had a new alarm system installed at his house, and outside spotlights as large and powerful as public streetlamps lit up his property at night. He replaced the clear glass in his front door with frosted glass so nobody could see through it. It was also rumored that Huey had begun to sleep with a gun under his pillow.

The Pennsylvania State Police Lab in Bethlehem filed a report after examining the evidence that was gathered at the crime scene. They concluded that there was no evidence of seminal material found on any of the items that they examined, but there were several hairs that were not consistent with the victim's hair so they may have belonged to the murderer.

Frantz built a case against Wayne Huey in order to obtain a body search warrant. He wanted Huey's fingerprints and samples of his hair. In order to obtain these items, he had to show probable cause.

In his request to obtain the warrant, Frantz brought up questions, as well as statements, that would cast suspicion on Huey.

If, according to Huey's statement, he had a bad feeling about his neighbor all day long, why did he do nothing until ten and a half hours later, after his wife arrived home from work? Why did he make his wife enter the house first? When he opened the bedroom door, Huey did not enter. He said that he "just knew it was Myrt, and he knew she was dead as soon as he saw her lying on the bed."

Wayne Huey would not have been able to see the face of the person lying on the bed from where he was standing. He did not check to see if she was alive or dead. He did not try to untie her. He just knew that it was Rupp, and that she was dead.

He also had a key to the Rupp house. She had given it to him after there was a fire at his house. The key was so that Mr. or Mrs. Huey could use the phone in the Rupp house if needed. Huey used the key to enter the Rupp house in order to take out her trash, but there were times when he would enter the house for reasons other than to take out the trash or use the phone. Knehtle and Aungst both remembered occasions when Huey suddenly appeared in the house.

During the investigation into the murder, cigarette ashes were found in the toilet. Rupp did not smoke cigarettes, but Wayne Huey did.

In a rider to the request for a search warrant, Frantz added other damning facts. On April 16, Huey left for work at 6:35 A.M. Between then and noon, when he was seen at Youngies Inn, nobody could definitely place him anywhere. As a supervisor at Empire Steel, he could leave the plant at any time without clocking out.

Wayne Huey said that he was at a pattern shop in Fleetwood that morning, but nobody at the pattern shop remembered Huey being there on that particular day. In a statement taken April 27 by Frantz and Chief Smith, Huey said that he was at his home that day at 10:57 A.M. That time on April 16 was within the estimated time period when Rupp was raped and murdered.

Frantz was able to obtain a body search warrant, and on August 15, 1979, Wayne Huey was forced to provide investigators with fingerprints, palm prints, and hair samples from his head, chest, and pubic area.

Specimens from Rupp's house, including clothing, shoes, bedcoverings, and the contents of a waste basket, were sent to the FBI's fingerprint lab in Washington, DC, for examination. To the dismay of the Muhlenberg Township investigators, there were no latent prints of value found on any of the items. Frantz had nothing to match Huey's prints against. To add salt to the wound, Huey's hair samples were found to be inconsistent with the foreign hairs found at the scene of the crime. The actual report stated that hairs taken from the scene were *too limited for suitable comparison,* and that when matched against Huey's hair samples, there were *no hairs found with sufficient characteristics* to deduce whether there were similarities.

Exactly one year after the presumed date that Myrtle Rupp was murdered, Detective Frantz received a phone call from Captain Conrad, of the Middlesex Boro Police Department (MBPD) in

New Jersey. Conrad told Frantz that an inmate named Thomas Carruth Jr. was currently incarcerated in Middlesex County Jail in New Brunswick. He said that Carruth had been admitting to crimes that he was involved in over the past year.

Carruth's method was to pick a house at random, usually on a quiet, dimly lit street. He would knock on the front door. When a woman answered, he would start a conversation with her and work his way inside the house. Once inside, Carruth would force the female down onto her stomach, disrobe her, and then tie her hands behind her back. Carruth told police that he generally used a drapery cord to tie up his victims. He would rape his victim and then use the cord to tie the woman's feet together while she still lay facedown on the floor.

Carruth was wanted in Plainfield, New Jersey, for armed robbery and in Middlesex Boro for sexual assault. Conrad told Frantz that Carruth might be extradited to Virginia in the near future because he was wanted there to face a homicide charge.

Knowing that Frantz was anxious to find the person responsible for the Rupp murder, Conrad said that Carruth had a good memory for details. If given particular specifics about a crime, Carruth would probably remember it. Frantz made arrangements to interview Carruth on April 22, 1980, in New Brunswick.

Detective Hadley and Lieutenant Meyer, of the Middlesex Boro Police Department, accompanied Frantz when he interviewed Carruth at the New Brunswick Adult Detention Center. During the interview, Carruth admitted to numerous serious offenses in several states, but he denied being involved in any crimes in Pennsylvania. He said that in 1979, during the months of March and April, he was in the state of Alabama. Carruth told Frantz that he had only been in Pennsylvania a few times in his life, and he had never been in the area near the city of Reading.

The unsolved murder of Myrtle Rupp had frustrated Muhlenberg Township investigators for over a year now, and they still had come no closer to finding the killer. It seemed that they had exhausted all avenues available to them, and although the case would not be forgotten, it was time to put it on to the back burner until some new evidence revealed itself.

11

July 14, 1979

The Cape Girardeau Police Department received a frantic phone call at 11:30 P.M. from a black woman who claimed that she had been sexually assaulted about thirty minutes earlier.

Patrolwoman Karen Sullinger received the assignment to make a preliminary investigation into the incident, and she drove to the home of Robelian Carter, located on North Middle Street. When Sullinger arrived, she found that Carter was in a state of shock. When Carter gave her account of the events that took place, her speech was barely discernable. Carter's body shook uncontrollably as she tried to relay the details through her tears and sobs. She gagged continually and actually vomited several times. Sullinger was able to pull the story out of her eventually.

Carter said that she had been asleep on the sofa in her living room and was shaken awake by a strange man. She described him as a white man in his early twenties, with a slender build and dark hair. She said that he was about five feet, eight inches tall, and he wore blue jeans and a dark shirt. Carter told Sullinger that she could not see her attacker's face because it was covered by a blue bandana. She couldn't remember what kind of shoes he wore.

According to Carter's statement, the man was holding a lawn rake, which she had left in the front yard, and he told her not to scream. He said that he did not want to rob her or hurt her; all he wanted was to have sex. She said that he told her that he was actually looking for her daughter, but she would do, instead. Carter's sixteen-year-old daughter, Denise, was babysitting at her sister Marcia's house at the time.

Carter said that her assailant gave her a choice. He told her she could "either take it in the mouth or in the butt," Carter stated. Then he unzipped his pants and pulled her head toward his penis. Carter tried to break free and make a run for the door, but the man grabbed her, dragged her into the bedroom, and threw her down onto the floor.

Carter said that the man then began masturbating and forced her to put her mouth on his penis while he ejaculated. When he was done, he told her not to call the police, and simply walked out the front door. Carter ran to the door and locked it behind him when he left, and then she staggered into the bathroom to spit the semen in the toilet.

She wanted to call the police immediately, but when she returned to the kitchen, she noticed that the phone cord had been cut. She went to the bedroom window and called out to her brother, Albert Carter, who lived next door. Albert heard her frantic screams and hurried over to find out what was wrong. When Albert found his sister in a state of shock, he helped her to his house and did his best to try and calm her down. It was from there that Robelian called the police.

By the time that Sullinger arrived, Robelian said that she had changed her clothes and had gargled repeatedly with mouthwash. Detective Donna Coombs was called to continue the investigation, and evidence technician Hellwete was called to process the scene of the crime. Hellwete found the rake lying in the front yard. Apparently, the assailant dropped it there when he left.

After reporting the incident to the police, Robelian Carter was too scared to return to her home, so she decided to stay with her son-in-law. Her daughter Marcia recalled seeing her mother gargle with straight bleach while she was there. After two days, Carter told her son that it was time to take her back home. She wanted to clean her living room.

July 17, 1979

Robelian Carter and her daughter Denise were asked to come to the CGPD one more time. Without any significant clues found at the crime scene, investigators hoped that the Carters might be able to provide them with some more information, now that things had calmed down a bit.

After asking them if they had any clue to the identity of the assailant, Denise Carter signed a written statement that read:

The only white boy that knows where I live and knows

that me and my mother are the only two that lives here is James Hager! I've been knowing him for two years and has been to my house twice.

Robelian was shown a photograph lineup of five different Caucasian men and was asked if any of them looked like the man who had attacked her. She picked photograph number three and identified him as James Hager.

Carter said that Hager looked closest to the man that assaulted her, but then she added that she couldn't be sure because the man was wearing a bandana over his face.

Six days later, police tracked down Hager and brought him into the station for questioning. He was read his rights before police questioned him. Hager denied having anything to do with the attack against Carter, and he refused to sign his waiver of rights. He did agree to provide the police with a sample of his blood, though, and two full vials were extracted from his left arm. It didn't make much difference, however, because there was nothing collected from the crime scene to compare it to. Hager was released.

Robelian Carter never mentioned the attack again, not even to her own family members. The attempt to bury the horrible memory would not work, however. The Carters would see that haunting blue bandana once more.

April 18, 1980

Special Agents Connell Smith and James Lummus, of the Federal Bureau of Investigation, attended a meeting at the Cape Girardeau Police Department headquarters, along with Detectives Dennis Dolan, B. J. Lincecum, Donna Coombs, and Patrolman Steven Niswonger.

Niswonger reported that he had received information from Calvin and Joy Jauch, of Cape Girardeau, that might be relevant to the Parsh and Cole murder cases. The Jauches told him Billy Watkins, a sales manager for the Springfield division of Cape Girardeau Ready Mix Concrete, had purchased a Charter Arms .38-caliber handgun several years ago from Willian Hindman, Joy Jauch's father. Hindman was contacted by the Cape Girardeau Police Department during the initial investigation into the Parsh murders in 1977. As an arms dealer, Hindman reported that he recently sold five of that particular type of pistol, and he provided investigators with the contact information of his customers. The Jauches told Niswonger that Hindman did not tell the police about a sixth handgun that he had sold to Watkins, who was Hindman's friend.

Joy Jauch told Niswonger that Watkins told her mother, June Hindman, that the Parsh women deserved to die. She added that when Watkins was in Cape Girardeau, he usually stayed with his mother-in-law on Lewis Street. Niswonger noted that the address was located approximately one block from the Parsh residence.

The Jauches also said that Watkins had made sexual advances toward June Hindman. Whether the Jauches were telling the truth or just being spiteful because Watkins was allegedly hitting on William Hindman's wife, there was no way that the investigators could ignore their story.

That same day, Cape Girardeau police detective

Coombs contacted Hindman, who lived on North
Sprigg Street. Coombs questioned Hindman about
any additional Charter Arms .38-caliber handguns
that he sold in 1977 and might have forgotten to
inform the police about. Hindman admitted that
there was one such sale that he could have overlooked. He didn't mention the name Billy Watkins,
however. Hindman told Coombs that he sold a .38-
caliber Charter Arms handgun, serial number
27143, to a man name Otis Williams. Hindman provided Coombs with the most recent contact information that he had for Williams. When she called
the telephone number, it was still current. When
Coombs inquired about the pistol, Williams told
her that he could not immediately tell her anything
about it, and he would have to check his records
to reference the disposition of the handgun.

There were no additional police records that ref-
erenced the disposition of that handgun or one
owned by Billy Watkins.

Rifling is a term used to describe the patterned
groove inside the barrel of a firearm, in order to
make the bullet spin as it flies through the air. The
purpose is to stabilize the projectile so it becomes
aerodynamic and more accurate during its flight
toward the target. Rifling is described by its twist
rate, which indicates the distance the bullet must
travel to complete one full revolution. Every firearm
has distinctive rifling that causes a bullet to spin
either left or right at a particular rate in conjunction
with its distance of travel. The grooves are the spaces
that are cut out, and the resulting ridges left on the

bullet are called "lands." These lands and grooves can vary in number, depth, shape, direction, and rate of twist. When investigators perform a ballistic check, they are analyzing bullets fired from a specific weapon to find out if the bullets have the same distinct signature of grooves, scratches, and indentations that match a bullet recovered in a crime scene in order to identify the firearm that was used. Every fired bullet contains a specific "fingerprint" and behavior that can be matched to the firearm that it came from.

The bullets recovered from the Parsh and Cole murder scenes were rifled with eight lands and grooves that had a right twist. In June 1980, they were sent to the FBI laboratory to be compared with evidence bullets from other cases involving the use of a .38-caliber weapon. There were no specimens that bore sufficiently similar microscopic marks to provide a conclusive match.

Nearly three years had passed, and although investigators had eliminated many suspects, they were no closer to finding the killer. That did not mean, however, that they were going to give up the search.

12

Shortly after the attack on her mother, Marcia Carter and her three children moved in with her. The small wood-frame house was located directly across from a sanitation landfill in an economically distressed part of the city. The four-room house was crowded with Robelian, Denise, Marcia, and a total of five small children.

When the police arrived at around 6:30 P.M., they reported that the residence was dirty, disarranged, and smelled bad. They came in response to a call that was made a few minutes earlier. Marcia Carter called to report that a man had broken into the house and sexually assaulted her by forcing her to perform fellatio on him. The details of the incident were eerily similar to those her mother had made a year and a half earlier.

Sullinger, who investigated Robelian Carter's assault, wrote down the statement as Marcia dictated it to her. Marcia said that she had just returned home from doing some grocery shopping, and she sat down on the floor in the living room with her family. She said she was changing a diaper for one of the children when a man burst into the front door and pointed a revolver at them.

"He asked for money. I told him we didn't have any. Then he asked for our purses and told us all to lie down on our stomachs."

Marcia told Sullinger that everyone was crying and screaming, but the man kept his voice very quiet.

"He kicked my foot and told me to get up. He took me into the bedroom. He made me take off all my clothes and he started kissing all over me. He told me either I would have to fuck him or give him a blow job."

Marcia said that she begged the man to leave and that they didn't have anything he could want. He told her that she would have to do one or the other, and she better make up her mind fast.

"He told me, 'With all those babies, I bet you have a good pussy.' Then he fingered me and forced his penis into my mouth. He came and told me to swallow it all, and I had better not drop any of it," Marcia said.

Marcia said that the man wore blue jeans and a red plaid shirt. She also said that he wore a blue bandana over his face, and surgical gloves covered his hands. She said that before he left, he cut the phone cord. Just as she had done before, Robelian Carter called out the window for help. Her neighbor discovered this time that his phone line had also been cut.

Evidence technicians recovered a pubic hair that

was foreign to Marcia Carter. They also collected a surgical glove outside, near the scene of the crime. In the meantime, Marcia was taken to SEMO Hospital for examination.

At the hospital, she had to tell her story once again. She was examined and it was noted that there were no signs of physical trauma, such as bruises or lacerations, on her body. According to the medical report, the attending nurse wrote that Marcia Carter was hysterical and rocked back and forth, hugging herself while her eyes remained in a fixed gaze. She stared straight ahead at nothing in particular.

The physician took a rape kit, pubic hair combing, and vagina and saliva swabs to test for semen. The specimens were tested immediately, but the results came back negative. Marcia said that she had rinsed out her mouth earlier. Her cervix and pharynx were also swabbed to be tested for any indication of a sexually transmitted disease. Carter's shirt was placed into the rape kit, along with the pubic combings. The package was given to Sullinger to keep as evidence. Marcia was referred to a social worker for future counseling, given some antibiotics, and then taken home.

The next day, Sullinger went to check in on the Carters. Marcia was lying in bed with a fixed stare at the ceiling. She looked like she was in a catatonic state. Robelian Carter told Sullinger that her daughter had been that way since the previous night. Marcia occasionally woke up screaming.

No fingerprints were able to be recovered from the surgical glove, so the only real physical evidence in police custody was a single hair that might have fallen from the attacker. Robelian said that when the intruder entered the house, he asked where Marcia's sister, Denise, was. Just like in 1979, Denise happened to be out when the assault took place.

With little else to go on, the Cape Girardeau investigators turned their attention once again to James Hager. They contacted his father, who told them that James would not be home until the following day.

December 30, 1981

Hager was obviously not happy that he was once again the target of a police investigation, but he agreed to come to the Cape Girardeau Police Department for questioning. He even signed his waiver of rights this time, acknowledging that he would be willing to make a statement without the presence of a lawyer. It was a short statement. When asked where he was on December 28, 1981, he replied that he was at home all day with his father and his little brother, Daniel. He said that he didn't leave the house at any time during the entire day. His story was corroborated by his father and brother.

Hager willingly provided head and pubic hair samples, and even consented to take a polygraph examination, which was administered by Sergeant John Brown. Brown sent the results of the polygraph to Sullinger, along with a statement: *It is my opinion, based on the polygraph examination of Mr. Hager, that he is telling substantially the truth.*

* * *

Investigators put together a short list of possible suspects that fit the description of Carter's attacker. There was no significant evidence to link any of them to the crime, but police had almost nothing else to go on. The list grew substantially shorter very quickly as white males that fit the description were eliminated through alibis. There was one name left, however: Malcolm Hicks. There was no reason to suspect him other than his description, and the fact that he lived on North Middle Street so he might have known the victim.

When questioned, Hicks told police that he was sleeping at his house on the date the crime was committed. He told them that he didn't wake up until 10:00 P.M., and from that time on, he watched television. He said that his mother and father were at the house while he was sleeping and that he never left the premises the entire day.

Notes made by Sergeant Brown said that Hicks fit the description and that he owned similar clothes. Brown also wrote that Hicks had the opportunity to commit the crime and had access to surgical gloves. These were broad statements that might include anyone, but Hicks was brought in for further questioning and agreed to submit to a polygraph examination.

After Brown administered the examination, he determined that Hicks was not telling the complete truth to certain questions such as:

"Do you know who received a blow job at [address on] North Middle Street on December twenty-eighth?" and "Did you receive a blow job at [address on] North Middle Street on December twenty-eighth?"

Hicks voluntarily provided pubic hair and saliva samples as evidence. In the end, his hair sample did not quite match the one found at the scene, and Marcia Carter could not positively identify Hicks as her assailant. He was finally eliminated as a suspect.

In May 1982, Sullinger wrote the Carters a letter to let them know that she was being transferred to a different division and that another detective would be continuing the sexual assault investigations. Although the new investigator kept the file open, no new leads developed and the case became dormant.

In the meantime, the crime wave in Cape Girardeau continued to spill over its river walls. In 1982, the tide of violence swelled to its greatest height and spilled over the city, drowning its population in terror and fear in a way that even the mighty Mississippi couldn't compete with.

1982

She just wouldn't die. For some reason, she kept on trying to breathe, even when I was strangling her.
—Timothy Wayne Krajcir

13

January 9, 1982

Ann Shares, an attractive thirty-four-year-old single mother, worked for the City of Cape Girardeau at the Division of Family Services. She was a well-spoken black woman with some education beyond high school. Shares was described as a polite and well-mannered lady, and a generally nice person.

Her ten-year-old daughter, Missy, attended school about six blocks from their home. They lived in a duplex on Themis Street. Unlike the Carters, they lived in a middle-class neighborhood, which was considered a safe section of town.

A typical day for Shares was that she began work at around eight o'clock in the morning. That meant that she had to leave the house about ten minutes before her daughter left for school. After her mother left, Missy would wait by the front door. Her bus stop was right across the street, so she would wait until she saw the school bus come down the road and then run across to catch it. Ann worked until around 4:30 P.M., so Missy would be home alone for no longer than an hour and a half to two hours in the afternoon. Shares worried about leaving her daughter home alone, but she didn't have much choice. That worry intensified to become all-out fear.

At around eight o'clock in the evening, a man burst into her house and held a gun to her head. Then he raped her and forced her to commit multiple sex acts with him in front of her daughter. He told her not to call the police because he knew where Missy went to school. If she reported him, he would be back to take care of both of them.

After the attacker left, Ann didn't know what to do. She wanted to call the police but was afraid for her daughter. She called her brother, Ben, instead. He came right over to comfort her. They decided that the best thing to do would be to report the crime. If she didn't, there was nothing to stop it from happening again and again under the same threat. Shortly after 10:00 P.M., the Cape Girardeau Police Department received the call and sent investigators to the scene.

Evidence technicians collected a blue coat that belonged to Missy. The coat had what appeared to be semen stains on it. They also collected a pair of brown rawhide shoelaces, which were used to tie up the mother and daughter. Other items that were taken as evidence included Shares's underwear, the bedsheets, and several crumpled-up pieces of paper that could provide possible fingerprints from the attacker.

Ann Shares was taken to St. Francis Hospital for examination so any evidence could be collected and put into a rape kit. She told the attending physician that she had not had sexual intercourse in the last twelve months.

There was no sperm found on the vaginal slides that were taken. No prints were able to be lifted from the pieces of paper that were collected. The only evidence that might be of use was that the semen found on the blue coat indicated that the perpetrator had an A blood type. Unfortunately, that blood type is the most common type among the general population, so the field of possible suspects was not narrowed significantly. Blood tests indicated that Shares had an O blood type.

January 10, 1982

Detective Sullinger met with Ann Shares the next day to conduct an in-depth interview and get as many details of the attack as possible, because she suspected that the man responsible might have also committed the Carter rapes.

Ann Shares explained that the garbage disposal under her kitchen sink had a leak and that she kept a bucket under it to catch the water. She decided to mop the kitchen floor and needed the bucket, so she went to toss out the water that was already in it. Shares decided that it would be easier to toss the dirty water out the kitchen door instead of having to walk all the way to the bathroom and flush it down the toilet.

She opened the door just a few inches, and before she could put one foot outside onto the porch, a man came bursting inside and held a gun to her head. Ann screamed and the bucket fell, spilling its contents onto the kitchen floor. He grabbed her and said, "Don't look at me" as he scooted behind her and out of her line of sight.

Shares was five foot, seven and weighed 135 pounds. She described the man as being several inches taller than she and physically fit. She said he had a ruddy completion, dark hair, and bushy eyebrows. He wore a red-and-black-checkered shirt, blue jeans, dark blue tennis shoes, with a white stripe, a black stocking cap, and a dark blue scarf over his face.

"I've been watching you for several weeks. I know that you used to live on the corner. I know you moved here several weeks ago. I know where your kid goes to school. I know that there's not a man around here," he told her.

Shares told Sullinger that the man's voice wasn't exactly feminine, but was soft and quiet.

Missy was in the garage playing with her puppy when she heard her mother cry out. She ran up the steps and into the kitchen to see a stranger holding a gun to her mother's head and holding his left hand over her mouth.

Ann described the firearm as a little gun, barely bigger than the man's hand, with a short, almost square-looking barrel. She thought it might be a derringer, like the ones she used to see on television.

When Missy came into the room, she was obviously concerned about her mother. The man continually told her to be quiet. He kept telling her that. Every other statement was "Be quiet."

Mother and daughter were instructed to lie down in the living room and put their faces to the floor while the intruder closed the drapes, switched off all the lamps, and secured the door. Once that was done, he seemed to become a bit calmer and told them to get up.

"He told us to start walking up the stairs. He was holding on to me real close and I was holding on to Missy. I kept telling her to be quiet and calm and not to agitate him," Ann said.

At the top of the stairs, he told them to go into the room on the right, as if he already knew the layout of the house. It was Missy's bedroom. Once inside the room, he told them both to get on their hands and knees and place their heads on the bed. Then he covered their heads with the bedspread and told them not to move. Afraid that a bullet might penetrate the back of their skulls, they remained still.

To Ann, it sounded like the intruder left the room for a moment and rummaged around in her bedroom. She was too scared to move and felt helpless because she needed to comfort her daughter. The man was back in less than a minute, anyway, and began digging through Missy's clothes dresser.

Ann felt the barrel of the pistol poke her and she was ordered to get up. "The kid can stay where she is," he said.

When Ann stood up, the intruder had already pulled his pants off and was sprawled out on the bed. He ordered her to strip for him. He wanted to see a show. Shares reluctantly did as she was told.

"I'm going to make you do some things you probably won't like, but just do them and you'll be okay," he told her.

"I told him that I was a Jehovah's Witness and that I just couldn't do some of the things he's asking," Ann said.

"You do it and you won't get hurt. You give me

any trouble, and you and the kid will get it and everything else," he told her.

He forced her to give him oral sex, and after he ejaculated on himself, he made her lick it off his skin. Afterward, he told her to stick her finger up his butt and suck him some more. Ann did as she was ordered, but all the while, she was thinking of a way to get to her own bedroom, where she had a hammer hidden under her bed. She needed access to a weapon, any weapon that she could use against this man. She kept trying to coax him into her bedroom. She used any excuse she could think of: "The bed there is more comfortable. I don't want my daughter to have to be exposed to this."

On this latter statement, the intruder seemed to get even more excited. He began to make comments about her ten-year-old daughter joining in. He said that if she was too tired to continue, her daughter would have to take over.

"He said something about that he thought she was hot. One minute he would tell her to look at what was going on, and that he was going to make her join in, and then when she would start talking, he would tell her that she was getting on his nerves and to be quiet. At one point, he said that he wasn't going to rape her, but he just wanted to have her undress so he could look at her," Ann said.

Still looking for a way to find a weapon, Shares told her assailant that she was sick and needed her medication. She told him that her pills were in her purse, which was in her bedroom.

The man had already taken her purse from the living room before they went upstairs. He said, "Your purse is right there on the bed," and he emptied it, found her medication, and gave her a pill. He was wise to the fact that Ann was trying to lure him into the other room for some reason, and he wasn't going to let that happen.

"You're going to do things my way," he told her.

The escapade seemed to go on forever. He forced her to perform oral sex on him for what seemed an endless period of time—but he was unable to ejaculate a second time. Still, he was excited enough to enter her vagina and raped her as well. Shares didn't think that he ever came inside her. He finally just got tired of not being able to ejaculate and gave up.

"After he finished, he got up and started messing around in Missy's dresser again. He told me to put my head under the bed, and I was just scared to death that he would kill me. I could see him shooting us both in the back of the head. I told him that I needed to go to the bathroom really badly and he let me get up, but said that he would have to watch me. Afterward, I told him that I was really cold and asked if I could put on a housecoat."

Shares's housecoat was in her bedroom, and she thought that she might finally be able to access a weapon to use to attack her assailant. The intruder escorted her to her bedroom and stood beside her as she reached into her closet to get her housecoat and covered her naked body. Then he led her back to Missy's room without giving her a chance to reach for the hammer hidden under her bed.

He told her, "I won't be back and I won't bother you again, unless you call the police. I know where your kid goes to school and I'll get you both if you do."

He made them both lie down on the floor; then he tied them up with rawhide shoelaces that he had brought with him.

"I'm just tying you tight enough that you can't follow me. After I get going, don't try anything for at least fifteen minutes. You can try to get loose, but don't call the police whatever you do."

They could hear the man walk down the stairs. It took another minute or two before they heard the front door open and then close. Uncertain if he had left yet or if he might return again, mother and daughter lay still for about another ten minutes, and then they loosened their bonds until they were free.

Ann Shares confided that this was not the first time that she was sexually assaulted. She said that she had been abducted, about five years earlier, with her daughter as they came out of Wal-Mart in Cape Girardeau. A white man with a knife grabbed them as they walked across the parking lot, and he forced them into his car. Shares said that the man drove to a secluded area and forced her to give him oral sex before he raped her in front of her then-five-year-old daughter, who was sitting in the backseat. She said that she was thankful that she and her daughter were not injured or killed, but she had been traumatized by the incident and had never reported it to the police. Shares couldn't remember the exact date that it happened, but she guessed that it was in November of 1977. After she was assaulted the second time in her home in 1982, Ann Shares never even realized, or suspected, that the crimes may have been committed by the same assailant.

14

Detective Sullinger mulled over Ann Shares's statement, hoping to find a lead to pursue. One part of it seemed to jump out at her. Her attacker told her that he had been watching her for several weeks. He was familiar with Shares's daily routine. He knew where her daughter attended school. He even knew that she had recently moved from her previous residence on the corner of Pinwood and Themis Streets. It seemed to Sullinger that the man probably lived in that area. It might have been a neighbor. At the very least, it seemed like it had to have been someone who knew Shares.

Sullinger hoped that with further thought, Shares might be able to pinpoint something about her attacker that was similar to someone she knew. At least that would give the police a place to begin searching for clues.

"Was there anything at all that seemed familiar to you about the guy?" Sullinger asked.

Ann pondered the question for a moment; then a thought spilled over her like a wave.

"There was something about him. He reminded me of my ex-husband, Bill. We separated. It'll be two years in April. He was giving me some problems for a while. Finally his mom and dad talked him into moving to Florida. He has a sister down there. That guy had this look. It was a general look, but it is the same look that Bill had sometimes. There was something about the guy that reminded me of Bill," Ann said.

Shares told Sullinger that she had dated Bill for two years and then was married to him for two years.

"I knew Bill pretty well and I kept thinking, 'Could this guy possibly be Bill?' Then I told myself no. This guy had the same hairy legs as Bill, but they were a little bit longer, and not quite as square. There was something about him, though. Bill's voice was kind of soft-spoken like this guy's," Ann said.

Sullinger had a stepping-off point now—a direction in which to move in the investigation.

Bill's legally given name was William Marvin Isbell. After searching through old police files, Sullinger came up with an application for prosecution for harassment and disturbing the peace, which Shares had filed against Isbell on August 7, 1980. At that time, Shares was still Ann Isbell and she was waiting for her divorce to be finalized. The couple had already separated five months earlier.

According to the report, Shares said that she was forced to move from her apartment at Village on the Green because Isbell would come around at odd hours and attempt to break in. She moved to an apartment on Pinwood Street, hoping that he would not be able to find her new address. At that time, she told the police that Isbell drove around the city until he found her car, and that was how he found her again.

When Shares filed the complaint, she told police that Isbell would come around to her apartment all the time and call her constantly to harass her about reconciling. She added that there were incidents when he would physically hold her prisoner and would not let her leave the apartment. She also said that Isbell was emotionally unstable and had attempted suicide three times in the previous three weeks.

Shares's claim was verified when Isbell's employer, East Missouri Action Agency, was contacted and they told police that he was on a thirty-day suspension for attempting suicide on the job. Records do not indicate the outcome of the charges that Shares filed against Isbell at that time.

Isbell sounded like a viable suspect. The Cape Girardeau Police Department sent a request to the United States Postal Service (USPS) for disclosure of Isbell's current known address. It turned out to be in Pinellas Park, Florida.

Despite the fact that Isbell had moved to Florida, it was difficult to overlook the similarities between the attack on Shares and the assaults against the Carters. The police needed a solid link between the cases, and they found it with Isbell. Shares was married to him. Marcia Carter worked at East Missouri Action Agency, where Isbell was also employed.

Another victim, Valarie Schetter, who reported that she was raped, was also employed there. In that incident, the alleged victim told police that two men forced her to have sex with them. She said that she had sex with one of them and then the other, and then both at the same time. She told police that she didn't scream or yell or anything, and that neither of them physically threatened her, but she felt intimidated by their presence. Police didn't investigate this incident as thoroughly, and one report dated May 24, 1982, indicated that it probably was really not a rape but a consensual sexual encounter.

A psychological profile of the unknown perpetrator in the Shares and Carter cases was prepared by Special Agent Karl C. Schaefer, the psychological-profiling coordinator for the Federal Bureau of Investigation.

Schaefer wrote that he believed that the same individual was probably responsible for the rapes of Ann Shares and the Carters. He defined the perpetrator as an anger-retaliatory rapist who committed a blitz type of attack against victims who were in the same age range or older than he was. He wrote:

Generally, the subject will be on foot and will commit his crimes near his residence or his employer. This type of subject removes and/or rips or tears the victim's clothing. He uses a lot of profanity. His attacks are usually preceded by a conflict with a woman in his life. The subject could be an acquaintance of the victim. The subject is typically impotent or has a retarded ejaculation.

The subject is selfish verbally and sexually to his victims and normally engages in oral, vaginal, and often anal intercourse. The subject likes to degrade and punish the victim, and will display anger.

Schaefer added that this type of person usually attacked a symbolic type of victim, which in these incidents was probably a black female who may have committed real or imagined injustices against him. His purpose was to punish, degrade, and humiliate his victims, and women in general.

According to Schaefer's profile, the attacker was probably married and involved in extramarital affairs, as well as conflicts with his spouse.

Schaefer also concluded that *he has an explosive, violent temper, and a possible mental health history. Educationally, he usually has a high school or less background, and was possibly kicked out or was a dropout with disciplinary problems. Often, he is involved in contact sports and likes to work off aggression.*

If he has an arrest record, it would be for assault and battery, disorderly conduct or burglary. Often he will abuse alcoholic beverages but has no drug abuse.

On a social level, the profiler believed, the perpetrator had an impulsive-type personality, with a quick temper. Schaefer described him as a self-centered loner who was a manipulative con man. He probably had multiple "drinking buddies," which were really superficial relationships, and he was most likely in the lower to middle class economically.

Schaefer assumed that the attacker would have an action-oriented job, such as a construction worker or a laborer so he could work off his aggression.

Finally he recommended that a woman officer be present during an interview if the subject was found.

The FBI profile was created to narrow down and help to identify potential suspects. Normally, it is a helpful tool in criminal investigations but it did little in this case to advance the efforts of the police department.

In May, before being transferred to another division, Sullinger wrote a final report on the disposition of her investigation. She included that there was one individual in the neighborhood near Themis Street who jogged and had a kind of bizarre personality. She wrote that he wore shorts in the winter, and in the summer he wore a huge amount of clothing. He also had been seen wearing a bandana often tied around his head. Since the time of the Shares rape incident, neighbors had not seen him. Area residents were told to notify the police if anyone spotted the individual.

Sullinger indicated that Isbell was currently the only good suspect in the case and that authorities in Florida were looking into the matter further. So far, the only information that they uncovered was that Isbell recently worked for the Parks Department and was fired. No reason was given.

For the next twenty-five years, there were no new developments in any of these cases that Sullinger initially worked on.

15

Margie Call
January 27, 1982

Marjorie Bertling Call lived in Cape Girardeau, Missouri, for nearly two decades, and worked there for twice as long. She obtained employment at a local Woolworth department store and kept a position there for over forty years.

She fell in love and married Ernest "Tink" Call in 1947. He worked in a shoe factory and then later got a job with the USPS. They lived their lives together in harmony, socialized with neighbors, had children, and worked hard to make ends meet. They produced two sons, Gary and Don, who eventually married and created an extension of family ties, which included members of the Bertling, Call, and Sewing families.

To Margie, family was everything, and she was the glue that held the three extended families together. She aspired to be a loving wife and mother, a grandmother, and a role model. In every one of those aspects, she was successful, and so she was happy with her life.

Don recalled a nearly ideal childhood growing up in the south side of Cape Girardeau. He attended Lutheran school with his older brother, Gary. Religion didn't dominate their life, but it played a significant role in molding a moral foundation and providing a regimented structure that could be relied on.

Don and Gary were both athletic, and there were always a lot of other children in the neighborhood to engage in activities with. Don joined a Little League team. He recalled that the now-famous radio personality Rush Limbaugh was also on his team, the Dodgers.

"He was a couple of years younger than I was but despite that, I didn't think he was a very good ball player," Don said.

With or without Limbaugh's contributions as a baseball player, in 1961, the Dodgers won the local championship, and Don still held on to that year's team photograph with pride.

The Calls eventually bought a house on the corner on Koch and Brink Streets, just blocks from where the Parshes lived. Don talked about the "cruising" route that was popular in Cape Girardeau among the teenagers. He also recalled the "lovers' lane" part of town, which was a parking lot that overlooked Capaha Park.

"They used to call it 'Cherry Hill,' but now it's referred to as the 'Fruit Loop' because the people that go there today are known for having a different sexual orientation than we did," Don said.

Don attended SEMO State University in his

hometown. He played on the college's basketball team, but he attained barely mediocre grades in his classes. His saving grace was a girl named Sharon Sewing, whom he met and started going steady with. They discovered that they lived only blocks apart as young children, but they never knew each other at the time. Margie never had a daughter of her own, and she quickly developed a close relationship with Sharon.

Margie didn't especially enjoy cooking, but when Don would have friends over, she and Sharon would cook up six or seven pounds of ground beef to make tacos for everyone. There was always an open-door policy at the Call house.

Margie was an avid card player. Pinochle and pitch were her preferred games. She even joined a "card club," in which she was the only Lutheran with seven Catholics. Don played billiards for money at a local pool hall and also liked to play cards, but his preferred game was poker and it involved cash.

Margie set a rule in her house that nobody was allowed to play cards for money. One day when she was off with Sharon for the afternoon, Don, Gary, their father, Tink, and several friends held a poker game at the house. Margie and Sharon came home early, and when they pulled into the driveway, Gary hollered, "It's Mom!"

Everyone at the kitchen table stood up. Tink grabbed all the money and ran to the bedroom. Even the "boys club" of the Call family feared the matriarchal wrath of Margie. According to Don, Tink made out because he never had to pay anyone back.

Don was drafted in 1971, but he was allowed to finish school before he was shipped to Vietnam in

1972. During his absence, the relationship between Margie and Sharon grew even closer. They would often take trips together to Memphis and spend the day shopping for bargains.

Margie and Tink were avid sports fans. Margie also liked to read a lot of different kinds of books, do crossword puzzles, and, of course, go on shopping adventures. When Don returned from Vietnam, the extension of families grew with his marriage to Sharon. They soon began having children of their own. Picnics and family reunions at the Call house became the highlight of Margie's life.

In 1978, Tink died of a heart attack at the young age of fifty-eight. This tragic loss made Margie's connection with her extended family more important than ever.

Don and Sharon had moved to Ashley, Missouri, which was about ninety miles away. Their son, Matthew John, was baptized on Sunday, January 24, 1982. A baptism dinner and family get-together was held at Margie's house. The house was filled with Calls, Bertlings, and Sewings, love and laughter.

Sharon had originally planned to stay at Margie's with her two young children for a few days because she had scheduled a six-week postnatal checkup with her doctor in Cape Girardeau on Wednesday. Instead, she decided to drive her family home to Ashley because Don had recently injured his foot and could not drive his car equipped with a manual clutch.

On Wednesday, January 27, which happened to be Sharon's thirtieth birthday, she loaded her sons into the car and returned to Cape Girardeau for her appointment. Sharon planned to visit her own parents for a short time before she went to the doctor. On her way to her parents' house, she drove past Woolworth's and noticed that Margie's car was not parked in front of the store, where it normally would be. Sharon assumed that Margie was either out running an errand for work or that she might have stayed home sick.

The same morning, a manager from Woolworth's attempted to contact Margie after she failed to show up for work, which was unheard of from her. After several failed attempts, Margie's brother, Albert Bertling, was called next, because his phone number was listed under her emergency call list and he lived relatively close by. Albert also had a set of keys to Margie's house. Albert attempted to contact his sister by phone several times without success. He became worried so he decided to drive over to her house. The place looked deserted when he arrived, but he approached the front door and used his key to gain entry. He found his sister's partially nude body lying facedown on her bed with her hands crossed behind her back as if they had been bound together that way. He immediately contacted the local police.

Albert knew that Sharon was coming into town and he called her parents to tell them what happened so they could warn Sharon not to stop by Margie's house. Without giving the reason for his abrupt departure, Sharon's father left the birthday celebration and went to meet Albert at Margie's house. When he returned, he delivered the grave news that Margie was murdered.

"I was wondering what happened and I was worried, but I could hardly believe that it was a homicide," Sharon said.

Don was called into the office of the principal at the school where he worked. He was used to this because he had earned all the qualifications to become a school principal himself and was often called in to confer about different situations on the school campus.

"Whenever I entered the principal's office, we would always discuss things with the door open. This time, however, he pulled the door shut, once I entered, and I thought, 'Uh-oh, what'd I do?' He told me that there was some bad news that was personal in nature. I immediately thought of Sharon's grandparents, who were getting on in years. He told me that was not it. I became frantic for a moment and asked if there was a problem with Sharon or our boys. His calm, quiet answer was no. Then he finally said, 'It's your mom.' He didn't provide any further details. I wondered if she was sick or injured. He didn't mention anything about an accident.

"Mom's brother, Albert, came to pick me up, but he wouldn't tell me what happened. I think he was having a difficult time dealing with finding his sister that way. During the drive to Cape Girardeau, I thought of a multitude of possible scenarios, and though I didn't want to admit it to myself, or dare to say it out loud, in the back of my mind, I knew that she was dead," Don said.

"We went straight to Sharon's parents' house, and just as I walked in, a television newscast was finishing a report about a recent local homicide. Sharon already knew, and as I looked into her eyes, I knew as well. My mother had been murdered.

"Albert never revealed to me in detail what he

found that day. Part of me was aching to know all the details, but another part of me didn't want to know. He never did tell me everything, and now that he has passed away, I guess I'll never know. I don't think I want to know, anyway," Don said. "It's better that way."

Sharon said, "The big question was how in the world, of all the people in Cape Girardeau, [did] this guy pick her? It was devastating."

Because there were nearly forty people in the house for the baptism party on the previous Sunday, everyone who attended was contacted by the police and asked to be fingerprinted so that any prints found other than family members' could readily be identified.

It took several days to make funeral arrangements, and an unexpected snowstorm kept Don and Sharon from returning home for another couple of days. They were still shocked and bewildered when they had to return to their jobs, take care of their own family, and continue on with their lives.

The world didn't stop when you stepped onto the trail of tears.

16

Corporal Brad Moore was the first officer from the Cape Girardeau Police Department to arrive on the scene. Albert Bertling was waiting in front of the house on Brink Street when he drove up. Moore went inside with Bertling, who directed him to the bedroom in the southeast corner of the house. Moore found the body of an elderly woman lying facedown, diagonally, across the bed. She was nude except for a pair of black leather knee-high boots and a pair of blue socks. Her clothes were lying beside her on the bed. Her hands were behind her back, and there were ligature marks around her wrists, as if they were bound in that position at one point.

Moore checked for a carotid pulse and found none. That was when he noticed that a rag had been stuffed in the victim's mouth and that there were also more ligature marks around her neck. Bertling had become increasingly distressed, and Moore led him back outside to the front of the house just as a patrolman, Leonard Minor, arrived. Moore asked Minor to stay with Bertling, interview him to find out everything he knew, and keep the area secure until other officers arrived. In the meantime, Moore notified police headquarters of what he had discovered, and then he began a search of the outside of the residence.

Bertling relayed how Woolworth's manager Pam Sander had contacted him at approximately nine-thirty in the morning after his sister did not show up for work. He said that he arrived at the house within ten minutes. He went to the carport entrance and found the door was closed, but not locked. Bertling told Minor that he stuck his head in the door and called out his sister's name. When he didn't get an answer, he went inside and found her in the bedroom. He said that he immediately went into the kitchen and used the telephone to dial 911. Shortly after calling the police, Bertling told Minor, he had received an incoming call on his sister's phone. He said that it was from someone he didn't recognize and they asked for a name he also didn't know. The person on the other end of the line then stated that he must have dialed a wrong number and hung up. Bertling was understandably upset at the time and couldn't remember the name of the caller or the person that he had asked for.

During his search of the premises, Moore discovered the apparent point of entry by the perpetrator. The bathroom windowpane on the south side of the house was broken in from the outside and the lower sash had been raised. Several items of women's makeup were found scattered on the ground outside the window. A rubber surgical examination glove was found lying on the ground by the southeast corner of the house.

Patrolman David Warren arrived and took charge
of the collection and preservation of evidence.
Moore assisted Warren in photographing the exterior of the house and helped to procure fingerprints from the exterior of the kitchen window. He
also assisted in photographing the interior of the
house and dusted for additional fingerprints.

The scene of the homicide was processed over a
period of several days, and a videotape was made to
record the evidence that was gathered. Police
found a used adhesive bandage in the backyard,
and there was a Benson & Hedges cigarette butt
near the northwest corner of the house. A tennis
shoe print was discovered on the carport pad. A
piece of leather shoe string was found on the bed
near Margie Call's body, and another piece of similar material was found in the toilet in the hallway bathroom. A yellow artificial rose, apparently
moved from one location to another within the
house, was found on the bed in the northwest bedroom, and there was an indentation on the covers
that made the investigators believe that someone
had sat or rested on the bed. Numerous hair samples were taken from various locations of the crime
scene, as well as from the victim.

As the scene was being processed, Margie Call's
body was transported to St. Francis Hospital morgue
by Ford and Sons Funeral Home. Michael Graham,
of the St. Louis County Medical Examiner's Office,
determined the cause of death to be from asphyxiation due to strangulation and smothering. Two
rape kits were completed on the victim's body. Acid
phosphates were present in her vagina, rectum, and
mouth, indicating sexual contact at those areas.

There were two pubic hairs found that were foreign to the victim. One was found on her neck and the other on her bed. Both were apparently pulled out and still contained the root. The hairs were determined to be dark in color, and had come from a Caucasian male subject. A seminal stain found on a pillowcase was examined and determined to have been left by a subject with a blood type of A, which was also shared by the victim, as well as a significant percentage of the population. At the time, little more could be determined because DNA technology did not exist.

One disturbing bit of information was examined and photographed, but it was not released to the media or the public. Margie Call's left nipple had been removed. It could not be determined whether it was cut off or if it was bitten off. The body part was never recovered, but it was believed that it was removed postmortem. This information was kept secret because it might later become a vital piece of evidence. Other than the investigators involved in the case, only the killer would know about it.

Investigators canvassed the area and were able to establish where Margie Call shopped, where she had her car maintained, what servicemen had been to her home, where she banked, and everything else they could find out about her personal life.

Neighbors reported seeing a brown late-1960s or early-1970s station wagon driving on Brink Street, near Call's home, at approximately eight o'clock in the evening of January 26. It was also seen still parked with its headlights on across the street from Margie's house, at about six-twenty the next morning. Nobody was able to provide a license plate number.

Further interviews with friends, neighbors, and coworkers established that Margie Call had worked a full day at Woolworth's on Tuesday, January 26. She left Woolworth's at around five o'clock and was home by quarter after. A neighbor, Aaron Perry, reported seeing Margie arrive home and noticed that she turned on her living-room and outside carport lights at that time.

A short time later, Margie was seen getting into her car and drove away from her residence again. Call normally played cards with her "card club" group on Tuesday nights, but on this particular evening, she had made alternate plans. Through more interviews, it was determined that Margie Call had driven to Penny Street, where she was invited to have supper with Eugene and Virginia Criddle. Another friend of Call's, Lorene Welch, was visiting from out of town and was also at the Criddle home that evening. The Criddles told police that Lorene left at about 6:30 P.M. and that Margie had stayed at their residence for about three more hours. When she left, she told them that she was going straight home.

Police questioned Linda Bollinger, who lived in the first house directly west of Call. She told them that at approximately 9:30 P.M. she had heard a banging noise. She turned her lights out and looked outside her window. She said that she saw Margie Call's car parked in the driveway under the carport light and that her living-room light was still on.

Rodney Enderle, who lived in the first house directly to the east of Call, told investigators that his dog started barking at around ten-thirty in the evening, but when he looked outside, he didn't see anything suspicious. Another neighbor, Debbie

Payne, said that she also looked out her window at about that same time and that she did not remember seeing any lights on at the Call residence.

Another neighbor, Mr. Leyerle, said that he left for work at 4:30 A.M. but didn't notice anything unusual at the Call residence. His wife told police that about a half hour after her husband left for work, she heard a noise coming from the direction of the Call house. When she looked outside, she noticed that the living-room light was still on, but wasn't sure about the carport light.

During the processing of the house, officers subsequently found the living-room light in the on position and the carport light in the off position.

Several neighbors noticed a brown station wagon parked in front of the Call house at about 6:20 A.M. One of those neighbors, Robert Nelson, said that it had square taillights and he believed it to be a late-1960s model Plymouth Satellite.

Of all the neighbors, family members, friends, and coworkers that were interviewed, nobody was able to provide a clue to a motive for the murder. Margie Call had no enemies to speak of. Her financial records were obtained, but there was no motive that could be determined that involved insurance or inheritance issues. Robbery was ruled out because nothing valuable was taken, not even the rings or earrings that Call was still wearing when she was found.

With assistance from the FBI, a psychological profile was created, which suggested that the murderer was a young, single, white male who lived within walking distance of Margie Call's house. It was believed that he may have been an introverted

loner who watched Call over a period of time, and
then raped and murdered her as a means of acting
out a sexual fantasy. The profile indicated that this
sexual fantasy might be related to the perpetrator's
recent loss of a close female relative.

Several specimens collected at the scene, including Call's purse and its contents, her boots, a pair
of gloves, the single surgical glove found outside,
and various paper items were sent to the Latent Fingerprint Identification Division of the Federal
Bureau of Investigation. Other items, such as arti-
cles of clothing, glass and carpet samples, items
from the bed and bathroom, and various hair specimens, were sent to the Regional Criminalistics Laboratory in Kansas City for examination. It took until
March 11 to receive word from the FBI that no
latent prints of value were observed.

By that time, Cape Girardeau detectives had interviewed close to three hundred people, including
sixty additional suspects that were picked using the
criteria of the psychological profile that was created. After all the time and manpower put in by
local, state, and federal authorities, there were still
no firm leads in the case, no motive, and not a
single palpable suspect. Investigators were becoming increasingly frustrated, and so were the members of Margie Call's family.

Don Call said, "There were a lot of thoughts and
theories about who killed my mom, but no substantial evidence to prove anything. I suspected a door-
to-door food delivery person who also provided
service to other local women who were murdered
previously. A few years earlier, Mary and Brenda
Parsh were killed in a similar fashion as my mother,

and they were buried in Alton, the same town that the delivery guy was from.

"My brother, Gary, and I plotted out a scheme to break into this guy's apartment. DNA testing wasn't a technology that was readily available at the time, but hair samples could be matched. We were going to break into this food delivery guy's apartment and get hair samples. We never did, though. We chickened out because we knew that we weren't going to be good criminals.

"We also knew that even though we suspected this guy, we had no proof to pin him to the murder of our mother. I'm six foot, three inches tall and weigh about two hundred ten pounds. My brother was about an inch taller than me and about the same weight. We thought about taking matters into our own hands when we would see him. I used to have dreams about a trial regarding my mother's murderer, but I could never see the face of the accused man. In my dreams, my brother would jump over the rail in the courtroom and begin to pummel this guy mercilessly," Don described.

It took another month for the results to come back from the laboratory in Kansas City. There was nothing useful that investigators could use at the time, and no physical evidence to match up to a suspect. The information and evidence were filed away for future reference.

In the meantime, Don Call's dreams continued to haunt him for many years to come.

17

April 25, 1982

Sometime before 9:00 P.M., Mary Lacey and Geraldine Drake went to visit their friend Ethel Smith at her house on South Hanover Street in Cape Girardeau. Drake brought her two children with her, and Smith had two children of her own at the house. The three women listened to some music, drank rum and Coke, and chatted while the children were left to amuse themselves.

It was supposed to be a light, happy evening of socializing with friends and having a few drinks. It turned out to be an event filled with terror, degradation, robbery, and sexual assault as an assailant conquered three victims at one time.

At approximately 9:30 P.M., Drake called the Cape Girardeau Police Department from the home of one of Smith's neighbors because Smith did not have a phone in her house. Sergeant Carl Eakins took the complaint, and according to his initial report, a man with a gun entered the house on South Hanover

Street, robbed three women, and forced them to have sex with him. Eakins wrote that Drake described the assailant as a white man, twenty-eight to thirty years old, about five feet, eight inches tall, and he weighed between 160 and 170 pounds. The report stated that the perpetrator wore a blue sock cap, a blue jean jacket, blue jeans, white sweat socks, blue tennis shoes, and he had a blue bandana over his face.

Eakins responded to the call immediately and was the first to arrive at the scene of the crime, where he was initially met by Geraldine Drake. He met all three women and had them explain to him what took place. Three other police officers, including William McHughs, were called to the scene to collect evidence.

A screen door on the rear porch of the house was found to be cut through. It was believed that this was where the intruder made his point of entry. Once he gained entry into the screened porch, the man easily gained access to the kitchen door, which was unlocked, according to Ethel Smith.

A white towel was also found lying under some bushes at the east side of the house. Smith said that the towel belonged to her and that it had been hanging on the clothesline outside, along with other laundry that she had hung out to dry earlier in the day.

The facts in Eakins's report did not correspond with some of the statements given by the three victims in a secondary report. Eakins wrote that one of the ladies was forced to sit on the assailant's lap while another was forced to suck his penis, and one of the victims was forced to engage in anal sex. It was between midnight and 1:00 A.M. on April 26, 1982, that McHughs took the official statements from Smith, Drake, and Lacey. In this second report, the ladies may have toned down the events that they claimed took place because after the shock of the incident wore off a bit, they were embarrassed about what had happened. It is also possible that the shock of the incident led them to exaggerate the stories in the initial report. Regardless of which report was most accurate, it was readily apparent that the three women had been involved in a traumatic, hostile, and degrading experience.

According to Smith's statement to McHughs, she was entertaining her friends when a man with a gun entered the living room from the kitchen.

Smith told McHughs that the man told them, "This is not a play gun. It is real." She also reported that the intruder told everyone present to lie face-down on the floor, and then he told the children to go into the adjoining room.

Smith said that the intruder told her and her friends to stand in a row beside the couch. He told her specifically to take off her clothes and turn around while he watched her. After a minute or so, he instructed her to spread her cheeks and sit on him. Smith said that when she sat on him, his penis wasn't hard and it was slight in stature.

After a short time, ". . . he told me to get up and put my mouth on him. He said, 'When I get ready to come, leave it in your mouth.' This was while he had my other friend pull off her clothes and was feeling her up as I was sucking on him," Smith stated.

According to Smith, after her assailant ejaculated into her mouth, he instructed her to stand beside the couch while he continued to molest her friend. Then he ordered her other friend to take off her clothes as well. Smith said that she spit out the man's semen while she bent over the couch between her friends. The intruder began to lick and kiss their butts.

"He said that he didn't want to hurt anyone, but if we didn't do what he said, he would go in the other room and slap one of the kids," Smith told McHughs.

She said that the man emptied their purses, took their money, and then checked in on the children to see if they were all right. Smith said that then, "he told us to stay put for at least five minutes, and that if we would get up, he would hear us."

Smith said that she and her friends remained still for about ten minutes after he left; then they got dressed and went to a neighbor to call the police.

The women said that the assailant was calm, soft-spoken, didn't use vulgar language, and he didn't act like he wanted to hurt them, although he was intimidating.

Drake's statement was similar to Smith's in many aspects but differed in others. According to Drake, the intruder initially entered the house and demanded money. She said that it wasn't until after he emptied their purses that he began his sexual assault on them.

Drake confirmed that her friend Smith was forced to sit on his lap and then use her mouth on him. It was during this time that she said that she was also told to undress. While Smith was kneeling on the floor with her mouth on his penis, Drake was forced to stand beside her friend as the assailant penetrated her vagina with his fingers. After Smith said that she thought she might vomit, the man told her to go back over to the couch.

Drake said that the man began kissing and licking her buttocks, and then turned his attention to Lacey.

"All I saw then was him feeling her all over. Then he told her to go back to the couch," Drake said.

Lacey's statement concurred with Drake's in that the intruder came in and demanded money initially, and he did not sexually assault anyone until the children were moved to another room.

"After examining our purses, he told us to line up against the couch with our heads down," Lacey said.

She peeked between her legs and could see their assailant sitting in a chair while he masturbated with one hand and he held a gun in his other hand.

"He called for the girl in the middle, Smith, to do exactly as he instructed or else he would take his frustrations out on the children. He told her to move in a circular motion, which she did, and then he told her to sit down on his lap, which she did. Then I don't know what acts he had her perform," Lacey said.

"I heard him call Geraldine next and tell her to take off her clothes. I wasn't able to see anything of what went on with her," Lacey reported.

Lacey knew that she would be next, and she was. The intruder called for her to strip her clothes off for him. That was all she said that was demanded of her, but it was more than enough.

The three women were shown six photographs from copies of driver's licenses of local men who were similar in description to their attacker. None of them could be picked out definitively as the assailant who attacked them. (Police records still incorrectly date the time of this photographic lineup as April 30, 1981, when, in reality, it was 1982.)

Fuel was poured onto the flames of fear that penetrated and paralyzed the women of Cape Girardeau when news of multiple sexual assaults and rapes began to pile up on top of the unsolved murders.

A letter regarding the sexual assaults of Drake, Smith, and Lacey, from Paulene Brown, of Marion, Illinois, was sent to the police department in Cape Girardeau, Missouri. She wrote the letter to the police, hoping that they would pass it on to the victims of the sexual assaults, because she thought it might help them to better cope with their experience by knowing that it had happened to others who had managed to survive and carry on with their lives. Brown wrote that she was a widow who lived alone, and when she returned home from church on March 28, 1982, she was attacked by an intruder who had broken into her house while she was gone and had waited for her to return. She wrote: *Perhaps there is nothing that I can say that will take away the fear and the memory of what happened, but knowing that someone else has experienced the same thing and is fighting the same battle that you are might help a little.* She added that her prayers included the capture of their intruder.

* * *

No physical evidence was left at the crime scene that would be enough to convict anyone. There was no motive. The victims could not identify their assailant through a photographic lineup. Forensic evidence technology was not as precise at it is today. Someone got away with a crime of humiliation and sexual assault of other human beings.

18

Eunice and Elza Seabaugh
May 1982

The year 1982 was prolific for rape in murder in the area. April was an especially busy month for law enforcement officials. In addition to the Cape Girardeau assaults of Drake, Smith, and Lacey, this was also the month that Carbondale, Illinois, police discovered the body of Deborah Sheppard. The recent rapes of Marcia Carter and Ann Shares, combined with the murder of Marjorie Call, produced an epidemic of panic among the citizens of the Midwest. The fear was escalated even further when reports of a burglary hit the newspapers in the middle of May, and the perpetrator was described similarly to the man who committed the other crimes in the area.

Eunice Seabaugh called the Cape Girardeau Police Department on the evening of May 17, 1982, to report a burglary. Patrolman John Casteel drove to North Fountain Street to do a preliminary investigation. He met an elderly couple who lived at the residence, and he took an initial statement from them. Two days later, he met with the Seabaughs again to get an official statement that would be placed into police records.

According to the reports of both Eunice, and her husband, Elza, the couple was listening to some record albums in their living room. Both the front and rear doors to the house were unlocked and the music was turned up a bit loud due to Elza's poor hearing. Despite that, Elza had eventually fallen asleep in his chair.

Eunice said that she looked up and saw a man standing in the doorway between the kitchen and the living room. She reported that he held a small black handgun, pointed in her direction, and told her to be still and get on the floor.

Eunice screamed and awoke her husband. The intruder again instructed the couple to lie facedown on the floor. As Eunice lay down in the middle of the living-room floor, Elza stood up from his chair in defiance.

"Give me your wallet," the intruder demanded. "I don't want to hurt anyone, but I'll shoot somebody if you don't give me your wallet."

Elza defied the gun pointed in his face and threatened the intruder.

"I'll cut your throat," he said as he reached into his pants to retrieve his pocketknife. Elza ended up cutting himself as he opened the blade, and in the meantime, the intruder turned the barrel of his handgun toward Eunice and threatened to kill her if Elza didn't comply.

Eunice grabbed her husband by his belt and pulled him down to the floor and then reached into his pants pocket and pulled out his wallet. She threw it toward the intruder.

According to the Seabaughs, the intruder emptied the wallet of its cash, then discarded it onto the floor.

"How many phones do you have?" the intruder asked.

There was only one, and the cord to the receiver was cut. The intruder told the Seabaughs to lay facedown on the floor for at least five minutes while he rummaged through their place to look for more money.

"Don't even look up, or somebody's going to get shot," he told them.

After about three minutes, Elza got up and walked to the bedroom to get his shotgun and then turned on the lights inside the house. Eunice also got up and walked to the rear door of the house and locked it. Then she exited through the front door and ran to her neighbor's house. It was from there that she telephoned the police about the burglary.

The Seabaughs described the intruder as a white male with a dark complexion. They said he was between twenty and thirty years old. He was about five feet, eight inches tall and had a slender build. They described him as having thick black hair of about ear length, thick black eyebrows, and dark eyes. They said that he was wearing a blue shirt, blue jeans, and a dark colored handkerchief or bandana over the lower part of his face.

Officer Casteel searched the premises for evidence. He found Elza's wallet under the living-room couch. In the yard outside, near the northwest corner of the house, he found Euncie Seabaugh's handbag, with its contents scattered on the ground around it.

Everything was bagged and taken to police headquarters to be processed for fingerprints.

According to the Seabaughs, a total of $131 was stolen, including a 1922 silver dollar.

The Seabaughs did not describe any incidence of sexual molestation or assault. They described their assailant as having a mild voice, and that he seemed to have a desire to not harm them, but would if he had to. They said that he seemed "cool" in his demeanor, and accustomed to accosting people with the intent of robbery.

Police combed the neighborhood asking if anyone had seen anything suspicious. One neighbor reported that he had seen a man looking at the Seabaughs' house prior to the burglary. He recognized the man as a pallbearer at a funeral they had recently attended and identified him as James Lovelace.

A background check on Lovelace showed that he was incarcerated three years earlier on drug-related charges. According to his parole file, his address was listed as Flat River, Missouri. His photo was similar to the description given by the Seabaughs—except he had blue eyes. Lovelace became the prime suspect.

When a composite sketch of the intruder was created according to the Seabaughs' description, their granddaughter said that she had seen the man a day before the incident. On May 21, 1982, the granddaughter spoke with police and described the man she saw as a tall, blond man, which contradicted the Seabaughs' description of a dark-haired man with dark, bushy eyebrows, and dark eyes.

Unfamiliar latent fingerprints were recovered from Elza's wallet. They did not match Lovelace's. Investigators had no other incriminating evidence and even fewer leads to follow up. From then on, the Seabaughs lived in fear, like prisoners in their own home. They always kept their doors locked. Elza began sleeping in the front of the house, while his wife slept in the back bedroom. They bought two big dogs for protection, and they contracted a six-foot-high fence, which was built around the perimeter of their property.

Eunice Seabaugh rearranged everything inside the house. She changed the position of the furniture and the placement of their clothes inside their closets and drawers.

"I resented him knowing where we kept things," she said.

Elza believed that her husband lost his dignity, pride, and self-esteem during the robbery because he was overpowered and unable to protect his domain.

Within a month of the incident, a woman was raped and murdered just a few minutes' drive from the Seabaugh residence. It wasn't until years later that Eunice realized how lucky they were to have just been robbed. When her husband died in 1991, Eunice moved to Warrenton to live with her daughter, Jean Austin.

19

Mildred Wallace
June 1982

Mildred Wallace never married or had a family of her own. She concentrated on her career and her community. As a result, she became relatively successful financially, compared to many of her neighbors. Without a daughter of her own, Mildred developed a close relationship with her brother's niece, Teresa Haubold.

"She was very classy and elegant," Haubold said. "Mildred was about the same age as my older sisters, and as a young teenager, I was very impressed with her. I wanted to be just like her. She always looked like she came straight out of Hollywood. Even at that young age, she would dress in a long mink coat," Haubold said.

Marge Suedekum, a friend of Wallace's, said that as a young woman, Mildred's captivating beauty was the first thing that everyone noticed about her, but once you got to know her, it was quickly understood that she was just as wonderful a person on the inside as she was easy to look at from the outside.

"She was just a radiant human being. If she was in the room, everyone knew it," said Suedekum.

In 1982, Wallace was the president of the Cape Girardeau Business and Professional Women's Club, and Suedekum was the club secretary. It was one of several local civic organizations that Wallace was involved with. She served as the president of the Zonta Club of Cape Girardeau, a member of the Executives Club, and she was on the advisory board of the Cape Girardeau Vocational Technical School.

Wallace was also a previous member, of the Girardeau Chapter of the National Secretaries Association, the American Business Women's Association, and the Missouri Extension Advisory Committee.

Five murders in the surrounding area over the same amount of years had gone unsolved and had created a feeling of fear and terror, especially among the female residents of Cape Girardeau, where four of the victims had lived.

After the murder of Margie Call in January 1982, Mildred established a civic group to provide a home-safety program that catered especially to women who lived alone. She also helped to establish a Neighborhood Watch group in her community. Haubold's father, Mike Stafford, was one of the block captains at the time.

"It was a terrifying time, because nobody knew why these murders were happening or who was responsible. People didn't used to lock their doors and windows, but everyone was locking them after that," Stafford said.

The town of Cape Girardeau was in a near state of panic. Women's clubs, like the ones that Wallace was involved with, wrote to the *Southeast Missourian* newspaper to urge women to create a buddy system, where friends would check on each other and report any suspicious activity in the community.

Strangers in town were looked on with suspicion by those who lived there. Mary Greaser, a member of the Zonta Club with Wallace, said that she would sometimes drive around the block before going home to make sure that she wasn't being followed.

Within six months of the Call murder, Wallace's beautiful voice would no longer sing out as part of the First Baptist Church choir, of which she was also a member.

In June 1982, she became the killer's next victim. Suedekum compared Wallace to Grace Kelly, who died the same year.

"I would have to go past her house every day on my way to work, and it stood there like a sore, always reminding me of Mildred and how she was killed for no reason. Like Grace Kelly, she was always thoughtful and gracious and never did anything hurtful to anyone," Suedekum said.

The Marquette Cement Company, where Wallace had worked as the office manager for thirty-three years, offered a $2,000 reward for information leading to the arrest and conviction of her murderer. Some of the civic organizations that Wallace belonged to followed suit by offering similar rewards in the hope that it would prompt somebody to come forward with information that might help to solve the case. Additionally in a matter of days, the Mildred Wallace Music Scholarship was established for use at Southeast Missouri State University's Department of Music.

20

Mildred Wallace had been in and out of her sister's house all day long on June 20, 1982. Wallace's niece, Jean Orsini, lived out of town but was in Cape Girardeau visiting her mother, Mrs. Mercer, who was Wallace's sister. After a long visit with her sister and her niece, Wallace carried a plateful of cake out to her car, at about 10:00 P.M., and then drove home.

The phone in the Mercer home rang shortly after eight o'clock the next morning. Orsini answered it. It was someone from the Marquette Cement Company who was inquiring about Wallace. Apparently, Wallace had not arrived at work that day. She was usually there by seven o'clock, and calls made to her house went unanswered. Concerned that Wallace might be ill, Mercer and Orsini drove to her house on William Street to check in on her.

When they arrived, they found that the outer storm door was locked, so they couldn't use Mercer's spare key to enter. After knocking repeatedly without a response, Orsini found a hubcap on the east side of the house and used it to break through the storm door window so they could use their key to unlock the inside front door. They entered the kitchen and called out Mildred's name, but the house remained quiet.

Now becoming even more concerned, they proceeded to the northwest bedroom, but they were not prepared for the scene that confronted them. Wallace was lying faceup across the width of the bed. Her hands were bound underneath her back. Her head hung over the edge of the bed covered in blood, and the carpet beneath was stained thick, where it had pooled. She was blindfolded with a terry cloth towel, and a pink nightgown was wrapped around her neck and shoulders. She still had on the red dress that she had been wearing the night before, but it was pulled up above her waist and her panties, socks, and shoes were removed.

Orsini pulled the bedspread down to cover the bottom half of Wallace's body. Then she searched for a pulse. Wallace's skin felt cold and clammy to the touch. There was no pulse to be found.

Horrified, and in shock, they left the bedroom and went to the kitchen to call for help, but when they got there, they saw that the phone cord had been cut. Mercer and Orsini rushed out of the house and ran to the next-door neighbor. They knocked repeatedly, but nobody answered the door there, either, so they got back into the car and drove back to Mercer's house. When they arrived, they looked in the local phone directory. The first emergency phone number listing that they found belonged to the Cape Girardeau County Sheriff's Office (CGCSO).

After getting the pertinent facts from Orsini, Chief Deputy Carl Friedrich notified the Cape Girardeau Police Department. Patrolman Ross was first to arrive at the scene. He observed the single-story white-frame house for a moment before he approached with caution. Ross noted the broken glass of the storm door and a set of keys still hanging from the lock of the inner door. When he peered inside, he noticed that a color television set on the kitchen table was turned on. He decided to call for backup before entering the house, and Sergeant John Brown arrived within minutes. They entered together and slowly walked through the house, careful not to disturb anything. When they found the body and determined that she was dead, they exited through the same door that they had entered. Brown and Ross secured the area until evidence technicians arrived to process the scene. While they videotaped the scene and collected any evidence they could find, city police canvassed the neighborhood to conduct interviews, and investigators from the sheriff's department visited Mercer and Orsini to verify any details they could provide.

Plenty of physical evidence was gathered at the scene. It was determined that the intruder entered a bathroom window on the west side of the house. The glass had been broken out and shattered pieces of it were scattered across the bathroom floor. Cosmetics normally kept on the windowsill were found spilled on the floor inside the bathroom, as well as on the grass outside the house.

Several drops of blood were found in the bathroom, and some Band-Aid wrappers were discarded on the floor. Investigators suspected that whoever

Timothy Wayne Krajcir is escorted from the federal courthouse in Cape Girardeau, Missouri after receiving thirteen consecutive life sentences. *(Author photo)*

Prosecuting Attorney Morley Swingle was successful in gaining convictions for five counts of murder, seven sexual assaults, and one robbery against Krajcir. *(Author photo)*

Brenda Parsh was a beauty queen and fashion buyer who attended Southeast Missouri University. She was murdered in August of 1977 with her mother, Mary Parsh. *(Photo by Richard McGougan)*

The home of Mary Parsh on Koch Street in Cape Girardeau, where she was murdered along with Brenda, who was visiting at the time. *(Author photo)*

The broken window where Krajcir entered the Parsh house
and then waited inside until Mary and Brenda arrived.
(Photo courtesy of the Cape Girardeau Police Department)

Mary Parsh didn't even have time to remove the keys from her
front door before she was accosted by Krajcir, who was waiting
inside. *(Photo courtesy of the Cape Girardeau Police Department)*

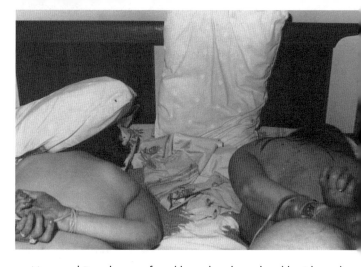

Mary and Brenda were found bound and murdered beside each other in August of 1977. *(Photo courtesy of the Cape Girardeau Police Department)*

Brenda Parsh *(left)* won the title of Cape Girardeau Watermelon Queen. Her friend Vicky Abernathy was runner up. *(Photo courtesy of Paul Stehr)*

Sheila Cole was a Lindbergh High School graduate who was attending Southeast Missouri University in Cape Girardeau when she was murdered in 1977. *(Yearbook photo)*

Sheila Cole's blue Chevy Nova was found in the parking lot of a Wal-Mart shopping center on Williams Street in Cape Girardeau.
(Photo courtesy of the Cape Girardeau Police Department)

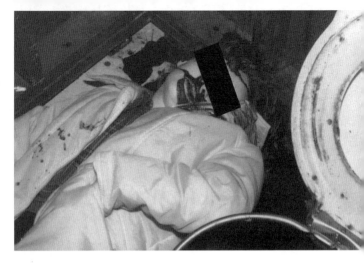

Sheila Cole was found in a rest stop along Interstate 3 in Illinois with two gunshot wounds in her head. *(Photo courtesy of the Cape Girardeau Police Department)*

Thirty years later, a memorial of flowers still marks the area where Cole was murdered. *(Author photo)*

The apartment building where Sheila Cole lived on Sprigg Street is directly across the street from the Cape Girardeau Police Department. *(Author photo)*

The restroom on Route 3 near McClure, Illinois where Cole was murdered has been torn down since the time of her murder.

(Photo courtesy of the Cape Girardeau Police Department)

Colonel Henry Gerecke retired as the Cape Girardeau Police Chief in September 1981. *(Author photo)*

Retired Cape Girardeau Police Sergeant John Brown was a lead investigator in the Parsh and Cole murders. *(Author photo)*

Marjorie Call stands in the kitchen of her Brink Street home where family and friends often gathered.
(Photo by Sue Sewing)

Krajcir stepped on the air conditioning unit in the back of the Call house to gain entry into a bathroom window.
(Photo courtesy of the Cape Girardeau Police Department)

Margie Call is framed by her sons Don and Gary after attending her husband's funeral in 1978. *(Photo by Sue Sewing)*

Margie Call holds her son Don at their home in Jackson, Missouri. Her husband Ernest "Tink" Call is in the background behind the car. *(Photo courtesy of Sue Sewing)*

Margie Bertling Call with her sister-in-law Rosebud Call as bridesmaids at the 1949 wedding of Hunter Jean Call Sewing in Jackson, Missouri.

(Photo courtesy of Sue Sewing)

Ernest "Tink" Call and his wife Margie in the 1950s before they moved to Cape Girardeau from Jackson, Missouri.

(Photo courtesy of Sue Sewing)

Deborah Sheppard attended Southern Illinois University, where Timothy Krajcir attended classes for criminal justice administration. He killed her in 1982. *(Yearbook photo)*

Joyce Tharp was kidnapped in Paducah, Kentucky and killed in Carbondale, Illinois in 1979. *(Yearbook photo)*

Mildred Wallace looked like a Hollywood movie star in her youth. In 1982, she became Krajcir's ninth murder victim. *(Photo courtesy of Teresa Haubold)*

Mildred Wallace organized a neighborhood watch program in her neighborhood shortly before she was killed. *(Photo courtesy of Teresa Haubold)*

Cape Girardeau police secured Mildred Wallace's house on Williams Street after her body was found inside. *(Photo courtesy of the Cape Girardeau Police Department)*

Krajcir cut the cord of Mildred Wallace's phone so she couldn't call for help. *(Photo courtesy of the Cape Girardeau Police Department)*

Rawhide bootlaces were a favorite binding device used by Krajcir on his victims, including Mildred Wallace. *(Photo courtesy of the Cape Girardeau Police Department)*

Krajcir said he put a towel in the broken window to block the breeze from alerting Wallace that an intruder had broken in.
(Photo courtesy of the Cape Girardeau Police Department)

Detective Jimmy Smith was a key force in finally solving the case for the Cape Girardeau Police Department. *(Author photo)*

Cape Girardeau Police Chief Carl Kinnison was elated to help bring closure to the families of Krajcir's victims.
(Author photo)

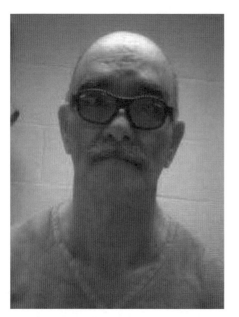

Timothy Krajcir waits for his arraignment hearing in the Cape Girardeau County Correction Facility.
(Photo courtesy of the Cape Girardeau Police Department)

broke in must have gotten cut on the glass when
entering the house. Further analysis confirmed the
blood type to be A positive. A beige towel had been
placed in the broken window from the inside.

A bottle of orange juice was found in the southwest bedroom. Nearby on the floor were several
faint shoe prints, possibly from a Sears-brand tennis
shoe. Investigators speculated that the perpetrator
took the orange juice from the refrigerator and
waited in this room for his victim to return home.

The cap of the orange juice bottle was lying on
the kitchen counter. A piece of carrot cake wrapped
in plastic sat beside it, along with a set of car and
house keys. A yellow phone hung on the wall, with
its receiver line cut and left dangling. Everything
else in the kitchen, living room, and other rooms
seemed to be in an orderly condition, indicating
that the house was not ransacked by a robber.

The northwest bedroom, of course, was not as
tidy, but still there were no signs that the room had
been ransacked. A white purse had its contents
dumped out onto the floor. No money was found
among the spilled contents, so if there was any cash,
it was probably stolen. There were several pieces of
jewelry, including a watch and some rings, that were
clearly visible and left behind. Robbery again did
not appear to be the motive.

Wallace had a gunshot wound, and the bullet entered the right temple of her head and traveled
slightly backward and upward before exiting the left
side of her skull. The presence of a high-velocity
blood spray on the items dumped from the purse
made it evident that it had been dumped prior to
the shooting.

Once a search of the body and bed was made, the deceased was wrapped in the bedspread, placed in a body bag, and moved to the morgue at St. Francis.

When the body was examined more thoroughly, no traces of sperm were found to reveal if she was sexually assaulted, but there was some seminal fluid found on the bedspread between her legs and under her buttocks. When tested, the seminal stains revealed that they came from someone with an A positive blood type. No other usable fingerprints were found. Her body was then stored at the morgue until it could be transported to the St. Louis County Medical Examiner's Office for a full autopsy. Despite the ligature found around her neck, there was no evidence of asphyxia, so it was determined that her death was caused by the gunshot to her head. The slug was recovered by crime scene investigators and taken to Olin's Winchester Ammunition Manufacturing facility in East Alton, Illinois, where it was examined by engineer Henry Halverson. Halverson determined that the projectile was a Winchester 125-grain bullet with a semi-copper jacket and a hollow-point lead tip. He surmised that the bullet was probably fired from a Smith & Wesson revolver because of the apparent right twist of the lands and grooves. The large amount of powder found around the wound would be characteristic of a .357-caliber bullet, but Halverson stated that he speculated it came from a .38 Special fired from a four-inch barrel, because a .357 Magnum would spread out more when it passed through bony material, such as a human skull. He made a point of telling the investigators that his determination that it came from a .38-caliber Smith & Wesson was only speculation, and that he would not rule out that it may have come from a Ruger, Rohm, or INA.

Fortunately, it was a bright, clear day, with a temperature of 76 degrees and a slight breeze. The exterior of the house was immediately processed for fingerprint evidence to prevent any evidence from being destroyed by the elements of the environment. Dozens of unusable fingerprint impressions were found. Others turned out to match Mildred Wallace's own fingerprints. There were two prints, however, which were clear enough to be used for identification purposes and did *not* belong to Wallace. One was a partial fingerprint and the other was a palm print. Both were found on the exterior of the north living-room window. Somebody must have leaned against the glass, probably to look inside the house. If the prints could be matched up to a particular individual, the police might finally have a suspect.

A size-9½ blue Sears Winner II tennis shoe, with three white stripes on each side, was later found at the intersection of William Street and South West End Boulevard, not far from the Wallace house.

Another piece of evidence that gave investigators hope had to do with the boot laces that were used to bind Wallace's wrists. The laces were similar to the ones used in the Illinois murders of Virginia Witte and Deborah Sheppard. The knots were also tied in a similar fashion. One knot had a loop tied with a granny knot; the other had two square knots topped with a bow. All of them appeared to be tied by somebody who was left-handed. It appeared that the unsolved murders that had spread terror throughout the region might be linked to a single serial killer, after all. The details of the case were entered into the FBI ViCAP program. Investigators hoped that they would soon receive a positive match to the submitted evidence and finally bring an end to this nightmare. They were disappointed.

Carl Kinnison, the police chief in Cape Girardeau, was a young evidence technician at the scene at the time of the Wallace murder. He spent the night alone inside her home on William Street in order to keep the area secure. More than twenty-five years later, he still recalled his feeling of fear as he sat in the dark at the kitchen table and envisioned the killer returning to the scene of the crime. In his mind, he kept picturing the scenario and thought about how he would respond if he ended up face-to-face with a killer. Would the killer try to kill him, too? Would he have the inner strength to kill another human being in order to defend himself? His senses remained acute, and every unidentified sound in the darkness made his body tense, while his mind struggled to keep from panicking. He needed to keep control of his senses, his mind, and his body in case he had to react to a potentially lethal situation. Needless to say, Kinnison did not get any sleep that night; fortunately, he did not have to encounter the killer making a return visit.

Several pieces of evidence were sent from the Southeast Missouri Crime Lab to be examined at the Department of Forensic Sciences in Huntsville, Alabama. They included: a red-stained cutting from the carpet of Wallace's bathroom floor, three small pieces of bathroom calking with reddish brown stains, pieces of the bathroom window, a Band-Aid cover and one plastic vial lableled BLOOD FROM BOX.

In the middle of July, criminalist Rodger Morrison
sent back a report of his findings. He wrote that the
carpet piece and the three pieces of calking each
contained bloodstains that reacted in a manner
consistent with having come from a male. Morrison's report stated that no further examinations
were conducted on those items, no examinations at
all were made on the rest of the items.

Hairs collected at the scene were sent to the
Kansas City Regional Criminalistics Laboratory for
examination. Chief forensic chemist John T. Wilson
sent back a report stating that he found one white
animal hair, numerous pubic hairs that matched the
victim, and hairs that matched the victim's head.
Wilson reported that no foreign hairs could be
identified.

When the news got out that Mildred Wallace was
murdered, the feeling of fear among the local population intensified even more, and the Cape Girardeau County Sheriff's Office issued seventy new
gun permits in a matter of weeks. Residents began
to look at every unfamiliar face in the city with suspicion. Rumors began to spread like wildfire. One
rumor was that Wallace had thrown cosmetic jars
out of her bathroom window in an attempt to at-
tract attention to her plight. It was also rumored
that Wallace had been receiving threatening phone
calls in the days preceding her death. It seemed as
though everyone had his or her own version of the
events that took place, and who might be responsible for the recent rash of rapes and murders. These
stories were passed on, altered, added on to, and
sometimes completely changed.

The police department was reluctant to release

information to the public because they feared it might impair their investigation, and the media was cooperative in agreeing to release only carefully worded press releases. Increasing anxiety and a lack of information added to the public's speculation about the facts.

One rumor became widely accepted and even infiltrated the ranks of the police department itself. It was speculated that the killer had been able to escape detection for so long because he had an intimate knowledge of police procedures and methods of investigation. He had gotten away with so many murders because the killer—it was rumored—was actually a member of the police department. The rumor opened up a possibility that investigators could not ignore; they began to investigate their own people.

In mid-July, Sergeant Brown met with the members of the Cape Girardeau Business and Professional Women's Club, of which Wallace was a past president. He told them that "rumors are rampant" and "we're not ruling anything out." He added, however, that rumors were proving to become a hindrance to the investigation. In regard to the rumor of a member of the police force being responsible, he said that eighty-three contacts in several states were notified and investigated before it was traced to a remark made by a woman who was having her hair done in a Cape Girardeau beauty shop. It was not based on any actual evidence.

Brown urged citizens to resist the tendency to profile people who might fit the characteristics of a suspected killer, and also not to ignore individuals who might not fit into that profile, because the real killer might be clever enough to avoid behaviors that drew suspicion. He also added that investigators were not certain that all the murders in Cape Girardeau were committed by the same individual, but none of the cases would be closed until the perpetrator or perpetrators are found.

The police did not want to exclude the possibility that different people might be responsible for the recent murders in Cape Girardeau, but they could not ignore the similarities in the cases involving Mildred Wallace, Marjorie Call, and Mary Parsh. All of the women were approximately the same age. Brenda Parsh was younger, but investigators believed that the killer did not expect her, and so he killed her in order to protect himself. All the victims lived near each other in similar middle-class neighborhoods. In every case, the intruder broke into the residences and waited for his victims to return home. All the women were found either nude or partially nude in their bedrooms with evidence of sexual assault.

Ray Johnson, the Cape Girardeau police chief at the time, was receiving pressure from the public to resolve these cases and put an end to the fear that penetrated the city. He realized that he needed help and asked for assistance from the St. Louis Metropolitan Police Department Homicide Division and the Federal Bureau of Investigation.

Johnson also used the media to help issue warnings that women who lived alone in the community should take precautions to prevent similar murders from occurring. He encouraged women to let friends or family members know when they expected to leave or arrive home and that they should check their

homes for evidence of a possible forced entry before
entering their houses. Johnson also suggested that
people should install outside lighting around their
homes and cut back any bushes or shrubs that might
provide a hiding place for someone attempting to
break into their residence.

The *Southeast Missourian* newspaper reported on
July 27, 1982, that George A. Williams, the police
commissioner in Marion, Illinois, brought up during
the most recent city council meeting the possibility
that there might be a link between several recently
reported sexual assaults in Marion and the murders
in Cape Girardeau, which was located about sixty-five
miles west.

Marion authorities would not release the details
of the attacks—except to say that one Marion
woman in her sixties was assaulted in her home on
the night of June 6, and another woman, also in
her sixties, was sexually assaulted in her home by an
unknown man on the night of March 28. The
March incident obviously referred to that of Paulene Brown, who wrote a letter to the Cape Girardeau Police Department after news of the attack on
Drake, Smith, and Lacey took place.

Cape Girardeau police chief Johnson said at the
time that "we haven't come up with anything concrete at this point, but we aren't ready to discount
the possibility of a connection yet." He added that
"they haven't had homicides there, just a number
of sexual assaults," but he emphasized that the
cases were still worth looking into, due to certain
similarities. He did not provide details of the similarities that he mentioned, and for some reason,
neither Johnson nor Williams mentioned or made

a connection with the 1978 murder of Virginia Witte, in Marion.

Despite the joint efforts of the police investigators in Missouri and Illinois with the FBI, nothing more than a general profile of a possible suspect was gained, and no actual suspects were able to be charged in connection with any of the crimes that were committed.

Hundreds of suspects and leads were eliminated, but authorities were still no closer to apprehending the murderer than they were in 1977 after the bodies of Mary and Brenda Parsh were discovered. This case had achieved one thing, however: the interdepartmental exchange of information between local, state, and federal authorities. Even though the results were not gratifying so far, it was a hallmark case in developing a cooperative link between jurisdictions that had in many ways considered each other adversaries instead of allies in the fight against crime. In the new millennium, it would prove to be a hallmark case in the use of technology, as well as cooperation.

1983

I'm not a Goody Two-shoes or some Good Samaritan, but I do have some good feelings.

—Timothy Wayne Krajcir

21

Sandra Schwartz
February 21, 1983

Detective Steve Strong received a phone call from authorities in West Memphis, Tennessee. Apparently, they had just arrested a man named Edward Louis Radouski and they were in the process of returning him to Cape Girardeau, Missouri, where he allegedly kidnapped a woman from the parking lot of the West Park Mall.

The next day, twenty-one-year-old Sandra Schwartz met with Detective Strong at the Cape Girardeau police headquarters to provide him with an official statement. She told him that she had just made some purchases at the mall and that it was around noon when she walked across the parking lot to her car, which was parked near the main entrance. Schwartz said that she was inside her vehicle and already had started the engine when a man suddenly pulled her door open and stuck something that felt like a gun against the side of her body.

"He told me to move over to the passenger seat or he would shoot me, so I moved over and he climbed into the driver's seat. Then he told me to put my head on my knees and my hands behind my back," Schwartz said.

Detective Strong wrote down all the details as Schwartz described them. Radouski handcuffed her and then drove to a less occupied section of the parking lot. She said that he got out of her car for a few seconds and then pulled up beside her car door in another vehicle. He moved her into his car and then used a T-shirt to wipe off everything that he touched inside her car.

Schwartz said that Radouski took $9 out of her purse and then asked her if she had a checkbook. She told him that she had it inside her car, so he went back to her car to find it. After he retrieved the checkbook, he got back inside his car and drove off.

"He asked me where the bank was, that I had the checking account at, and I told him that it was the Colonial Federal. Then he asked how much money I had in my account, and I told him that I didn't know," Schwartz said.

She said that Radouski stopped at a service station to call the bank and ask for a balance so he would know how much money he could write a check for. There was no answer. He became frustrated and decided just to drive to the bank, but on the way there, he realized that it was a holiday, so all the banks were closed. Radouski eventually agreed to move the handcuffs from behind her back to the front of her body. She said that he didn't know how to get to the interstate, so she had to give him directions.

Schwartz told Strong that Radouski drove on the

interstate for a while, and she heard on the car radio that it was almost one o'clock.

"He told me that if I follow his plan, I would live to see my husband again. He never told me where we were going or what the plan was. He just said that he would kill me rather than go to jail," Schwartz said.

According to Schwartz's statement, Radouski rifled through her purse once more and took the rest of her money. She said that it was about $23 total. Then Radouski began to ask her all kinds of personal questions. Was she a virgin when she married her husband? Had she been with any other men sexually? What kind of contraception did she use? Did she drink alcohol or use drugs?

"He told me that he attended church and that he didn't do this sort of thing every day, but he needed the money," Schwartz said.

When they reached West Memphis, Tennessee, Schwartz said that Radouski pulled off the interstate. He drove into the parking lot of a Holiday Inn and shut off the car. Then he used the handcuffs to secure her left arm to the steering wheel and told her that he would return in a few minutes. After Radouski got out of the car and walked toward the hotel, Schwartz said that she was able to wriggle her hand out of the cuff and pull herself free. She unlocked the car door and ran to a service station to get help. An attendant at the station called the local police, who drove out and arrested Radouski.

The case against Radouski was pretty airtight, and his method of grabbing a woman from the parking lot of the West Park Mall in Cape Girardeau sounded too close to the method used in the Ann Shares case to be a coincidence. But Radouski wouldn't confess to any other rapes or murders, and there was no concrete evidence to pin him to any crime other than kidnapping Schwartz.

Sergeant Brown and the rest of the people who had spent the last five years investigating the heinous crimes that plagued the area were convinced that the killer they were looking for was still out on the prowl.

Killer Captured

It's easy to slide through a system that's so overcrowded.
                              —Timothy Wayne Krajcir

22

Not long after the body of Mildred Wallace was found, Timothy Krajcir returned to Pennsylvania. His intention to do so was premeditated because he had informed authorities of his desire to return east, and his parole was transferred to Pennsylvania two days before Wallace was murdered. On his return, he initially lived with his mother for about a month; then he moved into a trailer with his half brother Bernard, "Bernie," at the Keystone Mobile Home Court in Laurys Station, a small town near where he once lived during his childhood. Krajcir's mother lived and worked in the city of Bethlehem, located about fifteen miles away.

Krajcir was never close to the other members of his family, so he spent much of his time cruising along the streets of Allentown—Pennsylvania's third largest city. Numerous sexual assaults throughout the south side of the city prompted local news coverage to dub the unknown perpetrator as the "Southside Rapist."

One of the reported incidents took place on

December 30, 1982, when a man broke into an apartment located on South Church Street. Mariah Simpson lived in the apartment with her two children, an eighteen-year-old daughter, Darlene, and a six-year-old son. Detective Barry Giacobbe was dispatched to the scene in order to investigate the complaint.

On arriving, Giacobbe noted that there was a door in front that provided direct access into the apartment, and another door that provided access to the apartment building. Inside this door was a hallway that led to other doors that gave access to all the apartments within the building. Both the inside and outside doors of Simpson's apartment building were locked, and there were no visible signs of forced entry at either location.

All the windows in the apartment were also locked, except for one in the living room at the front of the apartment. It wasn't a conventional double-hung window, but a slider window that opened sideways. Investigators decided it was through this window that the perpetrator had gained access to the apartment. While searching the premises, it was also discovered that the cords of both the telephones in the apartment had been cut. The investigating officer took an initial statement about the events that occurred and filed a report.

Allentown police detective sergeant Harold Boyer followed up on the incident on the following day. He had a special interest in the case because he knew the Simpsons personally. Just a year and a half earlier, Boyer had lived in the apartment across the hall from them.

The Simpsons told Boyer that a man broke into the apartment at about 4:30 A.M. Darlene was asleep in her bedroom when she woke up and went into the kitchen to drink a soda. When she returned to her bedroom, there was a man standing there with a pistol in his hand. He held the gun to her head and told her that if she would be quiet, she wouldn't get hurt. He made her undress and said that "he was a freak and only wanted to eat her out." According to the criminal complaint, the intruder told her as he fondled her butt, "You don't want me to kill your mother and brother." Darlene struggled against her assailant, and the commotion woke her mother, who was asleep about twenty feet away in another room. Mariah dialed 911 and notified the communication center that a man had broken into her apartment and was still there. The intruder heard Mariah, went into her room, and cut the phone line. He asked who she was talking to, and Mariah said that she was on the phone with her husband. The intruder brought Mariah into Darlene's room and made her undress and stand next to her daughter. He then resumed fondling Darlene while he masturbated.

Before leaving, the perpetrator stole Mariah's change purse, which she said contained approximately $15 in quarters. The only real usable physical evidence that crime scene investigators were able to recover was a palm print from the windowpane.

Boyer said that he was surprised but happy that the Simpsons weren't killed. He also said that he believed that both women were "holding back" when they described the events that took place. "I think they were too ashamed to come clean about everything that happened that night," he said.

Pennsylvania authorities would not release detailed

records of the incident, but to the best of Boyer's recollection, the Simpsons were able to describe their assailant with enough detail to have a likeness of his face drawn and published in a local newspaper, along with a plea to the public to help identify him. The image was enough to prompt other calls to the Allentown Police Department (APD). A man that looked like the Simpsons' attacker was observed at a nearby McDonald's restaurant eating a sandwich and drinking a milk shake. He was also observed walking along South Fourth Street.

After recognizing the photo in the newspaper, Georgia Johnson filed a criminal complaint of indecent assault. She said that she had just finished shopping for some groceries at the Acme, on South Fourth Street, when she was accosted. Johnson explained that at approximately 9:45 P.M. she walked across the parking lot, and as she attempted to enter her automobile, a man came up behind her and grabbed her buttocks. She was able to get inside her car and then quickly drive away.

After several unrelated sexual assaults and rapes were reported in South Allentown, residents became more observant of their surroundings. On January 27, 1983, a week after Johnson was assaulted in the Acme parking lot, Debra Moyer called the Allentown Police Department to report a suspicious vehicle parked on the outer perimeter of the Mountainville Shopping Center. She described it as a cream or yellow four-door Plymouth. Moyer told police that a man drove up in the car and parked. He stared at her for a long time from the parking lot as she sat in front of her home. After a while, he pulled away, and she noticed that the license plate on the back of the Plymouth was covered with masking tape so the numbers could not be read. Moyer said that the car stopped again in another part of the parking lot and the driver got out, walked to the rear of his vehicle, and began to peel the tape off.

Officer John "Jack" Ross drove out to Moyer's house on Baldwin Street to investigate the call. He hoped that it might lead to a break in the city's unsolved rape cases. As Ross spoke to Moyer, she pointed toward the Plymouth, which had just then begun to pull out of the shopping center parking lot. It was a yellow Plymouth Valiant.

Ross turned on the overhead lights of his patrol vehicle and pursued the car. He used his radio to call for assistance and engaged the police siren to gain the attention of the driver in the vehicle that he was following. Unlike the dramatic television and movie portrayals of how vicious killers are captured; there was no high-speed pursuit, no multicar collisions, no helicopters flying overhead, and no SWAT team shoot-outs. As Ross pulled the suspect's car over to the curb on South Church Street, Officer Diehl arrived for backup support in patrol car number eight. Ross cautiously approached the vehicle and found Timothy Krajcir in the driver's seat. He was quiet, complacent, and cooperative. He made no attempt to hide the loaded .25-caliber blue-steel pistol in his lap. Krajcir admitted that he did not have a license to carry a firearm, and Ross immediately confiscated the weapon, handcuffed Krajcir, and secured him in the back of his patrol car. Then he contacted Sergeant Boyer, who drove out to the scene to make the official arrest.

A National Crime Information Center (NCIC)

background check on Krajcir revealed that he was a former convict who had been involved in a crime of violence, so it was illegal for him to have a gun of any kind in his possession. He was soon incarcerated at Lehigh County Prison on North Fourth Street in Allentown.

It is ironic that when Krajcir decided it was time to return to his Pennsylvania roots and come home, he finally found the place where he truly belonged; in a locked cage surrounded by guards.

Boyer hoped to close the unsolved rape cases that recently plagued the south side of Allentown, so although Krajcir was only arrested for illegal possession of a firearm, he was questioned about the numerous sexual assaults that had taken place. After interrogation, Krajcir did not turn out to be the "Southside Rapist," but he did confess to the assaults of Mariah and Darlene Simpson and Georgia Johnson. In addition to carrying a firearm without a license, Krajcir was charged with robbery, burglary, criminal trespass, theft, receiving stolen property, aggravated assault, recklessly endangering another person, terroristic threats, and indecent assault.

Assistant public defender Michael Moyer was assigned to represent Krajcir, and he entered a plea of not guilty to all charges. On Krajcir's behalf, Moyer submitted an omnibus pretrial motion to suppress all statements made by Krajcir from being used at trial. The motion stated that Krajcir was unlawfully approached and that his automobile was searched without probable cause. It further stated that Krajcir made statements to the interrogating officer without being afforded full and adequate Miranda warnings. Moyer maintained that Krajcir

made his statements without having knowledge of
his right to remain silent and his right to obtain
counsel.

After his motion was denied, Moyer filed an application for an incompetency examination. In the
application, Moyer requested that a diagnosis of
Krajcir's mental condition be performed and that
a professional opinion be determined in regard to
his capacity to understand the nature of the criminal proceedings against him, as well as his mental
condition, in relation to the standards for criminal
responsibility.

Krajcir was housed on the third floor on the north
side of a recently built addition to Lehigh County's
prison facility in Allentown. The original structure
was a looming red sandstone fortress that stood at
Fourth and Linden Streets for over 125 years. The
fortress featured walls forty-five feet high and Spar-
tan cells that were extremely overpopulated.

While incarcerated there, Krajcir befriended a
fellow inmate, John Grello. Krajcir and Grello were
assigned to adjacent cells, numbers nine and ten.
On May 1, 1983, at approximately 10:30 P.M., the two
inmates cut the sliding fire door guide bar and
pulled the door out enough to make room for them
to squeeze through. The two men then crawled
down the rear fire tower and entered into the men's
recreation yard. They scaled a security fence and
then used a rope made of bedsheets tied together
to lower themselves along the north wall of the
prison and onto the city street outside the building.

Grello climbed down first and was observed by a
corrections officer (CO) who was making his rounds
outside the perimeter. The security guard used his

walkie-talkie to call to the front desk, and the transmission was picked up by the Allentown Police Department. They immediately dispatched officers to the prison, which was only two blocks away.

The CO then observed a second inmate climb down. He yelled up at him, and Krajcir lost his grip and fell. He landed on the roof of a parked car and then fell to the driveway. Krajcir was handcuffed and then taken to a nearby hospital to be checked for injuries. Additional charges were then filed against Krajcir in regard to his attempt to escape from prison. Grello was apprehended locally within days of his escape.

"If they would have escaped together, they would have made a dangerous pair," Boyer said. "Grello was a burglar. His whole family was a pack of thieves, but Grello held no value on human life. He'd kill you just as easily as look at you. He killed a guard while he was in prison. And Krajcir, he was just a dangerous guy that you didn't want to know. If they had teamed up together, there's no telling what might have happened."

Boyer recalled a previous incident in which Grello was surrounded by police after burglarizing a Laneco store on Cedar Crest Boulevard. "He scaled a drainpipe and made his way to the rooftop, like a monkey or Spider-Man. He was very agile." By Boyer's recollection of Grello's antics, it was probable that he was the mastermind behind his and Krajcir's escape from Lehigh County Prison.

While Krajcir remained incarcerated in Allentown and waited for his trial date, there was no doubt about his guilt for the crimes he was accused of. His mental capacity, however, remained in question. That would have to be evaluated first before he could be held responsible for his actions. A psychological evaluation might have an effect on his sentencing. Judge James Diefenderfer ordered that a psychiatric observation and examination of Krajcir be performed by Dr. Paul K. Gross.

After interviewing him, Gross reported that Krajcir was cold, detached, and devoid of almost all normal emotional attachments. Although Krajcir claimed that he would not harm someone he knew, he still showed no remorse for the crimes he committed— no empathy for any of his victims. Gross noted that Krajcir tried to explain his actions as the product of a difficult upbringing, and that he would transfer his feelings of anger toward his mother on other women. Gross commented that Krajcir never attempted to control his actions or retard his violent impulses. While Gross acknowledged that Krajcir displayed some sexually deviant behavior, he refused to say that Krajcir's actions were the result of mental illness.

Gross closed the statement of his evaluation by concluding that Krajcir suffered from severe sexual deviancy, and that he should be incarcerated in a prison where he could receive psychiatric treatment and possibly therapy that included prescribed medication. Even with this kind of treatment, Gross was not optimistic that positive results could be achieved by someone as far gone as Krajcir. He even suggested another alternative experimental treatment that was being used in patients who did not respond well to psychotherapy—a course of hormone therapy designed to reduce a patient's sex drive severely.

In July, Krajcir's attorney changed his defendant's

plea to guilty on all of the charges against him. On August 9, 1983, Judge James Diefenderfer imposed a sentence of not less than two years and six months, and not more than five years, with the specific directive that he needed continuous psychotherapy and psychiatric treatment. He received credit of 192 days for time already spent in custody. Krajcir's attempted escape from Lehigh County Prison guaranteed that he would serve the full extent of his sentence.

Krajcir was sent to the Pennsylvania State Correctional Institution at Graterford. The largest maximum-security prison in the state is located in Montgomery County, about thirty miles west of the city of Philadelphia. For the next five years, it would be home to Timothy Krajcir.

While Krajcir was falling down the prison wall in Allentown, Pennsylvania, Sergeant Brown was still tracking down leads to find a killer in Missouri. On August 4, 1983, he received an anonymous tip that a man by the name of William Cortez was responsible for the 1977 murder of Sheila Cole.

It wasn't much to go on. Brown didn't have a phone number or an address. He didn't even have a description of the man. All he had was a name, William Cortez. At least it was something. It was a new beginning that started out like hundreds of other previous beginnings. Brown hoped that this time it would finally lead to an end.

It wasn't much to go on, but Brown would attempt to identify the man named William Cortez. He would track him down, and hopefully prove once and for all that he was the one responsible for all the killings. Most important, Brown wanted to catch the man responsible so that the killing would end.

1984

I'm not a guy that doesn't have any feeling. I'm full of emotion, but it's become more so over the years as I learned more about myself. I've read all I could when I wasn't in therapy.

—Timothy Wayne Krajcir

23

By the time 1984 arrived, Sergeant Brown was still unsuccessful in his attempt to locate the whereabouts of William Cortez. He determined that Cortez actually did exist, and he even obtained a description of the man. Cortez was six feet, four inches tall. He weighed about 155 pounds. He had blue eyes and black hair.

Much of what Brown had learned about Cortez came from an interview he conducted with Debbie Clover, who lived on Good Hope Street in Cape Girardeau. Debbie Clover was a friend of William Cortez's wife, Bobbie Cortez. Clover told Sergeant Brown that Cortez told his wife that he had killed Sheila Cole in 1977. Bobbie, in turn, told Debbie about the incident. Clover said that she had not seen Bobbie or William Cortez in several months. She said that she had heard that William moved to Texas, but she wasn't sure if his wife was with him.

A couple of weeks later, on January 26, 1984, Special Agent Connell Smith wanted to confirm what Brown had discovered, so he went to conduct a second interview with Debbie Clover.

Clover told Smith that Bobbie Cortez was upset with her husband because he had recently beaten her up. It was when William Cortez was beating his wife that he told her that he had murdered the girl at the rest area in McClure. She supposed that it was his way of letting her know what he was capable of doing.

Clover said that Cortez lived on Spanish Street, and the apartment building had burned down since then. Clover added that she believed that Bobbie and William Cortez were now separated or divorced. She also told Smith that she had heard that William Cortez had recently returned to Cape Girardeau from Texas.

Further investigation revealed that Bobbie Cortez worked at the Candle Wick Lounge several years earlier, but when she was living with William at their Spanish Street address, she was unemployed and received public aid.

It took several months, but Cape Girardeau police investigators were finally able to track down William Cortez. Apparently, Debbie Clover was correct in her assumption that William Cortez had returned to the area. In fact, he moved into an apartment in the same area in which he used to live. Detective Curt Casteel was dispatched to interview William Cortez about his possible involvement in the kidnapping and murder of Sheila Cole.

Casteel questioned William Cortez for about an hour. Cortez told him that he did not recall telling Bobbie Cortez, or anyone else, that he was responsible for Sheila Cole's death. He added that he was an alcoholic at the time and was prone to making extreme, often untruthful statements. He said that he often told lies to impress his friends and to show how "macho" he was. Cortez told Casteel that he recalled the Cole case, because he had heard about it on television. He said that he did not know Cole personally and did not recall ever meeting her.

Detective Casteel requested that William Cortez submit to a polygraph examination, but Cortez refused. He indicated that he did not trust the instrument's accuracy and feared that his involvement in other crimes might be revealed.

After Casteel filed his report, Sergeant Brown forwarded the information to Special Agent Smith, who concluded that the interview failed to provide any information that might implicate William Cortez in the murder of Sheila Cole.

24

Lucas and Toole
March 1984

After more than six years of following leads that got Brown no closer to discovering who was responsible for the murders of Sheila Cole and the Parshes, he began to clutch at straws and hope for luck. He decided that he would travel to Jacksonville, Florida, to interview Ottis Elwood Toole, and then to Bay City, Texas, to question Henry Lee Lucas.

There was no physical evidence to link either man to the murders in Cape Girardeau, but Brown thought it might be possible that there was a connection. For about seven years, Lucas and Toole had traveled back and forth between the states of Florida and Texas on a killing rampage. If there was even a remote possibility that they may have diverted their normal path of travel a bit north, Brown wanted to make sure that it was investigated.

Before the March 1984 interviews, Brown did a bit of background research on Lucas and Toole and discovered that both of them were free men during the time that Cole and the Parshes were murdered.

For many years, Lucas was listed as America's, as well as the world's, most prolific serial killer after he confessed to his involvement in nearly six hundred murders. A Texas-based Lucas Task Force, claimed that number was closer to 350, and Lucas later claimed that he was only responsible for about 150 murders in all. The first murder that he was convicted of was that of his own mother in 1960, but he claimed to have actually committed his first murder in 1951, at the age of fifteen, when he supposedly strangled a girl who rebuked his sexual advances.

Based on confessions by Lucas, police officially cleared 213 previously unsolved murders, but ultimately he was only convicted of eleven homicides, including that of Toole's niece Frieda "Becky" Powell. After he was sentenced to the death penalty, he became more than willing to confess to anything that he was accused of, which put the credibility of many of his confessions into question. More than 150 death penalty cases came across George W. Bush's desk, who was then the Texas governor. In 1998, Lucas's was the only one in which Bush intervened and commuted to life in prison.

Lucas claimed to have engaged in cannibalism, bestiality, homosexuality, and heterosexuality. In the mid-1970s, he met up with Ottis Toole, and the two men became lovers, as well as accomplices in rape and murder.

Toole dropped out of school in the eighth grade after being tested with an IQ of 75 and being designated as mentally retarded. He claimed to have committed his first murder at the age of fourteen after driving a car into a traveling salesman who had propositioned him for sex. Toole admitted to multiple counts of murder, cannibalism, rape, necrophilia, and arson.

In April 1984, he was sentenced to death for a 1982 arson incident that resulted in the death of sixty-four-year-old George Sonnenberg in Jacksonville, Florida. He later received a second death penalty sentence for the murder of nineteen-year-old Ada Johnson. Toole's sentences were commuted to life in prison on appeal. After being convicted of four additional murders, he received four additional life sentences. For a brief time, Toole was housed next to Ted Bundy in Florida's Raiford State Penitentiary.

It was only a month before Toole was given his initial death sentence that Brown interviewed him in Jacksonville. On March 7, 1984, Brown and Sheriff Ferrell, of Scott County, Missouri, discussed several homicides with Toole with the assurance that he would not be charged with any crime. At the time, Toole was already awaiting trial on approximately thirty different felony charges.

During the interview, Toole said that he had killed approximately one hundred people by himself, and about sixty others with Lucas. He told Brown that he was usually intoxicated and under the influence of drugs during most of the incidents, so he couldn't be sure if he would be able to determine whether or not he or Lucas had committed any specific homicides that he was questioned about. He indicated that he met Lucas in the mid-1970s and had fallen in love with him.

Toole said that he frequently traveled across the country with Lucas, killing people as they went.

He told Brown that they had broken into bathroom windows of houses in order to burglarize the places, and then once inside, they would sometimes rape and murder a victim they found. He recalled that on many occasions he knocked makeup off the bathroom windowsills, which fell both inside and outside the houses. Toole said that he sometimes gagged his victims with pieces of their clothing and he usually tied them up. He also recalled cutting the phone cord in several houses. He said that he usually ended up shooting his victims in the head.

Toole said that there had been occasions that he and Lucas would approach a house while carrying an empty milk jug. They would knock on the door, and if a woman answered, they would claim that their car had overheated and that they needed water for the radiator. He said that they were seldom refused entry. Once they got inside the house, they would rape and murder the woman who let them in.

Their usual routine, according to Toole, was to wait in parking lots, including Wal-Mart, and then kidnap females as they returned to their cars. His descriptions of multiple rapes and homicides contained many similarities to the murders that had taken place in Cape Girardeau. Brown shared information with Toole regarding the Parsh, Call, and Wallace murders. Toole said that he did not remember any of those murders as ones that had been done by himself or with Lucas.

When Brown reviewed the Cole homicide with him in detail, including photographs, Toole could not recall that particular incident. He remarked that he did not remember ever leaving any victim fully clothed.

If Brown had wanted to clear the murders in his hometown from the books, he could have easily done so.

"Toole would have confessed to anything I wanted him to admit to if I would have gone a half block down the street from the prison and brought him back a four-dollar box of fried chicken," Brown later recalled.

A confession of that sort might have cleared the books, but it wouldn't have cleared Brown's conscience. He wasn't a lazy or corrupt cop, and he wouldn't compromise his morals. Even though other police cleared 213 cases from their files due to Lucas's confessions, Brown knew in his heart that there was no real evidence to connect Toole to the murders in Cape Girardeau. As much as Brown wanted to put an end to this investigation, he would not settle for less than arresting the real person or persons responsible for committing the crimes. He was not convinced that Toole had anything to do with them.

The next day, Brown and Ferrell traveled to Texas to interrogate Lucas. The interview was also prefixed with assurances that there was no intention to charge him with a crime. If honesty prevailed and closure could be brought to the victims' families, that would be enough. Lucas was already sentenced to death, so additional charges would not bring additional penalty. It was strictly a matter of finding out the truth, clearing the books, and bringing closure to a horrific case file.

Lucas discussed his crimes readily and appeared to have a desire to help. He gave a similar account to his crime activity, as Toole did, but as a more intelligent man, he recalled specific crimes in much greater detail.

When questioned about his activity in Southeast Missouri, Lucas said that he had kidnapped and robbed a girl from an automobile service station. He described her as a white female, approximately twenty to twenty-five years old, with blond, curly hair and no bangs, and wearing a beige sweater with a blue or beige blouse. He said that he drove north on Interstate 55 and then turned onto Highway 61. He told Brown that he raped and killed her and then dumped her nude body along the road near Pevely, Missouri. He recalled that he could see the Mississippi River from that location.

Lucas reviewed the homicide file of Cheryl Scherer, of Scott County, and indicated that he definitely was not responsible for her murder. After reviewing the files of Mary and Brenda Parsh, Sheila Cole, Marjorie Call, and Mildred Wallace, Lucas proclaimed that he was certain that he had not participated in any of those murders.

Lucas's confessions to crimes became criticized as outlandish when reports came in that he claimed to have killed Jimmy Hoffa and to have delivered poison to Jim Jones, prior to the notorious mass murder/suicide in Jonestown, Guyana. Most of the confessions that Lucas made were eventually challenged by the media. Brad Shellady investigated the life of Lucas for years and contributed to a book,

Everything You Know Is Wrong, edited by Russ Kick, in which he expresses his opinion that Lucas probably only committed one murder—that of his abusive mother. Supposedly, Lucas wrote a letter to Shellady that stated, *I am not a serial killer.*

Shellady reports that Lucas wrote him, *If they were going to make me confess to one I didn't do, then I was going to confess to everything.*

The fact that neither Toole nor Lucas confessed to committing the crimes in Cape Girardeau, combined with a lack of physical evidence to connect them in any way, failed to link them to the crimes. Nothing had been accomplished as far as getting closer to the resolution of the cases that had consumed Brown's life for nearly seven years.

Every morning Sergeant Brown would drive to police headquarters on Sprigg Street in Cape Girardeau. Despite the size of his current caseload, regardless of the personal sacrifices that he had made spending time away from his loved ones, and no matter how much time had passed by, one train of thought continued to consume him: Who killed the Parshes? Who murdered the young college student Sheila Cole? Who was responsible for the brutal murders of Marjorie Call and Mildred Wallace? These questions kept him awake at night. These questions coaxed him out of the warm bed that he shared with his wife so he could riffle through the card files of facts about the case. He kept his own personal file at home, and he would go back to it time and time again, hoping that he might see something that he missed the first hundred times that he read through it.

Brown had seen brutal things in his life, but he couldn't get the image of the bodies out of his mind. He would never forget the stench that filled his nostrils when he entered the Parsh house. He could taste the odor. It filled his insides and choked his throat and made his stomach wretch, and the taste of his own bile was less repugnant than the odor inside that house. And every morning Sergeant Brown would drive to police headquarters on Sprigg Street in Cape Girardeau, hoping that this would be the morning that he would find the person responsible for making him remember that for the last seven years. The first thing he would do was check the most recent NCIC reports to see if there were any hits for similar cases.

If the person responsible for the murders in Cape Girardeau was still on the loose, chances are that he would be responsible for even more murders in other parts of the country. It would only be a matter of time until the monster was finally caught. It was hard to believe that so much time had already passed. Brown didn't care who made the catch. He just wanted the shark pulled out of the water. He wanted closure for the victims—and a good night's sleep.

Over the next two years, a potential lead would occasionally look promising for a day or so, and then end up going nowhere. In July of 1985, Cape Girardeau County assistant prosecuting attorney James Hahn III informed Brown that a man named James "Jimmy" Kelly could be considered a suspect because he fit the psychological profile that was created for the potential killer. At the time, Hahn was known to be a nice enough guy, but he had a reputation for sometimes getting a bit overzealous about cases that had no merit. Brown followed up on the tip, but, as usual, it only came to a dead end.

Three months later, another lead looked somewhat more promising. When Brown arrived at work and checked the latest reports from NCIC, he came upon the case of James Smith, an inmate in the California State Penitentiary who was awaiting trial for three separate homicides. According to the information Brown received, Smith bragged to several other prisoners about fifteen murders that he supposedly committed in Missouri between 1975 and 1982. The time frame fit perfectly.

When Brown tried to get permission to question Smith about the unsolved murders in Cape Girardeau, the suspect's lawyer intervened. Smith had enough problems with three homicide charges pending. He wasn't going to confess to anything else. Nobody inside the prison came forward to confirm Smith's alleged bragging. Without any real physical evidence to link Smith specifically to the open cases in Cape Girardeau, Brown did not have a weapon to fight with against Smith's defense counsel. He couldn't even get an interview.

Meanwhile, back in Pennsylvania, Muhlenberg Township police had come no closer to discovering Myrtle Rupp's killer. When 1986 rolled around, seven years had passed since her body was discovered and the statute of limitations were such that if the person responsible was ever found and convicted, the only criminal charge that could be filed against him was the charge of homicide.

No new evidence had presented itself, and without

any new leads to follow, Wayne Huey remained as the
only prime suspect—despite the fact that the evidence failed to connect him to the crime six years
earlier.

A subpoena was served on Sterling Lee, Huey's son-
in-law and good friend at the time of the murder. The
subpoena obligated Lee to submit to a polygraph examination. The police wanted to verify if Wayne Huey
had made any incriminating statements to Lee in
regard to the death of Rupp. Lee said that Huey had
never made any such statements, and examiner Craig
Fink determined that the statements Lee made to the
police were truthful.

25

1988–1989

Just over eleven years had gone by since the bodies of Mary and Brenda Parsh were discovered. Investigators from every level of law enforcement had been involved in the case, and still no suspect was in custody. Detective John Brown, of the Cape Girardeau Police Department, was assigned to the case since the very beginning, and even though more than a decade had passed, he continued to search for the killer. In some cities, a cold case this old might have already been buried in the basement of the archives a long time ago. In Cape Girardeau, it still lived fresh in the minds of the residents who lived through a time they would never forget, a time when fear held the city hostage. Detective Brown's stamina and perseverance made him keep investigating, and the residents of Cape Girardeau, who did not forget the fear they experienced, made a point to keep reminding the police department that they still had a killer to catch.

Patrolman Earl Bruster received an anonymous telephone call from an elderly woman on November 22, 1988. The woman said that she had some information that had to do with murders that took place between 1977 and 1982. Bruster recorded the phone call and gave a copy of the taped conversation to Detective Brown.

In Brown's report, he wrote that the woman would not identify herself, but she believed that she knew who might be a good suspect for the homicides. She gave the name of Marvin Wallace and described him as a white male in his late sixties who used to be the owner of a furniture store in the city at the corner of Spanish and Independence Streets.

The caller indicated that she had heard rumors to the effect that Wallace had frequented Woolworth's and had flirted with the female employees. The flirtation, she said, included sexually suggestive and perhaps even obscene remarks. The caller was aware that Marjorie Call worked at Woolworth's at the time of her death.

After several unsuccessful attempts to get the caller to identify herself, she finally conceded to tell Bruster that she lived on Charles Street in Cape Girardeau. She said that she believed that Wallace sold his furniture business, and that he currently might be living in Sikeston, Missouri.

When asked why she thought that Wallace would make a good suspect, the caller replied that Wallace frequently entered residential homes in the city to deliver furniture. She went on to say that one time when he delivered a refrigerator to her house, he offered her $50 for sex and laid the money down on her bed. Brown's report never explained why Wallace would have been in the bedroom if he was delivering a refrigerator—perhaps Bruster never thought to ask. In any case, the caller said that when she refused Wallace's offer, he threw her on the bed and was about to rape her when a neighbor walked into the house.

By now, Brown was used to getting a lead like this, which he figured would go nowhere. There seemed to be a pattern of several leads that did not provide much hope and ended as expected, followed by a lead that promised hope and disappointed. It didn't matter if this one seemed like a futile effort; he was obligated to investigate them all.

It turned out that Wallace was the former owner of the furniture store and was currently living in Sikeston, just as the caller reported. The police department's communications division obtained information on Wallace's driver's license, got a list of all the vehicles that he currently owned, and found out that he had no criminal history.

Because there was never a report about the incident that the caller alleged, and since she wouldn't identify herself or the neighbor who supposedly witnessed the attempted rape, there was no reason to believe her claim. She might have been telling the truth, or she might have had a personal grudge against Wallace for some other reason. It didn't matter, because without evidence to suggest otherwise, Wallace was not a suspect. Brown also believed that Wallace was too old to fit the description of the killer.

As the pattern usually went, Brown's next lead proved to be a promising one that gave him hope. It centered on Robert McKinley Richards, a Caucasian male who was five feet, eleven inches tall and weighed approximately 160 pounds. It was learned that Richards had a penchant for uniforms—particularly, white ones for females. He was arrested in Tennessee by Hardeman County authorities and was identified as being responsible for the kidnapping and murder of Teresa Ann Jarvis Butler.

Brown contacted the FBI office in Tennessee to determine if Richards might be a viable suspect in the Cape Girardeau murders as well. Special Agent James Lummus sent Brown a synopsis of the investigation on Richards to date.

According to the information Brown received from the FBI, Butler was last seen when she left her job as a nursing student at St. Francis Hospital in Memphis. She left to go to her home in Shelby County. Approximately an hour later, her husband, Steve Butler, found her vehicle parked on a rural road with the headlights on and the engine still running. He reported that when he found his wife's car, the driver's-side door was open and a small portable radio, which she kept on the front seat, was still playing. His wife was nowhere to be found. There was a driving rainstorm at the time, and when investigators arrived at the scene, they were unable to find any evidence or clues to explain the woman's disappearance or the reason behind it.

Another Caucasian female nurse wearing a white uniform was driving in Hardeman County on July 22, 1987, when she was pulled over by a Caucasian male in a red pickup truck with a blue flashing light. She thought that it was unusual for a police officer to be driving a pickup truck, but he was dressed in a Shelby County Sheriff's Office (SCSO)

uniform. She also knew that Tennessee state authorities usually utilized blue lights on their vehicles.

According to the woman's statement, the "police
officer" told her that she was speeding and that she
would have to go to jail. He attempted to handcuff
her, and when she resisted, realizing that something
was wrong, he pulled out a pistol, which she noted
had blue bullets. She said that she continued to resist
the man's attempts to force her in his vehicle, and
eventually she was able to break free and escape. She
reported the incident to local authorities at her first
opportunity, and based on the information that she
gave them, Richards was located and arrested. At the
time of his arrest, Richards was still wearing a Tennessee sheriff's department uniform, and he was in
possession of an extensive amount of police equipment, including police radios.

Richards alluded to the abduction and murder
of Butler when he was questioned by Hardeman
County authorities, and during subsequent interviews by Shelby County detectives, Richards confessed to kidnapping Butler. He also told them that
he killed her by shooting her with a shotgun.

Richards explained that he had close ties to St.
Francis Hospital in that he dated several of the nurses
who were employed there. He said that he had
gained a special attraction to Butler. He described
how he followed her home one night to find out
where she lived, and then on a different evening, he
followed her home again. This time Richards knew
the path that she would take and was able to make his
plan in advance. As was his usual method, Richards
said that he was dressed in a police uniform and used
a blue light to pull Butler's car over to the side on a

deserted part of the road. Richards said that he told Butler that he was arresting her for driving too fast. He said that he then handcuffed her and put her in his vehicle, a 1979 light-colored Thunderbird. Then he claimed that he raped her, killed her with a shotgun, and disposed of the body.

According to the synopsis that Lummus forwarded to Brown, Richards was able to describe unique details that were only known by investigators who were close to the case—specifically, how he caused damage to the front grille of her 1986 Honda and how he kicked in the side fender, near the driver's door, with his cowboy boots when Butler tried to get back inside her car.

The report said that investigators were convinced that Richards was responsible for Butler's abduction and murder in Shelby County, but that he had not yet been charged by Shelby County authorities. One reason that Richards had yet to be charged was because his explanation as to how and where he disposed of the body was full of inconsistencies. At one point, he claimed that he covered Butler's body with leaves, and at another time, he said that he tied cinder blocks to her corpse and tossed her into a body of water. An attempt to locate the body was unsuccessful, even with Richards's guidance.

Federal Bureau of Investigation agents also believed that Richards was most likely responsible for the disappearance and presumed murder of seventeen-year-old Martha Green. According to FBI records, Green's brother drove to pick up his sister from her place of employment at the Holiday Inn on Interstate 40 and Highway 46 in Dickson, Tennessee. On the way home, they ran out of gas, and Green's brother left his sister in the vehicle while he walked to find some gasoline. When he returned, he found that his sister was missing. There appeared to be no sign of a struggle, but her purse was left in his car.

Another female reported that Richards gave her a ride to Memphis and told her about a time when he "killed a sixteen-year-old girl with long brown hair and brown eyes, and he buried her on a cove." Shelby County investigators placed Richards in Dickson on the day of Green's disappearance, and the description of the girl he supposedly killed matched Green's appearance.

During an extensive investigation, it was determined that Richards had issued nearly two hundred "courtesy speeding citations" in 1986 and 1987. It was also discovered that in addition to being an avid police buff, Richards was involved in bizarre sexual activities involving bondage and sadomasochism with two women from the Memphis area. Investigators were able to obtain statements from both of the women involved, but Lummus did not forward Brown the details of their relationship.

Investigators from the FBI believed that Richards was very mobile through western Tennessee and may have been active in Kentucky, Arkansas, Missouri, and Mississippi. At the time, authorities in Germantown, Tennessee, had a pending charge against Richards in connection with stalking a Kroger employee who was dressed in a white uniform. When he was picked up by Germantown police, Richards was dressed in a Shelby County sheriff's uniform and was armed with a shotgun.

According to the report, all the information was sent to the FBI Behavioral Science Unit for evaluation, and arrangements were made to bring polygraph examiner Don Wright to Memphis from Birmingham, Alabama, to interview Richards. It was concluded that "it appears that Richards has significant personality or possible mental difficulties." The report added that Richards was a serial murderer who was highly attracted to nurses and/or white uniforms.

Detective Brown read through the final report that Lummus had sent him until he reached the last page. He wanted to believe that the killer he had been hunting had been caught finally. Lummus told him that the FBI would continue to investigate any and all crimes that Richards might be connected with. He told Brown that he would contact him if they discovered any link to the murders in Missouri.

Brown's hopes were high but he was disappointed. The FBI never found any connection between Cape Girardeau and Richards. In the back of his mind, Brown already knew it. Richards was too young, anyway. There was no way that he could have been the monster responsible for the events that had taken place ten years ago. Richards was a monster. There was no denying that, but he wasn't the one that Brown was searching for.

In the meantime, Krajcir had completed his sentence in Pennsylvania, where he had been attending regular counseling sessions while he was incarcerated at Graterford. He would not walk out of prison as a free man, however. His arrest in Allentown violated the stipulations of his parole in Illinois after he was released from prison there in 1981 and labeled as a "sexually dangerous person."

Krajcir was immediately sent back to Menard Psychiatric Center in Chester, Illinois, in February 1988. By October of that year, he refused to continue his therapy. Krajcir remained incarcerated at Menard until 1995, when he was transferred to Big Muddy River Correctional Center in Ina, Illinois. In all that time, and for more than a decade after that, no one—except for Krajcir himself—had a clue about who was responsible for the savage rapes and murders that occurred at his hand.

It wasn't until 2007 that the mystery began to unravel and revealed itself.

2007

I regret doing all of it, but it was thirty years ago. I wish a lot of things could have been different, but that's the way it was. It's like I'm two different people. I worked for the ambulance service saving lives and here I was taking them.

—Timothy Wayne Krajcir

26

For a number of years, Detective James "Jimmy" Smith had been the unofficial investigator of cold cases for the Cape Girardeau Police Department. He would follow up on leads if they developed, and worked on the cases as time permitted. In March 2007, Smith was assigned to work full-time on homicides that were cold cases to make sure that they were brought up to date to meet modern forensic standards and advancements in DNA technology.

He was given three months to try and bring closure to the unsolved murders in Cape Girardeau that dated back thirty years. The investigators who were originally assigned to the cases had kept thorough records, and Smith went through the mountain of information with a fine-tooth comb. He worked in a coordinated effort with multiple law enforcement agencies to double- and triple-check the accuracy of the facts that were on record, but he needed more time. He was given an extension of an additional three months in June to work on the cold homicides. He was told that he would be allowed to work full-time on trying to solve the outstanding murders until September. After that time, the police department would not be able to justify the expense of having a full-time investigator work on the cases—unless there were some substantial results. Time passed quickly, and Smith had become frustrated that he had not gotten any closer to solving the crimes.

In August 2007, Smith viewed a television news release that revealed DNA evidence had linked Timothy Krajcir to the 1982 murder of Deborah Sheppard in Carbondale, Illinois. Smith noted that the incident took place at a time between the murders of Marjorie Call and Mildred Wallace. At that point, Smith said that he had exhausted all his other avenues and was "reaching for straws." He decided that he might as well contact Lieutenant Echols, of the Carbondale Police Department, to discuss whether Krajcir might have visited Cape Girardeau during that period in 1982. The two detectives began to work closely together, and they determined that there was a good possibility that Krajcir had been in Cape Girardeau on several occasions in the late 1970s and early 1980s due to his position with the ambulance service. They created a timeline to determine the periods when Krajcir was not incarcerated. They discovered that on each occasion when a homicide occurred in Cape Girardeau between 1977 and 1982, Krajcir was out of prison. After more than five months of frustration, Smith finally found a viable suspect worth investigating further. DNA links had pointed the way.

* * *

At sixty-two-years-old, Jimmy Smith could pass as a man ten years younger, despite his full head of completely snow-white hair and matching mustache and goatee. He was slender, fit, and agile. His normal expression was one of seriousness and professionalism, but on the rare occasion that he broke his demeanor with a wide smile, it made everyone near him smile along as well.

Smith was the son of an Arkansas farmer, and his family moved to Cape Girardeau when he was in the fourth grade. After he graduated from high school, Smith joined the U.S. Air Force. After serving in the military for four years, he returned to Southeast Missouri and procured employment as a patrolman with the Cape Girardeau Police Department. After a while, Smith left the force to take a job with the Ford Motor Credit Company, where he worked for several years. He eventually returned to law enforcement in the late 1980s when he accepted the position as chief deputy for the Stoddard County Sheriff's Department (SCSD). He said that he wasn't well accepted there, and he was told in 1990 that he was no longer needed in his position. Smith returned to the Cape Girardeau Police Department, and he became a member of the detective division in 1993. Since that time, he had received nothing but praise for his work.

Chief Kinnison described Smith as "Dick Tracy on steroids." He added that "he's a bulldog. He doesn't leave any stone unturned."

Prosecuting attorney Morley Swingle said, "He has a natural curiosity that makes him enjoy getting to the bottom of a case."

Smith, a father of four children, enjoys watching

television shows such as *America's Most Wanted* with them. He is a quiet man who gains self-satisfaction from his achievements without a need for continuous acknowledgment from others.

Lieutenant Echols, on the other hand, seemed to enjoy and encourage public praise for his work. He even began to toy with the idea of writing his own book about his part in the Krajcir investigation.

In contrast to Smith's appearance as a slim, stern, hard-boiled detective, Echols was balding and a bit pudgy. Despite having about twenty years of experience as a police officer, he looked as harmless as the Pillsbury Doughboy with a tan and a mustache. This may have aided in his ability to gain the confidence of suspects during interrogations because Echols did not appear to be an intimidating man. He was an intelligent man, however, and a very thorough investigator.

Echols developed a profile of Krajcir's method of rape and murder based on the Sheppard case. Cape Girardeau detective Tracy Lemonds compared the profile to unsolved rapes that occurred during the same period and found similarities that could not be ignored—particularly, the blue bandana that covered the perpetrator's face, as well as the physical description of a white male with dark hair and bushy eyebrows. There were also similarities in the way Sheppard and Wallace were raped and murdered.

Both women were sexually assaulted, and although Sheppard was strangled, while Wallace was shot in the head, there was a pink nightgown tied around Wallace's neck when she was found. In both cases, there was evidence that the intruder broke into the victims' residences and waited for them to return with the sole intention of attacking them. In both cases, the line to the victims' phone receiver had been cut. In both cases, all known acquaintances of the victims were eventually eliminated as suspects, leaving open the probability that both women may have been attacked by a stranger.

A report from the Regional Criminalistics Laboratory in Kansas City, Missouri, regarding the Wallace murder, also mentioned that boot laces used to bind Wallace's wrists were similar to those submitted as evidence in the rape of Ann Shares and the murder of Virginia Witte in Illinois. The report even mentioned that the type of knot and bow used was tied in a similar fashion in all three cases, and that the person responsible for tying those knots was most likely a left-handed individual. Timothy Krajcir was left-handed.

In October, Smith sent to the Missouri State Highway Patrol Crime Laboratory in Jefferson City DNA evidence that was collected from the Wallace case and preserved. Echols e-mailed the DNA match he received in the Deborah Sheppard murder to the Missouri crime lab as well. Smith was sitting at his desk when he received a call from forensic criminalist Stacey Bollinger. She told him that the two DNA profiles were very similar, and that the DNA collected from the Wallace crime scene would have had to come from Krajcir or one of his siblings. In order to get a more definitive match, Bollinger said that she would need a buccal swab from inside Krajcir's mouth. Smith obtained a buccal swab that Echols had previously taken from Krajcir and forwarded it to the laboratory. It was a match.

Using a recently developed technology that relied on a method called polymerase chain reaction (PCR), analysts compare sixteen core sequences of repeated DNA to see how many match. When all sixteen sequences are identified, it produces a one in 1.6 quadrillion match. The DNA found in the Wallace case produced a one in 720,000 match to Krajcir, which Cape Girardeau police chief Carl Kinnison described as a "cannot exclude match." It was still far from the one in 980 billion match that linked Krajcir to Sheppard.

Smith was excited to hear the news, but a one in 720,000 match might not be enough to convince a jury. Lemonds took the extra step of submitting a palm print that was lifted at the Wallace crime scene. The crime lab compared it to one taken from Krajcir and concluded that it was a definitive match.

Smith and Lemonds believed there was a strong probability that the unsolved murders of Mary and Brenda Parsh, Sheila Cole, Marjorie Call, and Mildred Wallace might have been committed by the same person, and now Krajcir was not only a person of interest—he became the primary suspect in all five cases. He was also the only suspect left that was worth investigating.

Smith immediately contacted Echols to inform him of the DNA results, and the Carbondale lieutenant arranged for both detectives to interview Krajcir. The date was set for November 14, 2007. In the meantime, the FBI, state police agencies in Mis-

souri, Illinois, Kentucky, and Pennyslvania, as well
as a host of county- and municipal-level detectives
across the country, began to examine unsolved
cases of rapes and homicides to see if there might
be a connection to Timothy Krajcir. He was immediately ruled out as a suspect in several cases in
which crimes took place during periods when Krajcir was incarcerated.

Echols contacted Marion, Illinois, police detective
Tina Morrow to discuss the murder of Virginia
Witte. Keeping Krajcir in mind as a "person of interest," Morrow began to examine the extensive files
gathered throughout the investigation of the case,
as well as four large boxes of physical and forensic
evidence. With the hope of building evidence to
support formal criminal charges, Morrow resubmitted some of the evidence to police labs for DNA testing. In addition to Witte's murder, Marion police,
with detectives from the Williamson County Sheriff's Department, also began to investigate three unsolved sexual assaults and robberies that occurred
in 1982 between the months of March and June.

In Pennsylvania, state police corporal William
Moyer also routinely investigated cold homicides in
addition to his current cases. He had been employed by the state police for about twenty years and
currently worked out of the barracks in Reading.
In May 2006, he began a case assessment into the
homicide death of Myrtle Rupp. With the assistance
of Sergeant Eric Grunzig, from the Muhlenberg
Township Police Department, Moyer reviewed all
the evidence that was collected during the original
investigation. He transported all the evidence to the
crime lab in Bethlehem, where forensic scientist

supervisor Joe Holleran could reexamine it for trace and DNA evidence.

Unlike the fairy-tale CSI world of television where results are returned in ten minutes, it took just over nine months before Moyer received a report back from the lab. That report indicated that a spermatozoa stain was detected on one of the items examined: a white bedspread that had been removed from the bed where Rupp's body was discovered. A sample of that stain was then forwarded to the DNA lab in Greensburg for further testing.

Muhlenberg Township police officially reopened the unsolved case of Myrtle Rupp. On November 2, 2007, personnel from the Greensburg lab contacted Moyer to inform him that they successfully obtained a DNA sample from the semen that was found on the victim's bedspread. The unknown DNA sample was entered into CODIS and came back with a "presumptive hit" linking inmate number C69201 from the state of Illinois to the case. The name of the convicted offender was Timothy Wayne Krajcir.

The state lab reported that in order to obtain a conclusive and definitive match to Krajcir, a new sample would have to be acquired for further testing. Moyer kept the Muhlenberg Township Police Department up to date on the investigation. Then he began to coordinate a trip to interview Krajcir and collect a current DNA sample from him at Big Muddy River Correctional Center in Illinois. However, Moyer would have to wait in line behind Jimmy Smith and Tina Morrow.

27

I don't want to spend another thirty years in here. What do I have to look forward to tomorrow? Why do I even want to wake up tomorrow? I've already made peace with myself. I'm just waiting for death. I'm done talking now, and if I die tomorrow, I don't care.

—Timothy Wayne Krajcir

November 14, 2007

Lieutenant Paul Echols and Detective Jimmy Smith traveled to the Big Muddy River Correction Center in Ina, Illinois, to interview Krajcir. Smith introduced himself. They had never met face-to-face. Krajcir was already intimately familiar with Echols because of the investigation into the murder of Deborah Sheppard.

After completing the formality of explaining to Krajcir his Miranda rights, and having him sign a statement that those rights were understood, Echols attempted to engage Krajcir in some small talk. He offered Krajcir of cup of coffee to make him feel more comfortable; then he eased his way into the purpose for the interview. He told Krajcir that he was seeking closure to several pending unsolved cases and wanted to know if Krajcir would acknowledge responsibility for them.

"I'll just run through some of the cases that I believe you were involved with," Echols said. "Two of them were in Marion, Illinois. One was in Johnston City, Illinois."

He went on to describe an incident that took place in March 1982 when an elderly woman came home from church and was confronted by a man who had entered through a window and was hiding in the bedroom.

"He came out and tied her hands, and then there was oral sex involved. And again, I'm just trying to bring closure to . . . This lady is still alive. Within the next few weeks, she moved out of that house. She couldn't live there anymore, and this is still a big deal with her," Echols said. "I would like to be able to tell her that the person who did this has some remorse. Can you do that for me?"

Krajcir grunted and shook his head.

"You can't do that for me?" Echols asked.

"I very seldom went over to Marion," Krajcir replied.

Echols moved on to another case that took place north of Marion in Johnston City. In this incident, a suspect entered the home of an elderly couple through the back door. He was armed with a gun and tied the couple up on the floor.

"There was not a rape in that case, although the suspect did masturbate onto her hands," Echols said.

Krajcir just grunted again and shook his head.

"I'm here shooting straight with you. I've treated you good. I just want to bring closure to these cases," Echols pleaded to Krajcir.

He went on to describe the second incident in Marion, which was very similar to the others. A man entered the house and tied the couple up. Then Echols changed direction and brought up a case that took place on North Almond Street in Carbondale, Illinois, in 1979.

Krajcir steered the conversation even further away from its focus by mentioning that he remembered a huge snowstorm that occurred around that time. Soon they were talking about the weather, and Echols struggled to bring the interview back on course.

He wanted to regain Krajcir's confidence, so he tried flattery. Echols told Krajcir that his decision to stay in prison deserved respect.

"You saved a lot of people heartache because of that. Had you stayed out and about, people might have gotten hurt. But the fact that you recognized that, and were willing to do what you could, what was within your control . . . that's admirable," Echols told him.

Krajcir didn't fall for Echols's attempt to befriend him. With an IQ of 125, Krajcir was an intelligent man and was not easily manipulated.

"Sorry, but like I said, the only time I went to Marion was in 1980," Krajcir told Echols. "One time I was gonna go over there and they had a tornado." The weather was always a safe subject to stick to, and Krajcir turned to it often.

Echols became increasingly frustrated.

"I don't know what else I can say. I—I—I have

lots of reasons to believe it's you. And—and it all fits," Echols stammered. "I'm just trying to bring some closure to these—"

"I can understand that," Krajcir said calmly.

"Two old ladies. I know you can respect that," Echols continued.

"Yes."

Echols was building up steam. "When these women suffer through these events like that, they never forget it. They look over their shoulder for the rest of their lives. You can imagine how they would walk around on the street, always wondering if the person they see over their shoulder is the person that attacked them. There is a . . . a . . . a . . . lack of trust with humanity in general. And—and if you did them, I mean, I'm looking for your help," Echols pleaded again.

Krajcir calmly replied, "Nah. I didn't do them."

Up to this point, Echols was no closer in getting a confession from Krajcir. Detective Smith decided that it was time to get involved in the conversation. He asked Krajcir if he had read or heard anything about the cases that they were talking about. Krajcir said that he had not, and that the only thing he watched on television then was sports.

Echols returned to his previous strategy of flattery in an attempt to put Krajcir at ease and gain his trust. He commented that someone had told him that Krajcir was the best basketball player in the prison system and that he played softball as well. Smith followed suit and said that he also played basketball and that it was his favorite sport. Continuing the small talk, Smith noted that he and Krajcir were only one year apart in age.

Echols, also trying to establish commonality between himself and Krajcir, commented, "Although, unlike you and I, he's (Smith) kept his hair."

With hopes that some small talk provided a bit of levity to the atmosphere, Echols decided to push forward. He told Krajcir that the Cape Girardeau Police Department had forensic evidence that needed to be tested, as well as photo lineups in several cases.

"I'm gonna talk to you about January 9, 1982," Smith broke in. "A nice-looking black lady and her daughter. She lived on the west side of town. Do you remember where the fairgrounds were located in Cape?" Smith asked.

Krajcir shook his head no.

"She lived in a new apartment building out there and she was preparing to mop her floor one night. She went to throw some water out the back door, and when she opened the door, someone forced their way in with a gun. Her daughter was ten years old. He forced them both to lie on the floor. He closed the blinds, forced them both upstairs onto a bed, and committed a sexual assault on the mother. She picked you out of a lineup. She was also a Jehovah's Witness, which should ring a bell with you," Smith related.

Krajcir shook his head to acknowledge that he had no recollection of the event.

Smith said that he personally knew the lady because he worked with her then, but at the time, he had no knowledge of the assault. Echols offered to refill Krajcir's coffee, but he declined. Smith continued talking.

"The ten-year-old daughter has since married and

left Cape and has been so affected by the incident
that she can't even come back. When her mom
visits, she's got to go to Indiana, where her daughter lives now. I think it's time that both these ladies
had a little comfort in their lives and realize some
closure in what happened to them."

"It's up to Tim Krajcir whether he decides to take
responsibility so we can put an end to this," Echols
chimed in.

"Uh-uh . . . didn't do it," Krajcir said.

Krajcir told Smith that he only traveled to Cape
Girardeau about once a month, because he was
going out with a girl named Marlene Smith whose
best friend, Nancy, was attending school there at
Southeast Missouri State University.

Both Smith and Echols had already completed extensive investigations to uncover and interview
anyone who knew Krajcir. They mentioned a woman
named Dottie, who worked with Krajcir at the Carbondale Ambulance Service. They also talked about
Beverlee Pappas, who had a lot of good things to say
about him and was astonished to discover that he
might be involved in the incidents that he was suspected of committing.

"It's like there are two Tims, and I can see that,"
Echols said.

"Yeah, I agree to that."

Krajcir said that the impulse to go out and commit
crimes was part of the "other Tim" when rationality
went out the window. He said that he did not have
a problem with alcohol or drugs, so he could not
blame it on that.

"I've been twisted since I was a little kid. I can't
blame it on anything else. The first six or seven years

of my life, I was left alone too much. It twisted me. It just got worse when I grew up, I guess." Krajcir said.

Krajcir said that he had two younger half brothers, Bill and Bernie, but no full brother because his paternal father, Mr. McBride, left when Tim was a year old.

Echols told him, "You're probably the smartest guy I've ever talked with on these sides of the walls, and it's interesting that you seemed to have been able to diagnose yourself. In that self-diagnosis, you've been able to remove yourself from society. I don't know anybody that has ever been able to do that. Most people will deny they have a problem and keep working to get out. I guess you realize that if you went back out, there might be a chance that you might hurt somebody again."

"I knew I would," Krajcir acknowledged.

"That reflects so much, but what do we do with the old stuff? What do we do with things that happened when you were out? Do we just leave them alone and leave them to linger until the people die? Or do we try to make something good out of something that was bad? What can you . . . what can you reap out of all of this and do good out of it? I mean, there's no doubt that the victims, Ann and her daughter, were . . . were somebody . . . a lady you raped. There's no doubt. Can you bring closure to that for her?" Echols asked.

"Wasn't me," Krajcir responded.

Echols reminded Krajcir that he denied killing Deborah Sheppard on the first day of his interview at the time, but he eventually admitted to the deed.

"I don't know how you feel when you acknowledge something like that, but I know what it does for the families. That's why we're here," Echols told Krajcir.

"You can't be locked up more than forever," Smith added.

"Help this lady and her daughter," Echols pleaded.

"I can't do it. It wasn't me. Someone that might have resembled me, maybe, but it wasn't me," Krajcir said coolly.

Frustrated again, Echols replied, "I'm not here to try to get you to confess to something you didn't do. I'm not here to clear off a bunch of cases."

Echols told Krajcir that he didn't think there would be any sense in pursuing further counseling sessions in prison if he couldn't come clean and be honest about these cases. Krajcir continued to deny any involvement, and Smith pronounced his belief that Krajcir was responsible for committing the crimes. He pursued the path of exploring Krajcir's youth and his upbringing.

"When I was four years old, I can remember pushing my younger brother off the porch and breaking his leg. When I was five years old, I went into somebody's house and trashed it," Krajcir said.

He said that he had been put on probation at about the age of eight years for stealing a bicycle, and that by the time he was fourteen, he started burglarizing homes near Allentown, Pennsylvania, and participated in voyeurism by peeking into windows.

Smith tried to make a connection with Krajcir by telling him that his father never had a kind word to say to him when he was a child.

"Yeah, but you had a father, and my mother was never there. You have to have something from a female or a father . . . some kind of attention. If you don't, you just go twisted," Krajcir said.

He contemplated that his deviant behavior might have been a result of trying to get back at a mother that was never present in his life. Krajcir told Smith that he never had a "normal" relationship with a female, despite a fleeting foray with marriage to a woman from Milwaukee that he met in 1962 while he was in the navy. Even then, they didn't live together. She continued to live with her parents in Milwaukee while Krajcir was stationed in Waukegan. The marriage lasted only a few months, but they produced one child before Krajcir was convicted of rape and attempted murder in 1963.

The interview continued. Smith asked Krajcir if he frequented any bars or businesses in Cape Girardeau. Krajcir told him that he went to Cape Girardeau on several occasions when he worked for the ambulance service in Carbondale, Illinois, but he never went there to party or socialize.

Smith attempted to appeal to any possible religious convictions that Krajcir might hold.

"I've done some things in my life that I haven't been real pleased with. We all make mistakes. We're all sinners, but we can also ask for forgiveness. An example of that is Mrs. Sheppard, who has forgiven you. I don't know if you get any comfort out of that, but you probably should. What do you feel about that?" Smith said.

"Well, I'm not real religious," Krajcir replied.

Echols continued with his strategy of trying to appeal to Krajcir's sense of morality by explaining that he wanted to bring a sense of relief to the victims of the crimes by letting them know that the person who committed them was incarcerated.

"I want to be able to tell these victims that the reason the perpetrator is incarcerated is, in part, because he accepted responsibility within his own heart and maintained himself to be incarcerated so that others can live their lives peacefully," Echols said.

Smith brought up the subject of Ann Shares, who was assaulted in 1977 and again in 1982 by the same assailant. During the first assault, she was crossing the Wal-Mart parking lot in Cape Girardeau with her five-year-old daughter when they were forced into a vehicle. She was forced to perform oral sex on her kidnapper while her little girl sat in the backseat of the car.

"She said both times it was you, and we believe her. There's evidence that's probably going to show that. You need us to bring you that evidence, don't you?" Echols said.

"Wasn't me," Krajcir replied.

Both Smith and Echols told Krajcir that evidence obtained from the crime scene would be checked for a DNA match against him. Krajcir continued to deny any involvement in the crime against Ann Shares; then he told the investigators that he was not going to talk to them further about anything else.

Smith quickly pushed ahead with his questions, hoping that Krajcir would not end the interview.

"There's a lady by the name of Mildred Wallace. She lived alone and was never married. She was a secretary at our local cement plant in Cape Girardeau. She lived on William Street. Do you know where William Street is?" Smith said.

"I think so," Krajcir replied quietly.

"She was sexually assaulted and murdered. Do you remember that?"

"No."

"Did you know that lady?"

"No."

"Had you ever been to her house?"

"No. I don't know anybody from Cape Girardeau."

Smith handed Krajcir a report that included a palm print identification that was lifted from a window of Wallace's house. It matched Krajcir's palm print and provided a positive identification to prove that he had been at the scene.

"I don't want to talk about it," Krajcir said.

"You don't want to answer any questions about it? Do you want to know what's going to happen?" Smith asked.

"It doesn't matter," Krajcir said, as if he were already prepared for the inevitable.

Smith tried to convince Krajcir that it did matter—maybe not to him, but it mattered a lot to the family members of the victims. Echols tried to find out what motivated Krajcir to commit the crimes. He asked if either of his half brothers ever came out to Missouri to visit him, and if they took part in the crimes with him. Krajcir remained tight-lipped. He occasionally let out a single syllable in the form of "no." When he ventured to say a few more words, it was only to let them know that he didn't want to say anything at all.

Smith told Krajcir that he was scheduled to meet with the prosecuting attorney the next day. He said this was a capital case and that it would be filed with a recommendation for the death penalty. He wanted to give Krajcir something to think about, and Smith hoped that he might want to negotiate his way out of a death sentence.

Krajcir seemed already resigned to the fact that he was going to be executed. He told Smith that he was done talking and that he would face whatever came. He said that if he had a life to look forward to, it might have made a difference to him.

"I don't have any life. I haven't had a life for twenty years. This is no life," Krajcir said, as if a sentence of death posed no threat, and, in fact, might even be welcomed.

"I don't want to spend another thirty years in here. What do I have to look forward to tomorrow? Why do I even want to wake up tomorrow? I've already made peace with myself. I'm just waiting for death. I'm done talking now, and if I die tomorrow, I don't care," Krajcir said.

Echols said that there were other pending cases against Krajcir, and that there were a lot of people feeling hurt and in need of closure. He asked Krajcir if he would at least listen to Smith go through some of the other cases in which he was a suspect. There was no need to talk about anything, just listen. It was an effort to keep the interview going, even if Krajcir wasn't going to participate fully. There was always a chance that something would ignite a desire for him to confess. The strategy worked for a little while longer. At least the interview did not end just yet.

Detective Smith began to give a brief outline of the crimes he was sure Krajcir was responsible for committing, without going into too many details. As he spoke, he handed Krajcir photographs of the victims.

Ann Shares was assaulted after being abducted in a Wal-Mart parking lot in November 1977. That same month, a young student attending Southeast Missouri State University was kidnapped from the same parking lot. She came out from the store after picking up some photographs she had developed. She never made it back to the blue Chevy Nova she drove there in. The following day, she was found murdered in Illinois. As he handed him a photograph of the body, Smith told Krajcir that she was shot twice.

Smith handed over yet another photo and talked about another victim, Mary Parsh. He explained that she, along with her daughter Brenda, were killed on a Friday night and found the following Monday. They were lying beside each other on a bed, with their hands bound behind them. They were both shot in the head.

Smith handed Krajcir a photo of a broken window at the back of Marjorie Call's house. He explained that this woman was strangled to death in her home and found the following morning by her brother.

Smith continued. He mentioned a nineteen-year-old girl who was abducted from the gas station where she worked in Scott City.

"I've never been in Scott City," Krajcir finally spoke up.

His response was exactly what Smith was hoping to prompt. Krajcir wasn't really a suspect in the gas station abduction, but the detective wanted to gauge Krajcir's reaction to being accused of a crime he didn't commit.

"Is there anything we can tell the victims on your behalf?" Echols asked.

Krajcir returned to his stance of refusing to talk any further, so Smith reminded him that he would be facing the death penalty. For the first time during the interview, Krajcir stuttered a bit when he said that he didn't believe it would make any difference on the outcome if he cooperated. This was the window of opportunity that Smith had been waiting for. Krajcir needed some assurance that his life might be spared.

Echols pleaded once more for Krajcir to take responsibility for his actions in order to ease the minds of the victims' family members.

"Nah—" Krajcir began, almost closing that window of opportunity again, but Smith spoke up quickly.

"If you had some assurance that you could negotiate yourself out of the death penalty, what would you think about that?"

Krajcir said that he would think about it.

Smith told him that the time to decide was now. He told Krajcir that he could make a phone call to the prosecuting attorney and see if he could negotiate a deal, and that it would have to include full disclosure to all the crimes he had committed. It was now or never. Krajcir agreed to let Smith make the call to hear what the prosecutor had to say. He needed a break, anyway. Krajcir wanted a drink of water and a chance to use the bathroom.

While Krajcir was escorted to the bathroom, Smith called the office of prosecuting attorney Morley Swingle. He told Swingle that he was currently interviewing Krajcir and that Krajcir might agree to provide full disclosure to all of the crimes he committed if an agreement could be reached to waive the death penalty upon his plea or conviction.

Confident that he had enough evidence to gain a conviction against Krajcir, Swingle told Smith that he would not waive the death penalty in exchange for Krajcir's confession. The inflated balloon of hope for obtaining a confession from Krajcir was suddenly punctured. When Smith returned to the interrogation room, he told Krajcir that he was unable to reach Swingle and that he and Echols would meet with the prosecutor to discuss the matter in detail at a later time. There was nothing further they could accomplish at that moment. At least the investigators were able to get Krajcir to consider confessing, and he agreed to speak with them again in the near future.

The next day, the investigators met with Morley Swingle at the Cape Girardeau police headquarters to try and persuade him to consider waiving the death penalty phase against Krajcir, if Krajcir would confess. A confession would seal Krajcir's conviction, and they knew that an additional sentence on top of the one that Krajcir was already serving for the murder of Deborah Sheppard would guarantee that he would never again see the outside of a prison facility for the rest of his life. Swingle wanted Krajcir to pay for his crimes with his life instead of becoming a continuing burden to society, but he tentatively agreed to waive the death penalty if, *and only if,* every single surviving family member of every victim agreed to it.

Over the Thanksgiving holidays, the surviving family members of Krajcir's victims were contacted. They all gathered at the police department for a meeting, and subsequently they all agreed to spare

Krajcir's life if he would provide them with the details of the murders.

Smith and Echols delivered a letter of agreement from Swingle to Patricia Gross, Krajcir's public defender, on November 26, 2007.

Confessions
of a Serial Killer

28

December 3, 2007

A follow-up interview with Krajcir took place about a week later, beginning at 6:44 P.M. at the Big Muddy River Correctional Center in Ina, Illinois. Echols and Smith were still the ones who interrogated him. Echols told Krajcir that prosecuting attorney Morley Swingle had agreed that he would not seek the death penalty if Krajcir would cooperate, but only on the stipulation that he would provide full disclosure of all his crimes. Krajcir agreed to hear the terms, and Smith read a letter from Swingle written to Krajcir's public defense attorney, Patricia Gross.

The letter stated that Swingle had evidence that would connect Krajcir to multiple murders in Cape Girardeau, Missouri. Swingle also added that he had successfully gotten the death penalty on four previous cases, and that one of those executions had already been fulfilled. The letter emphasized that Swingle wanted to pursue the death penalty in this case, but the survivors of the victims convinced him to waive the death penalty if Swingle could get a thorough and complete statement as to the details of each particular crime that Krajcir was suspected of committing. The conditions included disclosure of every detail of every crime, the ability to pass a polygraph examination in regard to his disclosure, and a guilty plea on every count in each and every case.

Swingle also wrote that he did not want Krajcir to confess to anything that he didn't do, but he must tell the truth about what he had done.

If he violates the agreement by lying to the officers, the agreement would be off and I would be back in the spot that I am in now, where I can seek the death penalty, Swingle wrote. He added that he would be able to make a case against Krajcir eventually and seek the death penalty without his confession, anyway.

At the conclusion of Swingle's letter of agreement, Swingle emphasized that Detective Jimmy Smith was not authorized to make any other promises other than what was outlined in the letter, and that the agreement, if accepted, was solely between Krajcir and Swingle.

"All we want is the truth," Smith said. "Any particular place you want to begin, Tim?"

"Let's begin where it started . . . when I first raped Ann Shares," Krajcir replied. And with those words, closure became an element that was justice delayed but not denied. Krajcir related an incident that, he said, took place in 1977, because he remembered that he had already been out of prison for about eight or nine months.

"I had a relationship with this one gal I knew. We broke up, and it was at that point that . . . the most stupidest thing in my life, which was to go out and rape again."

Krajcir said that the Illinois woman he was romantically involved with was married, and that he became depressed when she cut off their relationship, so he drove to Cape Girardeau to look for his next victim.

Through Smith's questioning, it was determined that Krajcir had arrived at the parking lot of the shopping area on William Street and Kings Highway, the same lot that Sheila Cole was abducted from.

"I said to myself, the first good-looking gal that comes up there by herself, I'm going to assault," Krajcir said.

He recalled that an attractive woman came from the store, and he abducted her and her young daughter while wielding a knife in the parking lot. The little girl sat in the backseat of Krajcir's car. He said that he drove to a dark area and told the woman to take off her clothes. She offered to give him oral gratification rather than have intercourse. He agreed, but then decided that he wanted to have intercourse, anyway. Krajcir said that he got into position to have sex with her but never did. He ended up taking her back to the parking lot from which he had abducted her and her daughter. He said that he gave the woman some money for her services, and he didn't remember the little girl becoming too upset about the circumstances.

"I think I apologized to her even. That was the first time I had done anything like that since I'd been released, and I don't think I felt good about [it]," Krajcir said.

Krajcir said that he had been to Cape Girardeau several times in the past when he worked for the Jackson County Ambulance Service, but only for job-related purposes to make trips to either Southeast Missouri or St. Francis Hospitals. He picked Cape Girardeau as his hunting ground because he didn't want to commit any crimes in the same town in which he lived. He said that he went to Cape Girardeau that day with the sole purpose of committing a rape, and he picked the Wal-Mart parking lot because he figured that he could find a lot of women to choose from there.

Krajcir went on to tell of another incident with similar circumstances that took place on January 9, 1982. He said that he traveled to Cape Girardeau again with the intention of committing rape. This time, instead of prowling the Wal-Mart parking lot, he chose the newly constructed West Park Mall located a few blocks away but still on William Street.

Ann Shares, thirty-four, came out of the mall with her ten-year-old daughter, and Krajcir honed in on them as he waited in the parking lot. Krajcir said that it was not his intention to specifically look for Shares, and it was just coincidence that she turned out to be the same woman he abducted from the Wal-Mart parking lot and raped several years earlier.

"I didn't recognize her, but I thought she might have looked familiar," Krajcir said.

Krajcir followed Shares to her home on Themis Street and parked his car about a block away from the house. He said he walked to the back of the house and watched her through the back door as she mopped the kitchen floor.

"I had been standing outside for a good thirty minutes. I was about half-frozen and getting ready to leave when she opened the door to shake out her mop or something. That's how I got in," Krajcir said.

Krajcir told Smith and Echols that he was wearing a blue bandana over the lower half of his face and he was carrying a .25-caliber semiautomatic handgun. He said that he bought the gun from a man who worked with him at a nursing home in Carbondale. Krajcir was unable to remember any further details about the gun or what manufacturer had made it. Echols asked him if it was the same gun that was taken from him in 1983 when he was arrested by police authorities in Pennsylvania. Krajcir replied that it was. Echols also asked if it was the same one that was used in the Sheppard murder, and Krajcir said that he thought it was. Strangely enough, Echols did not question the validity of that last statement. Sheppard's death was ruled to be caused by strangulation. There was no documentation to support any evidence of a gunshot wound in that case. Perhaps Echols merely mentioned the wrong victim's name during his question, but neither Krajcir nor the investigators made any further mention of it during the interview.

"Anyway, she said that I scared her to death, and I think she recognized me, but I still didn't think this was the same woman that I had raped before," Krajcir said.

As the interrogation continued, Krajcir told the investigators that he led Shares and her daughter upstairs to a bedroom on the right side of the hallway. He told the mother to take off her clothes. She put her daughter on the bed, covered her head with a blanket, and told her to be quiet and face the wall so she didn't have to watch.

"Did you threaten the daughter?" Smith asked.

"I never threatened a child, other than you know . . . I might have told the mother to do what I say or somebody will get hurt."

"Do you recall telling her that you knew where her daughter went to school?"

"I might have said that to use as a threat," Krajcir replied.

"Do you recall telling her that you knew she had recently moved there from down the street?"

Krajcir finally admitted that he had followed Shares previously with the intention of attacking her. He said that one time he was outside of her old house but didn't break in because there was a church function going on across the street and there were a lot of people around. He emphasized, however, that he wasn't particularly looking for her on the night in question, and he did not recognize her as a woman that he raped previously.

Krajcir went on to describe the details of what took place. He forced her to disrobe and began to fondle her. While he sat on the bed beside the daughter, he made the mother get down on her knees and put his penis in her mouth. He said that after she gave him oral sex for a while, Krajcir decided that he wanted to have intercourse with her.

"It was unreal, because at the time that I was having intercourse with her, she was telling me she was a Jehovah's Witness and that she would try and save me. That was kind of strange, but I remember her doing that," Krajcir recalled.

Krajcir then revealed that he purchased some rawhide bootlaces earlier in the day. He told Smith and Echols that he used them to tie up the mother and daughter after he was done having sex. Smith asked Krajcir if he had touched the little girl in any way that night. Krajcir said that he only touched her when he was tying her up. Then he added, "And when I got up to leave, I think I touched her on her butt."

The last question Smith asked regarding the Shares incident was whether or not Krajcir had worn a condom. He told them that he had not. With so many cases yet to address, the detectives decided to move forward. They asked Krajcir what he wanted to talk about next.

Krajcir took them back to 1977 once more. He estimated that it was early August. He told them that he broke into a basement window on the side of an insurance salesman's house on North Springer Street in Carbondale, Illinois. Krajcir said that he believed that the family that lived there was on vacation and that nobody was home at the time. Once inside, Krajcir said that he stole a .38-caliber Special police handgun and a box of ammunition. He said that he even fired it inside the house to make sure that it worked.

"After taking that gun . . . it was like a rush of adrenaline . . . an all-powerful feeling. How can you not be more powerful when you have a gun? God, I wish I had never picked that gun up," Krajcir said.

Krajcir said that he hadn't committed a lot of crimes prior to that point because he didn't have a weapon other than a knife that he carried with him. He said that he had never killed anyone *before* he had a gun. Krajcir told the detectives that the fact that he now owned a gun is what led him to commit the Parsh murders.

Krajcir said that he drove around Cape Girardeau one night on the prowl for a potential victim. He parked his car on Koch Street because the neighborhood wasn't well lit. Then he walked around and peeked into windows of the homes in the area.

"I went 'Peeping Tomin',' you know . . . looking in windows and stuff like that. And I noticed that she (Mary Parsh) was living by herself, as far as I could tell," Krajcir said.

He didn't attack Mary that night, but he returned a week later. When he noticed that the house was empty, he broke into a back bedroom window and waited. Smith and Echols needed Krajcir to tell them something that only the intruder would know in order to give credence to the confession. Krajcir told them that the window he broke into was not a standard window that moved up and down. It was the type that opened outward and was operated by turning a crank handle from the inside. It was improbable that he would know that unless he was the one who actually broke in.

Then Krajcir related the grisly details of how he confronted the Parshes when they entered the house. He made them kneel on the floor at gunpoint and then led them into the master bedroom. He described how he forced Brenda Parsh to perform oral sex on him before he raped her in front of her mother, Mary.

He said that he remembered cutting an electrical cord to tie them up with, because it shocked him a bit and put a mark on the knife he used.

Krajcir finally gave the detectives what they were waiting for. He told them that the phone rang while Brenda was being forced to perform oral sex on him. Krajcir let her answer the phone while he listened in. He told Smith and Echols that it was Brenda's father who called from the hospital where he was recovering from some kind of surgery. He let Brenda tell her father that she loved him, and then she hung up the phone and he went back to brutalizing her.

That phone conversation was never revealed to the public or the media. The only people alive who knew about it other than the investigators were Floyd Parsh and the murderer. Krajcir also told them that the phone may have rung before as well, but he would not let anyone answer it. That would have coincided with the claims of others, such as Richard McGougan and Brenda's sister, Karen, who said that they had tried reaching Mary by phone that evening.

Krajcir then described how he shot Brenda in the back of the head, then fired a second bullet at Mary, thinking that he had killed them both. He told the detectives that he rummaged through a purse on the couch in the living room and stole some money out of a wallet he found in a desk drawer in the den. Then he heard Mary crying and returned to the bedroom to shoot her again.

Krajcir next told the detectives that he wanted to tell them something that was directly related to what had happened.

"In 1963, they sent me to Menard Psychiatric Center. At the time, I was eighteen years old, and it was probably the worst place anybody could send any youngster. It was filled with criminally insane . . . every kind of sexual deviant that you can imagine. A couple of guys who were off of death row were really crazy. The whole population was that way . . . criminally insane. I don't mean normal people. I mean they were really criminally insane.

"Anyway, they kept me there for about five years. When I left, I was full of rage and anger. My first couple of years there were full of humiliations. If it wasn't for sports being allowed in there, I probably would have gone crazy. I think sports was the only thing that kept me sane all these years. I would sit in the yard sometimes and talk with Kenny Rogers. I think he's up in Dixon now for killing his wife and another young girl in Carbondale, and somebody else, but he was just there for assault and battery at the time.

"I was young and impressionable then, and one of the things that really stuck in my mind was when he told me, 'Tim, if you ever do anything, don't leave no witnesses.' For some reason, that just stuck in my brain. When I decided to step across the line again in '77, to go back to doing those kinds of things, Kenny's words were still in my head."

Echols asked if there was ever a time that he might have thought that the police would ever stop or capture him, and Krajcir told him no. After they believed they had enough information about the Parshes, Smith encouraged Krajcir to move on to another incident that he would be willing to talk about.

29

December 3, 2007

During the interview in which Timothy Krajcir agreed to confess to all of his crimes and provide police with the details of each incident, he told them that Cape Girardeau, Missouri, was his favorite location to use as a hunting ground for committing sexual assaults and murders. The local visitor's bureau would probably not publish that in their next brochure as an incentive to promote tourism, but it was a fact in the late 1970s and early 1980s.

Detective Smith, of the Cape Girardeau Police Department, and Lieutenant Echols, of the Carbondale Police Department, had already taken Krajcir's confessions to several crimes that he committed in Cape Girardeau; now they were prepared to hear some more.

Krajcir told them that he had found an area in Cape Girardeau near where the post office was located, which was dark and isolated enough for him to prowl without fear of being discovered. He said that he did his Peeping Tom thing there on several occasions and found someone whom he described as an older black woman who lived in the area with a family of girls. He decided that he would return one night to assault her sexually. He returned on several occasions, and one time, when he saw that the woman was alone, he entered the house through the unlocked front door.

"I went in, woke her up, and made her perform oral sex on me. She fought me a bit, and I grabbed her and threw her onto the floor. I didn't beat her up or anything like that, because then she started to cooperate," Krajcir said. He later added that "she was a sweet old lady who was so embarrassed about what happened to her that she never told anyone or called the police, as far as I know."

Krajcir wasn't sure how much time had passed, but he knew that he went back to the same house a long time later. He said that he broke in at about nine o'clock in the evening and grabbed a teenage girl. He made her undress and forced her to give him oral sex. Krajcir admitted that the house was full of children at the time.

"There were three or four kids there and the older lady was holding a baby, but they were in the front room and we were in the back room at the time. I just told everyone to stay where they were, and nobody would get hurt."

"The lady you mentioned holding the baby . . . Was that the lady you raped the previous time?" Echols asked.

Krajcir corrected Echols by saying that he had not raped her—he had just forced her to give him oral sex.

"And you took the daughter to the back room?"

"I threatened her with the gun."

When questioned about the other people who were present in the house, Krajcir said, "I didn't hurt nobody other than the sexual assault, and then I left."

There was another incident in the same area that Krajcir said he took part in. He said that he entered an apartment building and knocked on the door of one of the basement apartments. When a girl answered, Krajcir flashed a badge and told her that he was a police officer. Smith asked him where he obtained the badge.

"In a department store or something," Krajcir replied. "You can buy them anywhere."

Krajcir said that he was about to pull out his gun, but then the girl ran out the door and up the stairs to another apartment, so he got out of there as quickly as he could.

Krajcir moved on, without hesitation, to describe the scene of yet another crime he committed. He told the investigators that he had been to a National Food Store where he noticed a black woman who looked to be in her mid-twenties and might be an easy victim. He followed her home and discovered that she had two or three children. He couldn't remember exactly how many. Krajcir assumed that she was a single mother, because he could see no evidence of a man living at the house. He scoped the place out and didn't do anything that night, but he said that he returned about a week later.

Krajcir said that he saw two women in the front room of the house at that time, but not the one that he had followed there earlier. He walked to the back of the house; then he saw her come home, so now there were three women inside.

"All black females?" Smith asked, and Krajcir replied affirmatively.

Krajcir said there was a screened-in back porch on the house, but the door was locked. He cut through one of the screens and then entered the house through the kitchen.

"I don't think I mentioned this, but when I was locked up, I used to imagine sexual fantasies. I decided that when I got out, I would do whatever I fantasized about. If I could have two or three women or whatever . . . I think that's why I went in there," Krajcir said.

Wearing his blue bandana around his face, and holding a gun in his hand, Krajcir entered the front room where the three women were socializing. He said that the mother took her children into another room and closed the door so they wouldn't see anything. Then she told them to be quiet and behave themselves.

"I had three girls on the couch and had them take off their clothes," Krajcir said proudly, as if he had accomplished something worth remembering.

He said that he made them strip for him while he sat on the couch and masturbated; then he made the woman who lived there perform oral sex on him until he climaxed. He said that he fondled the other two women, but he never had sex with them.

"Did you force the woman to perform oral sex on you, or was she agreeable to that?" Smith asked.

"Well, she did . . . but I don't think she really wanted to," Krajcir said.

"But you had the gun, too?" Echols chimed in.

"Was it displayed?" Smith asked.

"Yes, I believe it was," Krajcir answered.

Krajcir said that when he was through, he asked the women if they had any money. When they told him that they did not, he decided that it was time to leave.

Smith and Echols decided that it was time to take a break. It was 8:36 P.M. on Monday, December 3, 2007.

30

December 3, 2007

During the course of an extensive interrogation in which Timothy Wayne Krajcir confessed to multiple murders and sexual assaults in Cape Girardeau, Missouri, he admitted that he had a .38-caliber handgun that he obtained by burglarizing a home in Carbondale, Illinois. Krajcir already admitted that he used that gun to murder Mary and Brenda Parsh. Next he would provide investigators Smith and Echols the details of the kidnapping, sexual assault, and killing of Sheila Cole. According to Krajcir, the same gun was also used in her murder.

Krajcir said that he had gone to one of his favorite hunting grounds, the Wal-Mart parking lot on the corner of Kings Highway and William Street in Cape Girardeau. He spotted an attractive, young Caucasian girl who just exited the store with a small bag in her hand. She was walking across the parking lot toward her car, a blue Chevy Nova.

Krajcir said, "She parked next to a pretty big

truck that blocked the view from the store. I came around and got her out of her car, and put her in my car."

He said that in order to get Cole into his car, he threatened her with his gun, and he told her that if she did what he said, she wouldn't get hurt. Krajcir said that he drove to his mobile home in Carbondale, Illinois. During the drive, he learned that Cole was a college student who lived with a couple of roommates. After they arrived at his home in Carbondale, Krajcir said that he forced her to give him oral sex until he ejaculated into her mouth.

Smith asked Krajcir if he had planned in advance to take Cole all the way back to Carbondale

Krajcir said, "No, that was probably a spur-of-the-moment thought. When I was in that mode, I didn't think straight. It was stupid on my part because any one of my friends could have come over. How would I have explained what was going on?"

Krajcir said that after he was done, he told Cole that he would drive her back to her car. He said that on the drive back toward Missouri, he decided to pull over at a rest stop, just outside of McClure, Illinois, so he could use the bathroom. It was dark and there were no other cars in the parking lot. Krajcir and Cole got out of the car and went into the bathroom together.

Krajcir informed his interrogators that his sole intention that evening was to find a victim to sexually assault—he did not actually plan to kill anyone.

"I didn't decide to kill her until we got close to Cape. I mean . . . it wasn't premeditated, but when we walked into that bathroom, I knew what was going to happen. Again it was that thought that stuck with me about not leaving any witnesses behind."

He shot her point-blank in the head, and then fired a second shot into her head after she fell to the floor. Krajcir said that he threw her purse into the trash receptacle in the bathroom, which is where it was found by the officers who initially investigated the crime scene. Revealing this bit of information helped to validate Krajcir's confession. He was also shown several photographs, which he recognized and identified as images of Cole's car and the bathroom at the rest stop where he killed her.

After he killed Cole, he said, he drove a little farther south until he reached the bridge that crossed the Mississippi River and led to East Cape Girardeau in Missouri. About halfway across the bridge, he said, he stopped his car, got out, and threw his gun into the water below. The crimes he committed that night remained unsolved for thirty years.

Confident that Krajcir's testimony was legitimate, Smith asked him to move on to another incident that he would be willing to talk about. Without knowing her identity, Krajcir went on to describe the details of his 1982 attack on Margie Call, who lived just a couple of blocks from the Parsh house.

Krajcir described Call as a woman in her later forties or perhaps early fifties. He said that she wore glasses, and that she also had dentures. He said that he spotted her shopping at Kroger supermarket in Cape Girardeau, and then he followed her home to see where she lived. After peeking in her windows, he

decided that she lived alone. Krajcir gave an accurate
description of the house.

He waited about a week before he returned. He
saw that nobody was home at the time, and he said
that he stepped on an air-conditioning unit at the
back of the house, where he broke into a bathroom
window. Pieces of shattered glass were scattered
across the floor, and he said that he may have
knocked over some toiletry items when he climbed
in the window. He was also able to tell Smith and
Echols that the door to the basement was locked.

Krajcir said that he broke into the house at around
eight o'clock in the evening and waited inside the
living room for about a half hour before Call came
home. He said that Call entered the house and went
directly into a bedroom in the back. When she came
out of the bedroom, Krajcir said, she headed for the
bathroom and noticed that the window had been
broken. She turned and ran toward the front of
the house, and Krajcir accosted her. Armed with a
.25-caliber semiautomatic pistol, he led her to a
second bathroom and fondled her before taking her
to one of the bedrooms, where it was warmer. Krajcir
wore his signature blue bandana to hide his identity.

Krajcir told the investigators that he forced Call
to disrobe and to give him oral sex. He said that
he did not remember having intercourse with her.
He told them that he tied her up with rawhide laces
and then strangled her to death with his blue bandana. He said that he placed his fingers on her
neck to check for a pulse in order to make sure that
she was dead.

By this time, Krajcir's capability for brutality had
accelerated dramatically. He decided that he

wanted to take a souvenir of his conquest, so he used the knife he carried with him to cut off Call's left nipple. He later decided not to keep it and flushed it down the toilet, along with one of the rawhide laces that he did not use. The bootlace didn't make it down the plumbing and it was recovered by the initial crime scene investigators. Still, the fact that Krajcir was able to provide this information gave further credibility to his confession.

There were a few facts that Krajcir was not able to correlate to evidence that was discovered at the scene. One of them was a latex glove that was found outside the house. Krajcir said that he wore brown cloth gloves. There was also the yellow rose, which was found on the bed of an adjacent bedroom from where Call was molested. Krajcir said that he had no recollection of leaving it there, and he wouldn't have done that, anyway.

Krajcir said that after he killed Call, he smoked a cigarette in the living room and stole the money that Call had placed in several church donation envelopes, which he had found. Then he left through the door that led to the carport. His crimes that night remained unsolved for twenty-five years.

31

Krajcir's confessions seemed never ending. The list of kidnappings, murders, and sexual assaults grew longer and more disturbing with the telling of each additional incident, and he was just getting started. Cape Girardeau had become his hunting ground, and Krajcir felt comfortable seeking his victims in familiar territory. He told Smith and Echols that he picked his next one at the same Kroger grocery store where he had targeted Marjorie Call.

Mildred Wallace wasn't actually his next victim, but she had become the next one from Cape Girardeau, and that was what Detective Smith was concerned about at the moment.

Krajcir didn't know Wallace. He never met her before that day in June 1982 when he killed her. Like his other victims, she was picked randomly—and without cause.

Krajcir said that he saw Wallace at Kroger grocery store and then followed her to her house on William

Street. He said that it was the first time that he ever saw this lady. He parked about a block away and walked back to the house. He watched her through the windows. A few minutes later, she put her coat back on and left the house again.

"I decided that this was a good opportunity to get inside the house. I smashed the bathroom window, and I remember that I cut myself . . . my left hand. When I got inside, I got a bandage out of her bathroom and put it on to stop the bleeding. I think I used a towel to cover the broken window, so she wouldn't notice the cold air coming in right away.

"She must have gone out to get a newspaper or something, because she was only gone about ten or fifteen minutes. I was in a room down the hall when she came into the house. She went into the bedroom and started to undress, when I came down the hallway and confronted her in the bedroom," Krajcir said.

Krajcir told Smith and Echols that he threatened Wallace with a gun and made her disrobe in front of him.

"I didn't realize that she was that old. I thought that she looked a lot younger earlier. There was a lot of oral sex, and then I did try to have intercourse with her, but . . . she didn't give me the impression that she was that old. I mean, I thought she was a younger-looking woman when I first saw her. She was real dry and complained that I was hurting her. Anyway, I pulled out and I wanted her to do oral sex again, to finish it," Krajcir said.

He told the investigators that he couldn't remember if he tied up this victim or not, but he recalled that she was lying facedown on the bed when he shot her one time in the head. Then he looked through the house for any money or valuables he could steal. He said that the only thing he took was about $30 in cash, which he found in her purse.

Krajcir said that Wallace asked him if he was the same person who killed Marjorie Call. He denied it. He also recalled that there was some type of device in place to block the kitchen door so nobody could get in.

The original crime scene investigators found an empty bottle of orange juice in the southwest bedroom, and the cap was left on the kitchen counter, but Krajcir told Smith that he didn't recall removing anything from the refrigerator. Krajcir did say that he wasn't positive, but that he might have cut the phone line. Investigators did notice that Wallace's phone line was indeed cut. Krajcir also remembered that he saw a typewriter in the far left corner of the front room of the house. Wallace did, in fact, own a typewriter similar to the one Krajcir described.

Krajcir said that he left the house through the front door and returned to Carbondale. While driving home on Route 3 in Illinois, he said, he pulled over near some railroad tracks and threw away his gun.

The brutal tale of Krajcir's rampage continued. He related an incident that took place just before Mildred Wallace was killed. It was around nine o'clock on a Sunday evening when he entered the home of Lola Nicholson and her husband. He tied the husband up, raped the wife, then stole some money and

the gun that he later used to kill Wallace. Krajcir also
talked about two other cases of deviant sexual assault
that he committed—one on April 11, 1982, in Johnston City, Illinois, and one on March 28, 1982, in
Marion, Illinois.

Krajcir began to describe the details of the incident
in Marion. He said that he broke into a woman's
house by cutting through a bedroom windowpane
and screen. Echols mentioned that it was an older
lady who lived by herself and went by the name of
Polly Brown.

Before Krajcir had a chance to provide the details
of the sexual assaults, the camcorder used to record
Krajcir's confession ran out of power. When it was
restarted, and a new DVD was inserted, Krajcir had
already finished his description of the events. The
transcript of the interview also contained a gap
when he spoke about the assaults in Marion and
Johnston City. Police authorities refused to release
the original reports of these incidents. Once the
recorded interview resumed, Krajcir went on to
relate some details of three more sexual assaults
that he committed in Mt. Vernon, Illinois.

"I followed a black woman home. She lived in an
apartment complex behind the Wal-Mart on the
west side of town. She was probably in her early twenties. Her mother was there at the time. And there
was a little girl there at the time. I took the other girl;
the one in her early twenties," Krajcir said.

"They knew you were there at the time? I mean,
everybody knew that you were in the house?" Echols
asked.

"Yeah," Krajcir said. "They left the door open. I guess that she was taking something in from the car and hadn't closed the front door yet. I just went in right behind her."

Krajcir explained that he entered the house and threatened everyone with his .25-caliber handgun. Then he took the young woman into the bathroom and forced her give him oral sex while the older woman and the little girl stayed in the living room.

"And there was another one in Mt. Vernon. She was a real good-looking white woman that I'd seen at the mall," Krajcir said.

Krajcir said the woman was about fifty years old. He said that he followed her to her home, near the Mt. Vernon hospital, but decided not to attack her right away. He told the investigators that he returned to the home about two weeks later. It was about nine o'clock in the evening, and he saw that she was alone.

"I tickled the screen door a little bit and it popped right open," Krajcir said. He said that she was sitting in a little sewing room when he grabbed her. Then he took her into the bedroom, raped her, and then forced her to give him oral sex. Krajcir couldn't recall if he tied up this victim, but he remembered that he wrapped her in a blanket before he left. He told Echols that he did not have a gun with him during this attack.

"And the third one?" Echols asked.

"A . . . come straight into Mt. Vernon near the post office. There's an apartment right across the street from the post office. There was an old woman that lived there," Krajcir said.

Krajcir described her as a white woman in her early fifties or possibly a bit older. He said that he crawled into the apartment through an open window so he didn't have to break in.

"I accosted her in the bathroom. She started screaming real loud. She kept on screaming and I couldn't stop her screaming. I just . . . I stabbed her once or twice with a knife, and then I made myself stop. I jumped back out through the window and ran. That's all I did," Krajcir said.

Echols asked, "So you never sexually assaulted her—just stabbed her because she wouldn't stop screaming?"

"Yeah," Krajcir replied.

Krajcir began earlier to mention another incident in Marion, Illinois, but Echols interrupted him. After more questions and more answers, Echols finally asked if there was anything else.

"Just the one you prevented me from talking about," Krajcir replied.

Krajcir didn't know her name, but he was referring to the May 12, 1978, murder of Virginia Witte in Marion, Illinois.

Krajcir said that he spotted an attractive woman who was about fifty years old at a grocery store in a strip mall off Route 13. It was the middle of the day, and he said that he followed her home. He said that a few minutes after she got home, he pulled his car into her driveway and parked right beside hers.

"I just knocked on the front door and acted like

I was delivering a package. I remember that there was some kind of little English bulldog or something inside. When she opened the door, I stepped in and threatened her with a knife."

Krajcir said that he forced the woman to give him oral sex and that he also had intercourse with her. At one point during the assault, Krajcir said, the woman actually managed to take the knife away from him, but then he regained control of the situation and the knife. Afterward, he said, he strangled her for several minutes, and as she tried to fight him off, he used his knife and sliced her across her stomach.

"She just wouldn't die. For some reason, she kept on trying to breathe, even when I was strangling her. I just went nuts. Back in '77 and '78, I think I just went a little crazy."

Krajcir said that he became frustrated that the woman wouldn't die, so he took another knife that he found in the kitchen and stabbed her with it.

"It was like one slice and . . . I felt her die. I felt the air or whatever it was leave her body, and I thought that she was dead. I just . . . I was gone."

Echols asked Krajcir if there was anything else he had to add or any other crimes that he had committed that they hadn't discussed yet.

"I imagine you want to talk about that one in Pennsylvania?" Krajcir asked.

Echols said, "I think what I'll do . . . I don't know all the details on that. I'll wait until they come and bring a letter waiving the death penalty. It's my understanding that their district attorney or state attorney is willing to waive that. And then they'll interview you for that, then."

Smith asked if there was anything else that Krajcir could remember doing in Cape Girardeau.

"No, I think we pretty well covered it, except for the fact that I exposed myself a lot of the time around the area of the post office."

Echols said that he had one more thing he wanted to cover before ending the interview. He told Krajcir that he was in contact with Pennsylvania and Kentucky authorities regarding crimes that he was suspected of committing in those states. He asked Krajcir if he would be willing to talk about an incident involving a young female near Lourdes Hospital in Paducah, Kentucky.

Echols was fishing to find information about the June 21, 1981, rape and murder of Anna Brantley. That incident took place shortly after Krajcir was released from prison for having sex with a thirteen-year-old girl. Krajcir assumed that Echols had referred to a different incident that took place in March 1979. Krajcir said that there was an attractive black female in her early twenties that he kidnapped in Paducah. Echols was also familiar with the unsolved case of Joyce Tharp, but Krajcir said that he didn't know the young lady's name. He claimed that he also didn't know that Tharp was preparing to graduate from Southern Illinois University in Carbondale, the same college that Krajcir attended.

Just as he had done with Sheila Cole, Krajcir abducted Tharp and took her back to his trailer at the Carbondale Mobile Home Park. He said that he sexually assaulted her and then strangled her to death

there. He told Echols that he waited until the next
night before he took her nude body back to Kentucky and dumped it near Noble Park in Paducah.

Krajcir denied any knowledge of or involvement
in the rape and murder of Anna Brantley. At 10:32
P.M., on Monday, December 3, 2007, Smith and
Echols turned off all the recordings in the room
and ended their questioning.

Three days later, Smith received the results from a
preliminary DNA test performed at the Missouri
State Highway Patrol Crime Laboratory that matched
Krajcir's DNA from a hair taken from the crime scene
at Margie Call's house in 1982. Another report that
came in later indicated that evidence collected from
the rape of Ann Shares was consistent with Timothy
Krajcir's DNA profile.

32

December 10, 2007

There are certain dates in American history that remain recorded in infamy. Pearl Harbor was attacked on December 7, 1941. The World Trade Center was attacked on September 11, 2001. Krajcir's deeds, although not remotely comparable in scope to those events in history, will forever remain ingrained in the hearts and minds of hundreds of people who were close friends or relatives of his victims. The impact of his actions probably affected thousands of people for at least a short period of time while they lived in fear of a sadistic murdering maniac who hunted and violated women in the most personal way imaginable. He stole their dignity. He stole their sense of security and even their sense of humanity. From the friends and family members of the victims he robbed, raped, and murdered, he stole a huge part of their lives. To them, December 10, 2007, is a date that will live in infamy just as significantly as those other dates where tragedy struck the lives of thousands of other American citizens.

This was the date that Timothy Krajcir finally pleaded guilty to killing Deborah Sheppard, and he was sentenced to serve forty years in the Illinois Department of Corrections, with credit for 112 days served. Because the Truth in Sentencing legislation did not exist at the time when Krajcir committed the murder, he was also eligible to have one day taken off his sentence for every day of good time that he served. That meant that Krajcir could potentially be released after serving less than twenty years for his crime.

There was something else that made December 10, 2007, even more relevant to those who knew and loved Krajcir's victims. A few hours after his sentencing in Illinois, Krajcir was officially charged in Missouri with the murders of Mary and Brenda Parsh, Sheila Cole, Margie Call, and Mildred Wallace. Even though Krajcir was already incarcerated, Judge Gary A. Kamp set the bail at $10 million.

A press conference was held at two o'clock in the afternoon to make the announcement. It was attended by about a hundred people, including friends and family members of the victims, as well as many of the law enforcement officers who worked on the cases over the years. Morley Swingle called it a historic day in the history of crime and punishment in Cape Girardeau.

"For the family members of the victims of these crimes, there can never really be justice," said Cape Girardeau police chief Carl Kinnison. He referred to Krajcir's arrest as bittersweet. "It's nice to bring some level of closure, but at the same time the viciousness of the offenses makes you hate to go back and relive it," Kinnison said.

As Swingle read off the names of the victims and briefly described the crimes that were committed against them, friends and family members did relive those moments and the courtroom was filled with tears, as well as moments of laughter as the survivors recalled loving moments with the ones they lost. At the end of the press conference, everyone in the room stood and applauded the officers who worked on the cases for thirty years.

Margie Call's niece Cathy Bertling Brown said that she had been waiting twenty-five years for this day. "I didn't think that anything was ever going to happen. It's wonderful to hear that we'll finally get some closure. My daddy found Aunt Margie. He's dead now, but I know that he can now finally rest in peace."

Margie's son Don Call said that he and his brother thought about their mother every day since she was murdered. "My brother died a year and a half ago, but I'm sure that he's watching this from somewhere," Don said.

Don Call saw Krajcir for the first time earlier that day when he traveled to Illinois to watch him plead guilty in the Sheppard case. He inadvertently held open the door for Krajcir as he was escorted into the courthouse. Don had to hold back a well of emotions when he realized that he was holding open the door for the man who killed his mother. Although he was thrilled to see Krajcir in shackles, he said, "Any thoughts of revenge . . . it's just not worth it at this point. This guy is already in his own hell somewhere."

Bob Weiss, a neighbor who grew up on Crest Oak

Lane, near Sheila Cole's family told reporter Don
Corrigan, of the *South County Times*, that "Sheila was
a quiet, sweet girl. She had a brother and a sister,
and they were all good kids. This kind of stuff
didn't happen to Crestwood kids. It was a big deal
back then if a bike was stolen in Crestwood.

"Her dad, Harold, and his son were friends of
mine, and her dad used to take us hunting," recalled Weiss. "It's a shame that Sheila's dad and
mom passed away before the whole situation was finally uncovered."

Frank Michniok, a neighbor who lived across the
street from the Coles on Crest Oak Lane, told Corrigan, "It's pretty sickening. This guy is a real sicko.
This kind of stuff just didn't happen back then.
Everyone was asking, Who would do this? How
could this happen to Harold's girl? There was just
shock on our street. I'm not surprised to learn
about all the details on this guy. It kind of makes
you understand why it has taken so long to uncover
what happened."

Michniok added that Sheila's father, Harold, was
a nice guy who was angry about what happened to
his daughter.

"He would drive down to Carbondale to see if he
could, by himself, find the man who killed his
daughter," Michniok said.

Detective Sergeant John Brown, who spent years
investigating the case since the very beginning, was
now retired from the Cape Girardeau Police Department and worked as a campus police officer at
Southeast Missouri State University. He was also in
attendance. He was elated to hear that a suspect

had finally been charged with the crimes that he spent a great portion of his life trying to solve.

"I can't think of anything that we failed to do. I always said that as I entered the pearly gates, I was going to ask St. Peter, 'Who committed those killings?'" Brown said.

Kinnison said that the murders remained unsolved for so many years because the killer was cunning enough to commit his crimes randomly, and he took care to cover his tracks. He added that Krajcir was an intelligent man who knew better than to boast of his crimes while he was in prison.

Detective Jimmy Smith said that because Krajcir was a student who majored in administrative justice, with a minor in psychology, he would know what police would look for and how to avoid detection. (Those are the courses that students take when they are preparing for a career in law enforcement.)

Krajcir picked his victims at random. In a murder investigation, spouses, relatives, and acquaintances are almost always investigated first, but because Krajcir didn't have any relations with his victims, there was no reason for police to look at him as an initial suspect.

Former detective McHughs said that one strategic decision Krajcir made was to hunt for his victims in a city where he did not live, so even after friends and relatives were eliminated as suspects, Cape Girardeau detectives continued to focus on local suspects.

"Our thinking was that [the killer] watched these women and got down a kind of routine, so we thought it was most likely someone who lived in the area," McHughs said. "I didn't even know what the term 'serial killer' meant. I thought it was somebody who went after Cap'n Crunch," McHughs added.

Krajcir was also clever enough to change his methods of murder: some of his victims were shot, some were stabbed, others were strangled.

McHughs said similarities in most of the murders—like breaking into homes, waiting for victims to return, and the way he tied their hands behind their back—led investigators to believe the killings were connected. But it was difficult to conceive that the killer might be a stranger who chose his victims randomly.

Despite all the methods of criminal investigation that Krajcir might have learned about in college, DNA technology was still a science of the future, at that time. Echols said that he had conversations with Krajcir in which Krajcir acknowledged that as the science grew, eventually this day would come.

"He said he was aware of DNA technology, and that because he was a part of that database, someday he would be matched. He knew it was coming," Echols said.

On hearing that official charges were being filed against Krajcir, Smith said, "It's absolutely the greatest feeling you can ever imagine."

Two days after the press conference, Detective Jimmy Smith had the pleasure of driving to the Big Muddy River Correctional Center in Illinois to present Krajcir with the warrant for his arrest.

33

The same day that Detective Smith delivered a warrant for Krajcir's arrest for rape and murder charges in Missouri, the prisoner at Big Muddy River Correctional Center received several other visitors. Investigators from Reading, Pennsylvania, and Marion, Illinois, traveled to the small town of Ina and spent three hours interviewing Krajcir. During the interview, they obtained a fresh DNA sample from Krajcir in order to use for new tests to confirm a definitive match to samples collected at crime scenes. They also collected fresh fingerprints and palm prints.

Corporal Moyer, of the Pennsylvania State Police, interviewed Krajcir and was accompanied by Trooper James Cuttitta, of the Frackville, Pennsylvania, barracks, and Lieutenant Echols, of the Carbondale Police Department. When Moyer asked Krajcir if he killed Myrtle Rupp, Krajcir came right out and told him, "I did it."

Krajcir went into detail about how he knocked on her door. When she answered, he flashed a fake badge and identified himself as a police officer. When he told her that he was investigating the burglary that she reported the week before, she invited him inside her house. That's when he pulled out a knife and forced her into the bedroom.

Krajcir told Moyer that he made Rupp undress and then raped her from behind. He said that he pulled his penis out of her vagina before he ejaculated; then he masturbated. Krajcir said that when he did finally ejaculate, it was either on the carpet or on the bed. He couldn't recall for sure if he tied Rupp up or what bindings he used if he did tie her up. He remembered that he strangled her, but he wasn't sure if he used his hands, a bandana, or something else. When asked why he killed Rupp, Krajcir told Moyer that he did not know. "She didn't deserve to die," Krajcir added. At the end of the interview, Krajcir wrote out a four-page confession to the rape and murder.

Krajcir's confession to Rupp's murder was not immediately released, but Detective James Pollock, of the Muhlenberg Township Police Department, admitted to the public on December 12 that they were looking into whether Krajcir might be responsible for any unsolved crimes in the Lehigh Valley. Lieutenant William Tepper, head of the police criminal investigations section at Troop M–Bethlehem, said that they weren't ready to officially call Krajcir a suspect, but they were aware of his MO and were looking for similarities in several cases.

The next day, investigators from the Marion Police Department announced that Krajcir was "a distinct person of interest" in the murder of Virginia Witte. They refused to confirm or deny whether Krajcir confessed to Witte's rape and murder. Detective Tina Morrow would only go as far as to say, "He has been interviewed."

Marion police chief Gene Goolsby added that "he provided several pertinent pieces of information regarding the Witte investigation."

When asked about Krajcir's demeanor during the interview, Morrow replied, "He's just a little different. You walk into the room with an open mind and try to collect as much information as possible."

Investigators from both Pennsylvania and Illinois turned over the results of their investigations to their state's attorney's offices. It would now be up to the prosecutors to decide whether or not to file charges against Krajcir.

Krajcir was having a busy week. He was transferred from Big Muddy River Correctional Center to the Tamms Correctional Center, a maximum-security prison in which inmates were confined to solitary cells and severely limited in their outside contacts. Illinois DOC spokesman Derek Schnapp said, "In light of the recent criminal charges that have been brought against Mr. Krajcir, we felt Tamms was a more appropriate place for him to be."

In Kentucky, McCracken County sheriff Jon Hayden made arrangements to speak with Krajcir, even though he was not yet linked to any specific crimes there. Hayden said, "I feel that we have a duty to go speak to him. For whatever reason, he's coming clean with his criminal acts and the murders he has committed. We owe it to the victims' families to make every effort to bring some type of conclusion. The proximity to our area is why we want to talk with him." Hayden added that his detectives were reviewing unsolved cases that dated back to the 1970s and that his department was reaching out to retired sheriffs and detectives who might have had some insight into those cases.

Lieutenant Jeff Surratt, of the Kentucky State Police Post 1, told the *Paducah Sun* that a few unsolved murder and missing person cases were being reviewed, but he would not discuss the details while the investigation was ongoing.

Paducah assistant police chief Danny Carroll said that investigative assistant Malinda Elrod had been assigned to review the department's unsolved murder cases from the early 1980s after hearing about Krajcir's confession to killing Deborah Sheppard. Based on the profile of Krajcir's methods for committing crimes in the region that Lieutenant Echols created, Elrod suspected that Krajcir might have been responsible for killing Paducah resident Anna Brantley during the same time period. She sent all the information she had regarding the unsolved case to the Carbondale Police Department. When Echols and Smith interviewed Krajcir, he denied having any involvement with the Brantley case, but he mentioned details of another rape and murder that were very similar to the unsolved case of Joyce Tharp. Carroll decided to contact Joyce's brother Vernell Tharp on December 11 to tell him of the possible connection to his sister's murder.

Two days later, the Carbondale Police Department sent Carroll a transcript and videotape of the interview they conducted with Krajcir. Carroll said that he wanted to review the information before he contacted Vernell, but he decided, instead, to alert him to the progress in the investigation because Krajcir's name was making national headline news.

"We wanted to head off any rumors that the family might be hearing. We wanted to give the family answers," Carroll said.

On December 13, Paducah police issued a written statement that they were reviewing unsolved cases and hoped to interview Krajcir if they concluded that he might be involved in any of them.

"We didn't know what impact publicity might have on our interview [with Krajcir]," Carroll said. "We felt that Krajcir had committed this murder, but we were reluctant to release any information until after we talked with him and were sure that he did this."

Carroll and Elrod finally interviewed Krajcir, on December 18 at Tamms Correctional Center in Illinois. During the four-hour interview, Krajcir calmly detailed how he kidnapped Joyce Tharp, assaulted her, and then strangled her to death.

Carroll said that Krajcir spoke openly, as if he were having a casual conversation. "It was as if he was talking about how his day was going. He gave us specific facts about locations and Tharp's appearance."

Krajcir told Carroll and Elrod that he traveled to Kentucky with the specific purpose of finding a victim. He was familiar with the Paducah area because he had made several medical runs to Western Baptist Hospital while he worked as an emergency medical technician (EMT) for the Jackson County Ambulance Service in Carbondale.

Carroll said that Tharp was "purely a victim of circumstance" that Krajcir picked randomly after spending several hours of peeking into windows in the Forest Hills area. Even the place where Tharp's body was dumped was probably picked at random. "I don't think he realized it was a church. It was probably the first dark and secluded spot in the area that he could find. He didn't want to leave the body in Carbondale because he was living there at the time," Carroll said.

As he had done before in Cape Girardeau, Krajcir agreed to confess to his crime only under the condition that prosecutors would not seek the death penalty against him. When Mt. Vernon, Illinois, police chief Chris Mendenhall raised questions about the truthfulness of Krajcir's confession to Tharp's murder, Carroll said, "I have no reason to believe that someone else was responsible for her death. He gave us details that were specific enough to totally confirm he was present and that he was responsible."

McCracken County Commonwealth attorney Tim Kaltenbach said that it was unlikely that he would file a homicide/murder charge against Krajcir because it appeared that Krajcir actually killed Tharp in another state. He added, however, that the Kentucky kidnapping statute allowed prosecutors to seek the same punishment as a murder charge if the victim did not survive.

Even though murder and kidnapping were both capital offenses in Kentucky, because of Krajcir's agreement with the prosecutor to waive the death penalty in exchange for his confession, the most time that he could be sentenced to serve was life without parole. Still, it was highly unlikely that Krajcir would have to face any charges against him in Kentucky in the near future because then-governor Matt Blunt, of Missouri, signed paperwork on

December 17 to seek the extradition of Krajcir to face charges of rape and murder in Cape Girardeau. The state of Missouri would receive priority over Kentucky because it had more crimes to prosecute. Authorities pledged to expedite Blunt's request so Krajcir would have to face a Missouri courtroom as soon as possible.

It was Christmas Eve in Williamson County when Illinois state's attorney Charles Garnati filed charges of rape and first-degree murder against Krajcir in connection with the 1978 slaying of Virginia Witte. The announcement of the charges essentially froze efforts to extradite Krajcir to Missouri. Cape Girardeau County prosecutor Morley Swingle was told that Krajcir would remain housed inside the Tamms Correctional Center until the Witte case was resolved. Rebecca Rausch, a spokeswoman for Rod Blagojevich, then-governor of Illinois, told Missouri officials that she understood that they were frustrated by the delay, but there were complicated issues to work through because Krajcir was already charged in two states and was eventually expected to be charged in two others.

"We understand Missouri's interest in bringing him to justice. We're interested in the same thing, but he will remain in Illinois for the time being," Rausch said.

In response to the delay in Krajcir's extradition, a press release was issued on behalf of Missouri governor Matt Blunt, which stated: *Krajcir is charged with the murder of five Missouri women. The people, our law enforcement community and the prosecutor in Cape Girardeau County are as eager as I am to see justice done for those crimes, and Krajcir's presence in Missouri is*

*essential to the administration of that justice. I am
frustrated with this delay, but am not jumping to any
conclusions. There is no reason to believe that Illinois
does not wish to see Krajcir brought to justice for all of
his crimes.*

2008

I wanted to put everything I had done behind me. I had to give full disclosure for several reasons. I told them things that they knew nothing about.
—Timothy Wayne Krajcir

34

January 3, 2008

In order to start off the New Year on the right foot, Detectives Smith and Echols decided to interview Krajcir one more time. By now, Krajcir had been moved to the maximum-security prison in Tamms. They just wanted to verify the facts that Krajcir gave them during his confessions in December. During that interview, Krajcir admitted that he committed two sexual assaults in Mt. Vernon, Illinois. According to an Associated Press article printed in the *Centralia Morning Sentinel,* police authorities checked their records dating back to the early 1980s in order to validate Krajcir's claim. The article reported Lieutenant Echols saying that "police here apparently have found no records of those cases, indicating perhaps that the victims did not come forward." Because there were no open files in those alleged attacks, no charges were ever filed against Krajcir for those incidents.

Smith and Echols drove to Tamms, and they met

with Krajcir, who was escorted from his cell to an interrogation room for a final interview.

They began by discussing the Sheila Cole case. Lieutenant Echols told Krajcir that the Illinois State Police crime lab detected three DNA profiles from Cole's clothing and evidence that was collected during her autopsy. Echols said that one of them belonged to Krajcir, one belonged presumably to Cole's boyfriend, and the third one was unidentified. The purpose for Echol's line of questioning was to find out if anybody else had accompanied Krajcir or aided him when he committed his crimes.

"I know that for a period of time you had a roommate, which would have been Rod Matticks," Echols said. "Is there any chance that Rod would have been involved with this?"

Krajcir said that Matticks would never have taken part in any of the crimes that he committed, and that if he would have had any suspicions about what Krajcir was doing, Matticks would have kicked him out of the trailer that they shared in Carbondale.

This was new information for the detectives. They did not realize that Matticks was actually the one who was renting the trailer and that he later let Krajcir move in with him. Krajcir said that he couldn't be sure, but by the time that he had killed Cole, Matticks had probably already moved out of the trailer.

"I don't think I would have brought her there if [Matticks] had still been living there," Krajcir said. Then he added, "Or maybe he was at work at the time."

Echols told Krajcir that the reason he was asking about his roommate was that Matticks had been arrested several years earlier for more than one count of indecent exposure, and he pleaded guilty to the charges.

"He's a licensed physician now. . . . That's why that question comes up. Was he ever involved in anything? Was he ever there?" Echols asked.

Krajcir told Echols once again that he always acted on his own and that Matticks had no knowledge of his activities.

Echols then turned to the subject of Joyce Tharp.

"In regard to the black girl that was abducted from Paducah. You told Assistant [Police] Chief Danny Carroll that when you went into her bedroom, she had on some type of sleeping mask over her eyes. The family didn't remember her sleeping with anything like that. Then you said that you actually kept that on her as you brought her to Carbondale."

"Well, I'm not real sure about that," Krajcir said.

"It's not like you're gonna mix that up. You remember everything else well enough. Are you sure that's not mixed up with any other case? That was definitely her?" Echols asked.

Krajcir said that he was sure, and she was the only one that he had abducted from Paducah, Kentucky.

Echols moved on to ask about Krajcir's activities in Mt. Vernon, Illinois. Before the detective even had a chance to ask a question about a specific incident, Krajcir began rambling on about how he broke into a basement apartment across the street from the post office and stabbed a woman in the bathroom. Krajcir said he heard that another man was arrested for the incident.

"So somebody could be in prison for that?"

Echols asked. "That's something you didn't mention last time. I'll have to check into that."

Smith and Echols continued the interview, and they asked questions about all the victims that Krajcir admitted to killing in Missouri and Illinois. Then they moved on to talk about Pennsylvania and Myrtle Rupp. Krajcir told the detectives that he wanted to be able to live back in Pennsylvania when he got older. He thought that by confessing to Rupp's murder he might get transferred to a Pennsylvania prison, where he would feel more connected to his childhood home.

Echols asked if there were any more bodies in Pennsylvania that he should know about.

"No. I don't think so," Krajcir replied.

"When you say, 'I don't think so,' that makes me wonder if there was . . . if there was anything else," Echols said.

Krajcir told him that there was nothing else in Pennsylvania.

Smith asked Krajcir about a girl who was abducted from a gas station located a few miles off the interstate near Scott City, in 1979, and was never heard from again. Krajcir denied having any knowledge of the incident.

Smith then mentioned a case in Indiana in which a young college girl was found murdered in a cornfield just off Interstate 70. Her hands were bound behind her back with the laces from her shoes. Her body was discovered on September 11, 1977.

Krajcir told Smith that it couldn't have been him because when he drove home to Pennsylvania on holidays, he almost always had at least one, and sometimes several, passengers with him. He said that he would go to the SIU student center and look on the bulletin board to see if anybody wanted a ride so they could pay for his gas. Krajcir said, he would usually find two or three students to travel with him. Besides that, Krajcir said, it was the wrong time of the year. He usually only traveled home during the Christmas season.

Smith moved on to ask other questions. As he interrogated Krajcir about what he had done with the gun that he had used to kill Mildred Wallace, he had to pause at one point to remind Echols not to answer questions on Krajcir's behalf.

Smith had been receiving a lot of calls from other police departments throughout the state of Missouri regarding unsolved cases. He questioned Krajcir about specific locations and incidents, but Krajcir maintained that he had already disclosed everything about all of the crimes that he had committed.

The conversation soon turned biographical in nature. Krajcir said that he was the oldest of three boys, all born from different fathers. His actual father, Charles McBride, was a marine. Krajcir said that he did not know what had caused his parents to separate, because he was only about a year old at the time. His mother was only sixteen years old herself. He said that he never had a chance to meet his biological father. One of his uncles told him that his father was a pharmacist and that he lived in Newark, New Jersey.

Krajcir said that his mother had to find somebody else to take care of her, so she hooked up with the father of his middle brother, Bill. Krajcir couldn't remember that man's name and that it didn't matter, anyway, because their relationship didn't last.

"She had to go out and find another guy. I was alone all that time. I think she met Bernie Krajcir when I was five or six years old."

Krajcir said that she had another son, his youngest half brother, Bernie Junior. He said that his stepfather worked in construction, and because of that, the family moved from town to town. It was when they lived in Wescosville, Pennsylvania, that Krajcir got into an argument with his stepfather and was kicked out of the house.

"Me and him didn't get along too good. We never did. One day I told my brother to go home and do something. To me it wasn't a real big deal, but when I came home, they were gonna make me go to my room and not have no supper. We got to arguing and we went to blows, and Mom threw a suitcase at me and said to get out. So I split," Krajcir said.

Neither Smith nor Echols bothered to ask Krajcir what it was that he asked his brother to do that day. Shortly after that, Krajcir joined the navy.

Krajcir went on to talk about how he met his wife, Barbara Kos, at the Eagles Club in Milwaukee and the fact that they had a daughter together. Then he switched to a memory that he had in the 1980s while he was serving time in Pennsylvania.

"I'm in Graterford Prison, right . . . doing my '84, '85. I was thinking about getting into this program to teach other guys how to get their GED . . . do math for them, help them, you know. They showed a movie about learning how to help people, and it was made in Syracuse University. This girl walks up to the camera and she's got a name tag on, right. And it said, 'Nancy Lee.' That's my daughter's name!

"And she was dark haired. She was about five-six, or five foot, seven inches tall. She looked like one of my aunts. The age was right. I just wondered if that could possibly be my daughter, you know. It was a weird experience."

Echols tried to steer Krajcir back on track by getting him to focus on the sexual assault and attempted murder counts that he was charged with while he was in the navy.

"Based on old reports that I read, there were more than two sexual assaults, but that's what you got charged with," Echols said.

"No, there was only two. There was the first one I ever did and then . . . the second one was the one where the girl got stabbed. And then the night I got caught, probably would have been the third one."

Krajcir explained that he was still a novice rapist at that time. He didn't follow the women home and then take the time to make plans to return later in order to commit the actual deed. Back then, Krajcir said, he simply looked into people's windows and picked his next victim on the spur of the moment. He said that he already began peering into windows when he lived in Pennsylvania, but he hadn't yet acted out his desires.

Krajcir went on to talk about his time in prison.

While he was incarcerated at Menard, he played basketball and softball. His softball team, the Cubs, was part of the Herrin Coalbelt League, which competed against other teams in the area. When he was eventually transferred to the minimum-security prison in Vienna, he got to travel all over Southern Illinois playing fast-pitch softball. This was also the time when he was able to take EMT classes and college courses at Shawnee. He was also allowed to leave the prison to work as an EMT at Cairo PADCO Community Hospital and at Union County Hospital in Anna, Illinois.

Detective Smith had to laugh when Echols commented that he was born in the hospital in Cairo, but he didn't remember the details of the incident.

Krajcir said that the inmates that worked at the hospital in Cairo would stay on the top floor in an old obstetric wing that was mostly empty. He said that they were only lightly supervised. Somebody would come by to check up on them every couple of hours or so.

"Only two guys rode the ambulance, and there were three of us on each shift. We'd let one man leave the hospital to do his thing . . . get a girlfriend . . . sneak out for a while. When we got an emergency, we'd fire up the siren on the way out to let him know that we were going for a run and to get his ass back inside the hospital. We all did that," Krajcir said.

According to Krajcir, the EMT convicts at Union County Hospital ran the same kind of three-man shifts, which they rotated so that one of them could always have some free time. Krajcir said that when he worked there, he began a sexual relationship with a licensed practical nurse (LPN) who worked at the hospital and rented an apartment about a half block away.

"When it was my turn, I would go to her apartment. When I heard an ambulance go out, I'd go back to the hospital. The women went nuts over the convicts. You wouldn't believe it. From the ugliest guy to the handsomest guy. Married women and younger women . . . it was unreal."

Krajcir said that he was not lacking for sex during this part of his life, which brought Echols to ask if sex was his motivation for raping women when he was released from prison. Krajcir's response was "sex was not the prime ingredient there. It's power and control. I mean, instant gratification is there, but it's so quick that it doesn't take care of the need. A week later, you can be out doing the same thing again."

When Echols asked Krajcir how he felt within himself for the next few days after he stepped over the line by raping and killing Mary and Brenda Parsh, Krajcir told him, "To be honest with you, I didn't think about it at all. As callous as it sounds, it's the truth. That part of me just wasn't there . . . to care about other people."

The next subject that was explored was Krajcir's reason for moving to Carbondale. After being paroled, he moved there to attend classes as Southern Illinois University. He worked as a student employee for the SIU Health Service.

The university had its own ambulance service, but they soon turned it over to the county, which developed it into a professional ambulance service. At least half of the people that worked for SIU

Health Service ended up working for the newly established Jackson County Ambulance Service. One of their new employees was Timothy Wayne Krajcir.

It was through his work at the ambulance service that Krajcir began to make connections with members of the Carbondale Police Department. He got to know several of the officers well enough that they invited Krajcir to play a few games as a member of their softball team. That ended, and so did his job, when he was arrested in February 1979 for indecent liberties with a child.

"What did you do between the time you got arrested and the time that you went back to prison? I mean, obviously, there was the murder out in Temple, Pennsylvania. There was also the abduction and murder of the girl from Paducah. But what were you doing besides that?" Echols asked.

"Not much" was the extent of Krajcir's response.

Additional questions prompted Krajcir to say that he lived with a man named John Crosby at the Carbondale Mobile Home Park. He drew unemployment compensation and did anything with his days or nothing at all.

Krajcir got bored and may have wanted to avoid returning to a life behind bars, so he decided to travel back to Pennsylvania and live in the wooded hills far away from the rest of society. He said that he had accumulated close to $2,000 and drove to Belleville, Pennsylvania, where he went on a shopping spree for camping gear.

"I bought a tent, sleeping bags, a compound bow . . . everything. I backpacked it into the mountains of Pennsylvania. I put down a foundation for a cabin, dug me a root cellar, and practiced with the bow every day. I was gonna stay there. I was there for about two month and realized that I was just too much of a social person. I wasn't going to be able to handle it."

Krajcir returned to Illinois and was subsequently placed back into the psychiatric center at Menard.

"All the crazy people were gone by then, and it was a lot different than it was the first time," Krajcir said.

He began attending counseling sessions there, but he admitted that he was just going through the motions to make it look like he wanted treatment.

"I went along with it. It was easy to trick them into believing that you were getting well. It's easy to slide through a system that's so overcrowded," Krajcir said.

Further questioning covered Krajcir's release from prison a short time later and his return to SIU to finish his four-year degree. He said that he used school grants to pay for a car and then he drove back to Pennsylvania. He moved in with his mother in the city of Bethlehem for a period of time, and he obtained a job in a nursing home. Krajcir eventually moved to the Keystone Mobile Home Court in Laurys Station to live with his youngest half brother, Bernie.

Before the end of the interview, Echols asked Krajcir about a woman named Lucille Fligor, who was killed in the basement of her home in Carbondale. Before Krajcir had a chance to respond, Echols said, "I don't have all the details, but I trust that you've told me that Deborah Sheppard is the only murder you did there."

Krajcir told Echols that he had "to go to the bathroom real bad." The conversation quickly moved on to two burglaries that Krajcir admitted to committing, and then the interview ended abruptly.

35

Timothy Wayne Krajcir left a long trail of victims in his wake. The number of victims of sexual assault and murder is substantial, but it pales in comparison to the number of other victims of his crimes. The friends, family members, and loved ones of those he assaulted and killed were also victims, and they have struggled for decades to come to grips with the senseless and heinous crimes that Krajcir committed.

There is one man who also paid dearly with his life and became another possible victim of Timothy Krajcir's behavior. He wasn't robbed, raped, or murdered, but he still had his life taken from him, and he died in an Illinois prison cell in 1996 after being convicted of a crime that many people felt he was falsely accused of. Krajcir admitted to committing the crime that resulted in the arrest and subsequent conviction of Grover Thompson, a forty-six-year-old Mississippi man.

It had been drizzling throughout most of the evening, and on the night of September 7, 1981,

Thompson took shelter in the lobby of a post office in Mt. Vernon, Illinois. He had recently visited a relative in Milwaukee and had decided to rest for a while. He had plenty of time before he would catch the next bus back to Mississippi.

Across the street, in her basement apartment on Broadway, Ida White, seventy-two, was getting ready to take a bath before preparing to go to sleep. She undressed and walked into her bathroom. When she tried to pull aside the shower curtain, she was surprised by a man who had been hiding behind it. He reached out and grabbed White. She screamed and he covered her face and mouth with his hand. The intruder told her to be quiet and threatened her with a knife. White continued to scream and struggled against the intruder. She tried to grab the knife, but the blade sliced into the palms of her hands. Then she felt the steel blade penetrate her breast. White saw her own blood spill out of her body and became dizzy. The man stabbed her several more times until she fell to the floor—her screams finally silenced.

White's neighbor Barney Bates claimed that he heard her screams. He said that he broke down a door between their adjoining apartments and rushed in to help her. He later told police that he saw a black man climbing out of White's window. In an effort to stop the attacker, Bates said that he grabbed the man's T-shirt, which tore as he ran off. He told the police officers who arrived at the scene that the man was wearing either a dirty white or gray T-shirt. According to the police report, there was blood splattered everywhere.

Ida White survived her attack. An ambulance

took her to the emergency room at the Good Samaritan Hospital. She had lost a lot of blood, but her wounds did not damage any critical organs. After she was stabilized and treated, White was admitted to the hospital and recovered there for thirty days before being released.

As the police were about to leave the scene of the crime, they were informed that a black man was sleeping in the post office across the street. When they found him, Thompson had no blood on his clothes or body. A torn red-and-orange shirt was among his belongings, and a piece of it was tied around his waist as a makeshift belt. He was also carrying a pocketknife. Thompson was subsequently arrested and taken to the Mt. Vernon Police Department (MVPD) where Bates identified him as the attacker—even though court documents state that Ida White *never* identified Thompson as her attacker.

Stephen Swafford was assigned as Thompson's public defender. Even after twenty-six years, he believed that Thompson was wrongly convicted. He said that Bates wasn't given much of a choice when it came to identifying Thompson. There was no photo array of suspects and no lineup. The police simply said that Thompson was suspected of committing the crime, and Bates concurred that Thompson was the man that he saw earlier at White's apartment. Swafford said that Bates probably got that idea put in his mind through the suggestive identification procedure used by the MVPD.

At the trial, an expert in forensics testified that blood was found on the blade of Thompson's knife, but the amount was too small for analysis. There wasn't even enough evidence to identify blood type.

"There should have been more blood on the knife. There should have been blood splatter on his clothes and on his body, but none of that was present. The eyewitness account was not corroborated by any physical evidence," Swafford said.

Another inconsistency emerged during the trial. Bates testified that the attacker's shirt was red and orange. In his earlier statement to police, he told them that it was dirty white or gray.

Thompson's nephew S. T. Jamison said that his uncle had trouble walking for the last ten years because he was hit by a car in the early 1970s and both his legs were shattered. When Thompson was called to the stand, he shuffled his feet forward with obvious difficulty. He hoped that the jury would see that he was physically incapable of climbing in and out of White's window.

When Swafford addressed the jury, he pointed out the fact that Thompson's disabilities would have made it impossible for him to commit the crime. He described Thompson as a weathered and beaten man, with eyes that looked old and tired. He said that Thompson was just a homeless man with limited mental function who was guarded, baffled, and confused. He said that Thompson was forty-six going on sixty.

There were several inconsistencies in the testimony provided by Ida White during the hearing. First she said that her attacker escaped by smashing out the window and jumping out headfirst. Then she said, "I thought he went out headfirst, but I guess he didn't. I didn't really know how he did go out."

During Swafford's redirect examination, he

asked White, "Do you know what he knocked the window out with?"

White replied, "No, I don't. I thought he just knocked it out with his hands, but really I didn't see anything."

White was apparently hard of hearing, because the attorneys often had to repeat their questions to her. White said that she had been in the apartment for about six hours before she was attacked. When asked if she had heard any noise in her apartment during that time, White said that she had not. She added, "If I had heard a noise, and there is noise going on there in the apartment house, I don't pay any attention to it."

She later testified that she screamed for Bates to help her when she was being attacked. When she was asked how she knew that Bates was at home, White said that she heard noise from inside his adjoining apartment.

Not much of White's testimony could be credited as evidence that she actually observed herself. She only knew the approximate time of the attack because the friend she was on the telephone with later told her what time they ended their conversation. White said that she never really got a look at her attacker because he was behind the shower curtain, which covered most of her view of him. She said, "I think he was colored."

Swafford asked, "You could not tell for sure who the man was?"

White admitted that she could not remember what her attacker looked like. Then she said that Bates got a good view of him and that he identified him.

When Swafford asked White if she had any

previous problems with any black people, prosecutor Watkins objected and claimed that the question was irrelevant. Swafford defended the relevance of his question by telling the judge that White claimed a person who may have been black entered her apartment. "I think that whether or not there are other black persons with whom she has had problems is certainly relevant, especially when the question of identification is involved," Swafford said.

The judge ruled that the objection would be sustained, and Swafford was not allowed to pursue his line of questioning.

White couldn't even answer how many times she had been stabbed. "You'll have to ask the doctor," she said.

With a lack of physical evidence, and White's questionable testimony, the entire case boiled down to the testimony of Barney Bates. The all-white jury deliberated for less than four hours and came back with a guilty verdict on the charge of attempted murder. Thompson was sentenced to serve forty years. He died of natural causes while still incarcerated after serving fourteen years of his sentence.

According to the *St. Louis Post-Dispatch,* Caterina DiTraglia, an attorney with the Federal Public Defender's Office in St. Louis, said that jurors tend to believe eyewitness testimony above forensic evidence, and when DNA evidence began exonerating death row inmates, about 80 percent of the wrongly accused people had been convicted because of eyewitness testimony. DiTraglia added that "when a person views a lineup, studies have shown that what police say before and after they view the lineup changes their memory of the crime." Swafford believed that was exactly what happened in the case against Grover Thompson.

Twenty-five years after Thompson was convicted, Timothy Krajcir cut a deal with Cape Girardeau County's prosecuting attorney Morley Swingle to confess to and give full disclosure of his crimes in exchange for Swingle's promise that he would not seek the death penalty against him. During Krajcir's confession, he provided the details of two sexual assaults that he committed in Mt. Vernon. He also confessed to stabbing a woman in her basement apartment on Broadway, across the street from the Mt. Vernon post office. Krajcir said that he thought that he did that in 1981, and that it probably occurred during the late summer, because he wore a T-shirt at the time.

Swafford watched a video of that interview and said that Krajcir drew a diagram of White's bathroom and recalled that she had been talking on the phone shortly before he attacked her. At Thompson's trial, White testified that she had called a friend before she got ready for bed that evening.

Krajcir said that when the elderly woman entered the bathroom and saw him, she began to scream and wouldn't stop. Lieutenant Echols, of the Carbondale Police Department, said that Krajcir described White as a "feisty old gal," and when she wouldn't stop screaming, he stabbed her several times until she fell quietly to the floor. Krajcir said that he exited back out through the bathroom window, ran to his car, and drove away as quickly as possible. He told police that he threw his bloodstained T-shirt out the window of his car as he drove along Interstate 57, returning to his home in Carbondale. Krajcir said that he would be willing to take a lie detector test to prove that he was telling the truth.

He also told detectives that he remembered hearing that another man had been arrested for the attack on White, but he didn't pay much attention to it. He figured that since he actually committed the crime, police would not be able to link any evidence to Thompson.

According to a newspaper article published by the *Southeast Missourian,* Echols said that he couldn't think of a reason why Krajcir would lie about committing the crime, because he had been truthful in all his previous confessions.

In January 2008, Mt. Vernon police chief Chris Mendenhall said that Krajcir's confession was "bogus." He said that he thought Krajcir learned of the details of the attack from Grover Thompson when they were both incarcerated at the Menard Psychiatric Center. Although records show that Krajcir and Thompson did serve time there during the same period, there were about four hundred inmates there at the time. Krajcir said that he did not recall knowing Grover Thompson, and that they would not have been in the same social circle because most of Krajcir's friends were athletes.

Rather than admit that they may have arrested and convicted the wrong man, Mendenhall insisted that Krajcir was not truthful in his confession. Mendenhall said that Krajcir lied about the circumstances involving the attack against Ida White, and because of that, it should raise doubts about Krajcir's confession to the other murders in Illinois, Missouri, Pennsylvania, and Kentucky.

In February 2008, the *St. Louis Post-Dispatch*

reported Swingle as saying, "I don't understand why [Mt. Vernon police] are just sticking their head in the trench and saying, 'We're not going to look at this.' Krajcir has admitted to so many things—why would he tack on something he didn't do? They should reopen the investigation. It would be the professional, responsible, and ethical thing to do."

In March 2008, KFVS12 Heartland News reported that the Mt. Vernon Police Department finally decided to reopen the Ida White case and planned to resubmit some old evidence to see if the wrong man had paid for the crime.

Krajcir said that Thompson made a convenient victim for the police, and he was glad to hear that the case was being reexamined. Krajcir added that he would like Thompson's family to know that Grover Thompson was an innocent man.

Mendenhall responded via e-mail to questions regarding the disposition of the case in January 2009. His response left doubt as to whether or not the MVPD was actually looking further into the case. He wrote, *There is no one working here that investigated the case. The officers, the witness, the State's Attorney and the jury apparently felt the right person was arrested. I have reviewed the case file, but was not working here when that occurred.*

In response to the question of how Thompson got convicted if White never specifically identified him as her attacker, Mendenhall wrote, *White's description of her attacker matched Thompson. We interviewed her employer who stated that White was very adamant that he was black, as well as Bates who had contact with him.*

Mendenhall wrote that Bates was recently interviewed by an FBI agent who became convinced that Grover Thompson was the attacker. He did not reveal the identity of the agent who supposedly interviewed him, and since Bates had been dead since 1996, there was no way that any interview with him could have been done recently.

All the evidence we currently have still points to Thompson, not Krajcir, Mendenhall wrote. He has continued to maintain his belief that Thompson might have casually discussed the incident with Krajcir while they were incarcerated at the same Illinois prison psychiatric ward, and that during his confession, Krajcir passed the story on as one of the crimes that he had committed.

During an interview with the Channel 12 Heartland News, Echols said that one of his fears was that there was a good chance that Thompson had been convicted and spent time in prison for charges he was not guilty of.

"[Krajcir] even told us that he wouldn't confess to something he hadn't done. Lord knows he's done enough. He doesn't need to make things up," Echols said.

36

January 4, 2008

A McCracken County grand jury formally indicted Timothy Krajcir on charges of burglary and kidnapping in connection with the Joyce Tharp case, but prosecutor Tim Kaltenbach said that it could be years—if ever—before he might appear in a Kentucky courtroom.

"I don't think we're going to be getting him tomorrow, but in the next several years, when the other outstanding cases against him become final, we'll be able to bring him to Kentucky. If it was one of my relatives that he killed, I would want him to answer in a court of law, even if it didn't mean more time on his sentence. I think it was important to take the first step, and we did that by charging him today," Kaltenbach said. "As long as he is securely in prison, I'd just as soon have another state pay for him," Kaltenbach added.

January 9, 2008

Williamson County prosecutor Charles Garnati agreed to waive the death penalty in the case against Krajcir in exchange for his confession in the 1978 rape and murder of Virginia Lee Witte, of Marion, Illinois.

Two days later, prosecutors in Reading, Pennsylvania, formally charged Krajcir with first- and second-degree murder in connection with the 1979 rape and slaying of fifty-one-year-old Myrtle Rupp in Berks County. It would be some time before Krajcir would have to face the charges against him in Pennsylvania, though. First he had to be extradited to Missouri, where he would be tried for the murders of five women in Cape Girardeau. At the time, Lieutenant Scott Compton, spokesman for the Illinois State Police, said that the extradition process was already under way and could take place within a week. In reality, it took about three months.

Berks County, Pennsylvania, district attorney John Adams said that it would be in the best interest of the Commonwealth of Pennsylvania if Krajcir was not extradited to his state to face the charges against him. Adams said that he would do his best to arrange for Krajcir's court appearance to take place without having to physically bring him to Pennsylvania.

"If all parties agree, Pennsylvania state law allows for criminal proceedings to take place even if the defendant is not actually present, unless the case goes to trial, and as long as all parties involved agree," Adams said.

Because Krajcir did not request a trial in the previous cases in which he was convicted, Adams hoped that Krajcir's arraignment, preliminary hearing, pleadings, and sentencing could all be handled without the expense, time, and manpower required to transport him to, and house him in, Pennsylvania. Officials there wanted to handle the entire proceeding through a live video feed, and technicians spent the entire next day testing video equipment at the Berks County Courthouse. Krajcir already admitted that he committed the crime, so authorities did not expect to have to take the charges against Krajcir to trial.

As everything else was going on, employees from a doctor's office in Cape Girardeau hung a wreath of flowers at the roadside rest stop near McClure, Illinois, where Sheila Cole's body was discovered thirty years earlier.

January 14, 2008

Larry Broeking, Krajcir's public defender in Illinois, told Garnati that he expected his client to plead guilty to all the charges against him, and he did not expect any complications. However, in the case involving Witte's death, Broeking said that Krajcir—not prosecutors—would have the choice of whether he wanted to be sentenced under 1978 statutes, which carried a possible twenty-to-forty-year prison sentence for a murder conviction, or the current law that was punishable by up to sixty years.

Broeking expected that Krajcir would opt for sentencing under the older statutes because he was already in frail health and was recently saddled with a forty-year prison sentence for strangling a college student, Deborah Sheppard. Cape Girardeau detective Smith confirmed that Krajcir had recently undergone surgery to remove his pancreas, and that Krajcir told Smith that his failing health was one of the reasons that he decided to confess to his crimes.

"Odds are that he will die in prison, anyway, regardless of what happens now," Broeking said as murder charges continued to mount against his client.

On Friday, January 18, 2008, Krajcir pleaded guilty to killing Witte. Garnati laid out his case and provided the gruesome details of how Krajcir followed Witte home after seeing her while they both were driving. He explained how Krajcir forced his way into her house, raped her, strangled her for several minutes, stabbed her repeatedly, and then slashed her torso with a knife. Williamson County judge Phillip Palmer sentenced him to forty years in prison for his crime, and Krajcir would serve his time consecutive to the forty-year sentence he received for the 1982 murder of Deborah Sheppard.

"For all practical purposes, this is a life sentence for Mr. Krajcir," Palmer said.

Detective Morrow said that she was glad that the court was able to tie up loose ends for Witte's loved ones and finally create closure for the community. "Today the court made this place safer for everybody, and I think the community in general feels a sense of renewed security," Morrow said.

March 11 and 12, 2008

During a brief hearing on a Tuesday morning in Alexander County, Krajcir waived his right to contest his extradition to Missouri in front of Illinois state's attorney Jeffrey Farris. The next day, he was transferred from the Tamms Correctional Center in Illinois to the county jail in Jackson, Missouri. Cape Girardeau County sheriff John Jordan said that Krajcir would be housed by himself in the older, more secure part of the jail. Jordan said, "We can keep a better eye on him there." He added that the reason for putting Krajcir in isolation was for Krajcir's own protection, as well as for the safety of the other nearly two hundred inmates that were housed there. Jim Suhr, of the Associated Press, quoted Jordan as stating: "I certainly don't view him as a celebrity. I basically view him as an animal."

Krajcir appeared in a Jackson, Missouri, courtroom in front of Judge Gary A. Kamp for his arraignment in the murders of five Cape Girardeau women via closed-circuit video feed from the county jail where he was housed.

Prosecuting attorney Morley Swingle added additional charges against Krajcir, including the rapes of four other women and the robbery of another. Public defender Chris Davis was appointed to represent Krajcir, and a preliminary hearing was set for April 4, 2008.

37

I've done a lot of terrible things to this community, and I imagine there is a lot of anger and hate here toward me. But believe it or not, I'm the type of person that likes to be liked.
—Timothy Wayne Krajcir

April 4, 2008
Federal courthouse in Cape Girardeau, Missouri

Approximately fifty people filled the federal courthouse in Cape Girardeau. They included members of the media, but most of them were friends and family members of the women that Krajcir had killed. Also in attendance was one woman, Marcia Carter, who was sexually assaulted in 1981 but had survived the attack. They all came to see Krajcir face-to-face, hear him confess to the crimes he committed in Cape Girardeau, and watch him get sentenced. They came with the anticipation of obtaining a sense of closure to the painful memories that had plagued them for over twenty-five years and the hope that they would finally be able to move forward with their lives.

With his ankles and wrists shackled and tethered to a chain that looped around his waist, Krajcir was led into the courtroom heavily guarded by federal agents. He wore bright orange prison pajamas, white socks, and open-toe sandals. Thick, rubber-framed prison-issued glasses were perched on the nose of his pasty white face and frequently slid forward, nearly falling off his bowed head. The courtroom, which had been noisy with conversations, was suddenly blanketed with silence.

Circuit judge Ben Lewis explained to Krajcir what his legal rights were and asked him if he understood those rights. Krajcir confirmed that he did. The charges against him were read out loud and included five murders, seven sexual assaults, and one robbery. Krajcir pleaded guilty to all thirteen counts against him.

With a hint of a lisp in his soft-spoken effeminate voice, Krajcir described the details of each crime that he had committed in Cape Girardeau. He told the court how he raped and murdered Brenda Parsh and then deliberately shot her mother, Mary, in the back of the head. He told how he kidnapped, sexually assaulted, and then shot Sheila Cole, with the intention of killing her. Krajcir provided the details of how he forcibly raped Ann Shares. He said that he willfully, knowingly—and with premeditation—killed Margie Call by strangulation after he raped her.

At that point, the shock and horror felt by those who attended the hearing had built up to the point of needing some release. Most of the people in the courtroom were part of Margie Call's extended family. Many of them began to cry. Their muffled sobs could be heard through the tissues they used to wipe their tears. However, Krajcir's confession of guilt had just begun.

Krajcir then gave an account of how he raped and murdered Mildred Wallace by shooting her. He described the incident in which he sexually assaulted Marcia Carter at gunpoint. He went on to tell how he broke into Ethel Smith's home and then sexually assaulted Smith and her two friends, Geraldine Drake and Mary Lacey. Finally he gave the details of the time that he broke into the house of Eunice Seabaugh and robbed her of approximately $130.

When Krajcir was through telling the tale of the brutal, deviant, sexual attacks and murders he had committed in Cape Girardeau between 1977 and 1982, he turned and shuffled back to his seat on the left side of the courtroom. Before he would decide on what sentence he would impose on Krajcir, Judge Lewis then offered the opportunity for friends and relatives of the victims to come forward and address the court in regard to how their families had been affected.

Don Call, Margie's son, was the first to step forward. "None of these victims did anything to deserve what happened to them. Margie Call was my mother. We called her 'Mom,' not mother. My wife, Sharon, grew very close to Mom and became the daughter she never had. The fact that we have an extended family, including the Calls, Bertlings, and Sewings, has given us the strength to carry on despite our grief. The overwhelming question we have asked ourselves is 'Why was our mother murdered?' Now we know that it was simply because she was at the wrong place at the wrong time," Call said.

Don Call had to pause for a moment as he choked back some tears. He said that he and his now-deceased brother, Gary, had lived with an overwhelming feeling of guilt ever since the time of their mother's death because they were not there to protect her. Once he regained his composure, he continued to address the court.

"Mom was prevented from fulfilling her life as a grandmother. She had four grandchildren at the time and would have had two more since. She also missed out on two great-grandchildren. She used to pick her grandchildren up from school, take them shopping, and read stories to them at night.

"She missed all the ball games, all the track meets, and all the graduations. Mom missed my daughter's high-school valedictorian speech. I have been consumed with sorrow, rage, and anger for twenty-five years because Mom had no reason to die," Call concluded.

Krajcir reacted by slumping forward and nodding his head slightly as if to express that he understood.

Another speaker who came forward to address the court was Margie Call's niece Cathy Bertling Brown.

"My dad was the one who found Aunt Margie. He never closed his eyes at night without seeing her. I remember that she always gave us a silver dollar at Christmas. I still have all of mine," Brown said as she broke into tears and was unable to continue.

Marcia Carter survived an assault by Krajcir, which took place in 1981. She also attended the hearing and was brave enough to come forward

and express her thoughts as she stood within a few
feet of her assailant.

"It was difficult to come here today because it
brought on a lot of old feelings, but I have to let it
all come out. I'm glad to finally know definitively
who did this to me. This man came into my house
twice, once to attack my mother and then again
when he assaulted me. There were six children between the ages of nine months and seven years in
the house at that time. It sent me through a lot of
changes I shouldn't have gone through. There was
a cloud over my head for the last twenty-five years
that I couldn't get rid of.

"The experience made me become closer to my
children. I hoped that my children would not remember what happened, but they do. I can't even
talk to my oldest son about this because he is so full
of rage.

"For years I couldn't even eat with the same uten-
sils as the rest of my family because I was afraid I
might have contracted some kind of disease. I felt
dirty, useless, and allowed myself to be abused.
Hopefully, today this cloud will rise and go away.
I'm not going to be afraid anymore," Marcia Carter
told the court.

Just before the hearing, while waiting in the hallway of the courthouse, Margie Call's nephew
Chuck Bertling was still struggling with the wording
of the testimony he wanted to present. In his notes,
he referred to Krajcir as a "thing," but his wife was
persistent in having him change that to "person."
Throughout the hearing, Bertling continued to
make several changes in his notes. Eventually it was

his turn to get up and address the court. He would speak from his notes and his heart.

"I am here on behalf of Margie Call and her family and friends. Margie was just a normal person with two sons and a job that she had for most of her life. Our family was always close, and she was one of the driving forces in that. She loved her children and grandchildren, and I'm sorry that they did not have the opportunity to enjoy her love and affection. As kids we were always welcome in her home, and we spent many happy hours there.

"The cowardly act by this *person* was devastating to the family. For years we have gone through disappointment, anger, and frustration. Thanks to the justice system, that is now over. While this has been a horrible event in our lives, it has also drawn our family closer together. We have held hands, hugged, and cried together for years, and now we do the same thing in joyous celebration. We request that this *person* never sees the outside of a prison cell again," Bertling said.

As Bertling turned away from the judge to return to his seat, he stopped in front of Krajcir, looked him straight in the eye, and said, "I hope that you rot in the fiery halls of Hell for eternity!"

A total of seven people got up to speak about how they were affected by Timothy Krajcir's crimes. Each and every one of them provided compelling testimony to show that Krajcir's victims extended well beyond those that he terrorized, raped, and murdered. With each crime that Krajcir had committed, dozens of others were affected in a conductive way.

Before passing sentence on Krajcir, Judge Lewis asked him to approach the court and make any final statements that he might have. After Krajcir stood and approached the judge's bench, he turned toward the people seated in the courtroom and began to speak.

"I'd like to say a couple of things," Krajcir said softly.

Lewis quickly ordered him to turn back around and address him, not the people. Krajcir turned to face the judge, as he was told.

"I've been locked up for the last twenty-five years, and deservedly so. I just want to let the families of the victims to know that I heard what they said. I spent the first eight years of my incarceration in intense therapy trying to learn why I did the things that I did. I learned a lot of answers, but I have more to learn. I would like to apologize to the victims, their families, and the people of Cape Giradeau for the terror that I caused."

Krajcir said that he was "blown away" that he was offered an opportunity to avoid the death penalty, and that he didn't know if he could have been as generous if he were put in the same situation. He said that he intended to get back into the prison sex offender program and do everything in his power to help prevent anything of this nature from happening again.

"From my heart, I'm terribly sorry for what I've done. I feel your pain," Krajcir told the court.

It was now time for Judge Lewis to pass Krajcir's sentencing.

"It is difficult to have to prescribe a sentence commensurate with the evil, pain, suffering, and terror that you've inflicted," Lewis told Krajcir. "You have a preapproved agreement to avoid the death penalty, so the only available action is that you be incarcerated and never draw a breath as a free man."

Lewis said that he was surprised that Krajcir showed what appeared to be a genuine appreciation for the wrongfulness of his acts. He added that he hoped that Krajcir would live with that pain for the rest of his days. Then he declared his sentence.

Krajcir received a life sentence on all thirteen counts against him. Each count would be served consecutively and he would not be eligible for parole in less than fifty years on each count. That meant that he would serve a minimum of 650 years in prison before he could receive conditional release, and that could only take place after completing the eighty years he was already serving for his conviction of two murders in Illinois.

After the hearing was over, many of the relatives and friends of the victims said that Krajcir's ending words of regret for what he had done did not assuage them. Vicki Abernathy, Brenda Parsh's long-time friend, said that she did not believe that Krajcir felt any true remorse. Chuck Bertling was still so full of anger that he didn't care if Krajcir was remorseful or not. He just wanted him to suffer. Don Call said that he hoped that Krajcir was as remorseful as he appeared, but it didn't really matter in the end.

38

Now that the cases in Illinois and Missouri were finally brought to a close, it was time for Timothy Krajcir to face the charge of homicide in connection with the rape and murder of Myrtle Rupp in Pennsylvania.

A preliminary hearing date was set for April 22, 2008. Berks County district attorney John Adams said that he expected Krajcir to plead guilty, as he had in the other cases in Missouri and Illinois. Glen Welsh, Krajcir's public defender, confirmed that sentiment.

When the time for the hearing came, Krajcir was still incarcerated in the maximum-security prison in Tamms, Illinois. He appeared before district judge Dean Patton via closed-circuit television. During the hearing, Krajcir provided biographical information about himself. He told the judge that he was born in West Mahanoy City, grew up in Ironton, attended Emmaus High School, and briefly lived in Muhlenberg Township.

When Judge Patton asked about his criminal history, Krajcir replied, "How far back do you want me to go?"

Although he didn't mention the killings he was recently convicted of, Krajcir recalled his 1963 arrest in Illinois for attempted murder and rape, his arrest in 1979 for indecent assault, and his 1983 arrest in Allentown, Pennsylvania, for indecent assault, firearms violations, and an attempted escape from Lehigh County Prison.

Krajcir gave up his right to appear before his accusers in Berks County and waived his preliminary hearing, which meant that his case would be sent to Berks County Courthouse. Judge Patton set aside June 19, 2008, as the date for Krajcir's formal arraignment, which would also be conducted through a closed-circuit video feed.

"He'll probably receive another life sentence here, but most likely, [Krajcir] will never serve any of his time in Pennsylvania," Adams said, referring to the fact that Krajcir would have to first complete the thirteen life sentences that he was previously sentenced to serve.

Verna Hartman, Myrtle Rupp's sister, said that she used to get regular updates on the investigation in 1979, but then the phone calls stopped until about a year earlier when Corporal Moyer told her that they might have cracked the case.

David Rupp, Myrtle's nephew, said that over the years he had heard rumors about the police getting close to making an arrest, but he had never heard of Krajcir until just recently. David showed up in the courtroom to get a glimpse of the man accused of murdering his aunt.

Hartman remembered the shock she experienced

when she first learned that her older sister had been killed. "It was completely devastating," she said.

Hartman said that Myrtle Rupp had attended Pine Grove High School. She described her as a well-respected person in her profession and a member of the Reading Chapter No. 251 Order of the Eastern Star, a group Hartman equated with the Masons, only for ladies. Hartman said that her sister enjoyed watching stock car races and meeting her on Saturday mornings for breakfast at the Reading Fairgrounds.

Christmas was Rupp's favorite holiday season. There was always a big Christmas party at the Rupp house, but because she had no children and few relatives of her own, most of the attendees were acquaintances and family members of her husband, Charles, who was a bus driver for the city of Reading. Charles died of a heart attack about five years before Myrtle was killed, and according to Hartman, her sister kept to herself after that and dedicated her time to her job.

"The parties stopped, but she still loved to bake Christmas cookies, and she always looked forward to a day of Christmas shopping with me," Hartman said. "We did more talking than shopping, though, often spending as much as three hours chatting during lunch while we were out and about. Those are the times that I miss the most."

June 13, 2008

Some people consider Friday the thirteenth to be an unlucky date. There is a lot of mythology and

superstition surrounding both the number 13 and
Friday. One commonly accepted origin for this
mind-set dates back to 1307 when the Grand Master
of the Knights Templar, Jacques de Molay, and sixty
of his senior knights were arrested on Friday, October 13, by King Philip IV of France. On that day,
thousands of Templars were arrested, tortured, and
finally executed.

On Friday, June 13, 2008, Timothy Wayne Krajcir faced the sentence imposed on him by Berks
County judge Linda Ludgate. Unlike the Templars
in 1307, Krajcir knew that he would not be executed. His sentence was the result of a plea agreement between the district attorney John Adams
and public defender Glen Welsh. Following the
precedent set in Illinois and Missouri, Adams
agreed not to seek the death penalty for Krajcir in
exchange for his confession. Instead of death, Krajcir was sentenced to life in prison for the rape and
murder of Myrtle Rupp.

Judge Ludgate's decree of punishment did little
to quell the anger that had built up in Myrtle
Rupp's nephew over the greater part of his life.

"I'm not sure that another life sentence for Krajcir really serves justice here. If he doesn't deserve
the death penalty, who does?" David Rupp asked
Ludgate.

When Rupp was given an opportunity to address
the court, his voice was shaking, but he made his
point clear.

"It is my hope that by prolonging his life in prison,
it affords the possibility that he encounters someone in the prison population exactly like himself—
someone who will one day arbitrarily decide to make

Timothy Krajcir his next victim. As that someone strangles the last breath of life from Krajcir's pathetic, repulsive existence, perhaps Krajcir will reflect on what he had done, not only to Myrtle but to all his other victims. That is precisely how Timothy Krajcir deserves to die. That would be justice."

When Verna Hartman had her chance to speak, her words were not filled with as much malevolence. She told Ludgate that God required her to forgive Krajcir.

"That's very hard to do. I have to forgive because it allows me to let go of it. If I stay angry with him, it destroys the rest of my life," Hartman said. "It was hard to hear the whole thing, detail by detail, but I'm relieved that it's over. I do feel better."

Although Rupp and Hartman had a difference of opinion about whether life imprisonment was a harsh enough sentence for Krajcir, they did agree on one thing: they were both grateful to Corporal Moyer, all the investigators involved, and District Attorney John Adams and his staff for not giving up on a murder that had haunted them for almost thirty years.

Epilogue

I have felt emotional about my victims at times, and I'm not the same person I was thirty years ago. They told us in therapy to try to feel what our victims and their families were feeling, and I've done that. But I can't say for sure that I wouldn't do anything again.

—Timothy Wayne Krajcir

Timothy Wayne Krajcir's story did not end here. Even though he was convicted and sentenced for killing Myrtle Rupp in Berks County, Pennsylvania, he was still being investigated for possible involvement in connection with other unsolved crimes in the state.

Retired state police detectives Joe Kocevar and Jerry Procannon were working at press time with Lehigh County district attorney James Martin's office to find out if Krajcir might be responsible for at least one other murder that took place near the city of Allentown. Nobody involved would reveal any details about the most recent investigation until they had enough proof to either make a solid case against Krajcir or dismiss his involvement altogether.

During his December 3, 2007, confession to Smith and Echols, Krajcir mentioned that the .25-caliber pistol he used in previous crimes was the same one that police in Pennsylvania confiscated from him when he was arrested in 1983. Inquiries about the status of that gun and whether a ballistic check was made to compare it to other murders were returned with a refusal by the Lehigh Country District Attorney's Office to provide any details because of the ongoing investigation. Even if Krajcir was found to be responsible for one or more other murders in Pennsylvania, chances are that he would not receive the death penalty because Illinois is already footing the bill for all the expenses associated with Krajcir's incarceration.

At press time, Krajcir still had to face the charges against him in Kentucky for kidnapping Joyce Tharp. McCracken County Commonwealth attorney Tim Kaltenbach also refused to comment on Krajcir's case because it was still pending, but Paducah assistant police chief Danny Carroll said that Kaltenbach had begun the process to extradite Krajcir to Kentucky to face the charges against him. "There is no real ambition to expedite the matter, since Krajcir isn't going anywhere for the next thousand years," Carroll said.

Because Tharp was actually murdered in Carbondale, Illinois, Kaltenbach said that he would not pursue prosecuting Krajcir for the homicide charge. On October 30, 2008, Jackson County, Illinois, state's attorney Michael L. Wepsiec said that he did not anticipate ever bringing Krajcir to court to face charges for the homicide of Joyce Tharp.

"What's the point? He's already confessed," Wepsiec said.

After being asked if he was concerned about repercussions from Tharp's family members if Krajcir was not sentenced for the murder, Wepsiec said that he felt bad for Tharp's friends and family but "there are other victims and crimes in the world, and we need to focus on them. What's another life sentence going to do?"

After Krajcir was sentenced in Cape Girardeau, Missouri, Morley Swingle said that the death penalty was an effective weapon in a prosecutor's arsenal that can be used to help solve cases by provoking confessions. The confessions made by Timothy Krajcir and the resulting convictions for his crimes were evidence of that, but now that that weapon had been disarmed in Krajcir's case, the wheels of justice seemed to be gathering rust once again. They were turning much slower. The desire to bring closure to the remaining victims' family members appeared to no longer be a priority because the justice system already has their man behind bars. It made sense to taxpayers, who are not intimately involved, that money and police resources should not be wasted in an effort to chase after old cases that ultimately would not add any significant penalty against a convicted killer who was already behind bars and would never reenter public society to pose a threat to anyone else. But to those

who have suffered the death of a loved one, it was a
matter of principle to hold the person responsible to
be accountable and acknowledged as the person who
committed the crimes. Should the members of Joyce
Tharp's family be able to see the man who killed her
be convicted and punished for committing that
crime, or can they be satisfied knowing that Krajcir
had already been sentenced to serve more than thirteen lifetimes in prison for the other crimes that he
committed? Is it worth the time and expense to reexamine the case of Ida White, and do Grover Thompson's family members deserve to see him exonerated
if Krajcir was proved to be the one who actually attacked her in her apartment? Is it just a waste of time,
money, and resources to acknowledge the true facts
and bring comfort to a few individuals at the expense
of many? These questions can be debated and may
never be resolved.

One thing was certain. The justice system would
someday either find enough time to prosecute Krajcir for all the known crimes he was responsible for
committing, or he would die in prison while waiting
to be sentenced. One thing that was not certain was
that all of the crimes that Krajcir had committed
throughout his lifetime would ever be discovered and
revealed as something that he was responsible for.

The thirty-plus years spent investigating these unsolved rapes and murders had become a hallmark
case for criminal investigation and law enforcement
for several reasons. It resulted in a cooperative
effort between local, state, and federal authorities.
It revealed a need for a national fingerprint database and tested the newly developed ViCAP system,

which has evolved since to include a much broader base of information about convicted criminals.

The investigation into the Krajcir murders had become a template that provoked investigators across the country to reopen old unsolved cases and update them using recent DNA technology. This resulted in not only solving cold cases by bringing criminals to justice, but also to prove the innocence of people who have been wrongly convicted of crimes they did not commit.

Steven Barnes walked out of an Oneida County courtroom in November 2008 as a free man after a judge ruled that advanced DNA testing cleared him of rape and murder charges for which he spent nineteen years in prison. His case was just one of many that have recently been turned around after the investigation into Krajcir's case set the standard for updating previous crimes.

Daniel Williams was convicted in 1973 of murder, rape, kidnapping, and deviate sexual intercourse. Williams is about the same age as Krajcir, and also lived in Allentown, Pennsylvania. His attorney, Gary Asteak, said that a jury convicted him based on circumstantial evidence, and now he hoped that by using new DNA technology, his client would be exonerated after thirty-five years of unjust incarceration. Similar cases were being brought into courtrooms across the nation.

If any good can be salvaged from the tragic atrocities that Krajcir committed, it might be that technology and cooperative investigative methods have been improved to make the American system of justice more accountable and more thorough.

* * *

Detective Sergeant John Brown retired from the Cape Girardeau Police Department after serving nearly thirty years. Much of his time on the force, both on and off duty, was consumed with trying to solve the murders committed by Timothy Krajcir. He has been employed as a security officer at Southeast Missouri State University.

Illinois governor Rod Blagojevich was impeached in January 2009 for abusing his power for personal and political benefit after being accused of attempting to sell the U.S. Senate seat left vacant by President Barack Obama. The Illinois Senate voted unanimously to oust Blagojevich from office, marking the first time in the state's long history of political corruption in which a chief executive had been impeached and convicted.

Detective Jimmy Smith was honored by the Cape Girardeau Police Department as the 2008 "Officer of the Year." He has continued to investigate cold cases and unsolved murders in addition to his regular duties.

As you read these words, Timothy Krajcir continues to be locked up behind bars inside the Tamms Correctional Center in Illinois, but he is still alive. He doesn't have to get up every morning to go to work. He gets three square meals each and every day. He has a home that he does not have to worry about being foreclosed on. He enjoys free medical benefits.

All of this is paid for by taxpayers, including surviving friends and family members of his victims.

I've been twisted my whole life. I feel sorry for what I did, but you have to understand that I'm not like you. If I was like you, then it wouldn't have happened.
                                        —Timothy Wayne Krajcir

MORE MUST-READ TRUE CRIME
FROM PINNACLE